2002

W9-BBZ-413

Ashley's Garden

ASHLEY'S
GARDEN

One Family's Journey from
Grief to Spiritual Restoration
in the Aftermath of the
Oklahoma City Bombing

Kathleen Treanor with Candy Chand

Andrews McMeel
Publishing

Kansas City

02 03 04 05 06 RDH 10 9 8 7 6 5 4 3 2 1

Library of Congress Cataloging-in-Publication Data
Treanor, Kathleen.
    Ashley's garden : one family's journey, from grief to spiritual restoration, in the aftermath of the Oklahoma City bombing / Kathleen Treanor with Candy Chand.
      p. cm.
    ISBN 0-7407-2223-9
      1. Treanor, Kathleen. 2. Oklahoma City Federal Building Bombing, Oklahoma City, Okla., 1995. 3. Terrorism victims' families—Oklahoma—Oklahoma City. 4. Bereavement—Oklahoma—Oklahoma City. I. Chand, Candy. II. Title.

HV6432 .T74 2002
976.6'38—dc21
[B]
                                                                        2001055201

Book design by Holly Camerlinck

Attention: Schools and Businesses

To Ashley,
whose ministry continues,
even after death

Contents

Acknowledgments

To my husband, Michael—it was your statement "I only wish Dad had written a book about his life" that encouraged me to write this story. I offer *Ashley's Garden* as a gift to our children, and grandchildren, for generations to come.

And to my family—you've been the well from which I've drawn my strength, and the subject of so much of this story. Without your understanding, and encouragement, I would never have made it through.

I would be remiss if I didn't offer a thank-you to the many people I've come to know, and have worked with, at the Oklahoma City National Memorial. This group embodies a cross section of the entire tragedy, as well as the recovery effort. Each showed a wealth of compassion and selflessness never before equaled. Even if you are not mentioned here by name, please know your love was felt and shared in this story.

To all the rescue and recovery personnel across the nation who dropped everything, and risked life and limb to help in the aftermath of the bombing—I realize you don't see yourselves as heroes, that you were simply doing your job. But on April 19, 1995, after a few seconds of evil, 10,000 angels rose up to bear the burdens we were unable to carry ourselves. I will never forget you.

To my church, Reverend Rex Haymaker and his family, you have been a true source of inspiration and salve to my open and raw wounds. Thank you for putting up with me and for praying.

Without the determination and support of my coauthor, Candy Chand, this book would have probably lain in a drawer and been forgotten. Candy, I know you believe you did very little, but you moved mountains for me. I would never have known where to begin, or even how to get this in front of a publisher, if it weren't for your help. I can never say thank you enough for your friendship and joyous spirit. I am glad we found each other, my friend.

And last, to my agent, Peter Rubie, and my editor, Jean Lucas. Peter, thank you, from the bottom of my heart, for believing in this project and for your never-ending determination to see it through to the end. And, Jean, thank you for taking a chance on an unknown and letting me share Ashley's story with the world.

Preface

Loss: For some, it arrives in small, bearable packages; for others, it's nothing less than torment. On April 19, 1995, Kathleen Treanor came face-to-face with a heart-wrenching dose of spiritual destitution when her four-year-old daughter, Ashley, became a victim of the Oklahoma City bombing.

For millions around the world, Ashley's story invoked an intense emotional response. Kathleen's daughter, not a part of the day-care center, where so many children lost their lives, had a tragic, unforeseen appointment with destiny.

After the bombing, Kathleen kept detailed journals, documenting her grief, anger, and unspeakable loss. She took great care to record events to which the media had limited access—the search for the truth, the trials, as well as the emotional aftermath. It is from these journals *Ashley's Garden* was born—reaching out and offering hope to anyone willing to open their hearts and listen.

Ashley's Garden is more than a story of grief; it is a story of grace born anew. Through faith Kathleen was lifted up and brought back from the shadows of death to experience joy once again. *Ashley's Garden* is a story of hope, of healing, of restoration, flourishing like the delicate flowers found blooming in its fertile soil.

—Candy Chand

One

Preparing the Soil

The seed of God is in us. Given an intelligent and hard-working farmer,
it will thrive and grow up to God, whose seed it is; and accordingly,
its fruits will be God-nature. Pear seeds grow into pear trees,
nut seeds into nut trees, and God-seed into God.

MEISTER ECKHART

I arrived at my office at 8:00 A.M. sharp, grabbed a cup of coffee, then quietly sat down to work. At 9:02, it happened. A sudden explosion rocked Oklahoma City. And my world would never be the same again.

Life's journey had lead me down countless winding roads. At times the path was smooth before me. But on occasion my pilgrimage was marked by sudden twists and turns. On April 19, 1995, I was brought to an unthinkable place, thrown head-on into tragedy by the loss of my four-year-old daughter, Ashley, in the worst act of terrorism inflicted on American soil up to that time.

Through my grief I went over the tiniest details again and again, retracing each step of my way, desperately seeking answers. It was clear, the path to this point had been long and wide.

While some go through life with little bumps and bruises, others experience enormous afflictions. So it was with my family. Throughout the devastation, images of years gone by seemed to pass before me like a surreal motion picture. Suddenly, I saw myself—just two or three years old—watching Mama crying hopelessly in the kitchen. I rushed to her side, offering comfort, but my older sister, Darlene, quickly dragged me down the hall. She explained, as best she could, Mama was sick, Daddy was taking care of her, and we just needed to stay out of the way.

After that day, she went away for a long, long time. I was reluctantly passed between neighbors, aunts, and friends while Daddy worked and my older brothers and sister went to school. Every day I asked when Mama would be back, but no one answered.

Finally, the moment arrived. She was coming home! My first sight of her was difficult at best. She was painfully thin, aged by mental illness as if years and not months had gone by. I was almost afraid to get too close. Eventually, I embraced enough courage to reach out once more. I climbed onto her lap to offer a hug, but even then my young mind realized everything had changed. Before the breakdown Mama's life had been filled with laughter and joy. Now it would be months before I saw her smile again.

But there were good times too. Mama often took me to church. Since we lived in the country, going along meant having other kids to play with. I cherished those moments and looked forward to Sundays with great anticipation.

On occasion, I'd pretend to be sick so I could stay home from school, and Mama would take me along to her gathering place, where she'd meet several ladies at the little country schoolhouse to sew clothing and quilts for foreign missionaries. I'd sit, as happy as could be, comfortably perched under the quilting frames, watching their hands tenderly work on intricate designs.

I grew up strong and independent. As a teen I dated Michael Treanor, a local boy I'd known for years. We were in love. We spoke of marriage. Life seemed perfect.

But soon, despite my love for family and hometown memories, I yearned for new adventures. By the time I was eighteen, unable to contain myself any longer, I headed off to Oklahoma State University in Stillwater, approximately an hour and a half from home. This distance, I determined, would give me the opportunity to test my wings, try out my independence, yet keep me relatively close to my loved ones.

It wasn't long before I experienced a newfound sense of freedom. I didn't want anything to keep me from a carefree life. Despite my godly upbringing, I threw my values to the wind, abandoned my spiritual belief system, and turned to a life of partying and decadence. Sometimes, in quiet moments, I felt I was akin to the prodigal son. Of course, as young people do, I also felt invincible, completely primed for experiencing all life had to offer. Sure, at times, I had fun. But now I realize I compromised my very character by living a life I knew was wrong. In order to avoid feeling guilty, I simply stopped coming home on weekends. I could no longer bear to see the disappointment in my parents' eyes.

Although I loved Michael, in time I began to see our relationship as holding me back. I made a decision to leave him, freeing myself from more than church values. There was no doubt about it; I was going through an identity crisis. Clearly it was classic behavior for someone my age, but it was still devastating in its consequences. Even though Michael and I were engaged, I hastily broke off our relationship. I told him I didn't love him anymore and there was someone else in my life. I knew if I didn't make the cut deep, Michael would cling to any shred of hope left. I needed time to figure out who I was before I settled down into a lifelong commitment. I wasn't ready for marriage, and I knew it. Yes, I was cruel, but at the time I felt it was my only way out.

Soon, though, this "freedom" became a harsh reality, and I realized I'd received more than I'd wished for. After a few failed relationships I knew I'd never find anyone who loved me as much as Michael did. I began to regret sending him away and desperately tried to get him back. But my attempts to contact him hit a fierce dead end. Michael's mother, LaRue, told me her son didn't want to speak to me. One day she explained Michael was engaged, the wedding was just around the corner, and he didn't need me interfering with his future.

Over the years I'd come to love LaRue. I missed her, and her family, almost as much as I missed Michael. We had so much in common, and I'd grown to love her as a mom. In retrospect, I realize she was simply trying to protect her son. But her words still cut like a knife. I knew I deserved it, but that didn't stop my heart from aching.

Within six months of our breakup, Michael married someone else. On the day of his wedding, I attempted to see him one last time. I took him a gift and caught a brief glimpse of him at the church, putting the finishing touches on his tuxedo. Reality hit me right between the eyes— I was too late. The love of my life was gone, and I would have to live with my mistake forever. As Michael recited his vows, I sobbed quietly behind the church window. My heart was crushed, and I had no one to blame but myself. After that, nothing seemed to matter. I buried any prospects of future happiness and began to walk forward in a lifeless, methodical way.

Before long things went from bad to worse. During my senior year in college, I watched from a distance as my mother succumbed to her mental illness and was hospitalized once again. It had been years since her last breakdown. I struggled with feeling helpless about my mom, I struggled with regret over losing Michael, and I struggled to stay in school. In spite of it all, in the fall of 1985 I obtained my degree in fine arts and set out to find my place in the world. I landed in Tulsa, where I was determined to survive on my own. However, moving to a city where I had no friends or family didn't make life easy.

I landed a job as club manager at the local Ramada Inn. It was there I met Steve, the food and beverage director. He was funny and attentive, and we quickly became friends. Before long we started dating.

Unfortunately, about six months later the hotel underwent a corporate takeover. We were terminated without notice or severance. I had nowhere to go, I was desperately lonely, but I was also determined not to tuck my tail and run home to Mama and Daddy. Steve and I decided to combine our resources by moving in together. It was a big step for me, but not for Steve. He was eleven years my senior and had two boys from a previous marriage. I wanted to settle down and start a family. Steve never offered marriage, but I assumed that in time he would.

Within a few weeks we both found jobs in fast-food management. The work was a real blow to my ego, but it would serve its purpose—to ward off bill collectors until I could find more suitable employment with another hotel or, better yet, as a graphic designer. We decided I'd forgo purchasing health insurance through my employer, and Steve would get it through his work instead. Then, he changed jobs to work for another company.

After we'd been living together for less than four months, I became ill. I was tired, losing weight, and couldn't keep my meals down. I had no idea what was happening. I went to my doctor. After the initial examination she asked several questions about my menstrual cycle. Suddenly I became concerned. Just a few months earlier I'd been diagnosed with cervical dysplasia, a precancerous growth, but I'd had surgery to remove it. Up to that minute I thought it had been successful. Had the disease returned? Would I ever have children?

"Is it cancer?" I asked with a trembling voice.

"No, I don't think that's it. Let me check on the results of these tests," the doctor replied. She stepped out of the room and left me alone to cry. I desperately wanted to have children. It had been several years since I'd been to church, but without hesitation I began to pray. "God, I know I've turned away from you over the past few years, but I need you now. I know I don't deserve it, God, but if you would see fit to let me have children, I'll do my best to raise them as you'd want me to. Please don't let her tell me it's cancer." Tears slid down my cheeks.

Soon the doctor returned. "What is it?" I asked, not hiding my fear.

"Well, actually, it's good news . . . I think, anyway. You're pregnant!"

The air went out of my lungs, and the room started to spin. "*Not yet,*" I wailed. "I can't be pregnant now. I've been faithfully taking the pill. How did this happen?"

She looked at me, her eyes reflecting sadness. "Sometimes it just does. If you don't take your pill at the same time every day, if you miss a day, or if you're just very fertile at the time, the pill may not work. You fall into that 1 percent of people who can't, or shouldn't, take the pill without other forms of protection." I tried to digest all she was saying. "Listen, if you don't want this baby, please consider adoption before you think of abortion. I have women calling me on a daily basis who would love to be in your situation. If you're interested, I can help you."

I shook my head. "Abortion is out of the question. But I don't have all the answers yet. I need time to think." Call me naïve, but the possibility of pregnancy had never crossed my mind—even with the symptoms staring me in the face.

I cried all the way home. How did my life get so out of control? I'd made so many irresponsible decisions, and now I was trapped. I knew Steve wasn't the love of my life. I liked him, but that was all. The only man I'd ever loved was out of my reach forever. I also knew my relationship with Steve was nearing the end. Now everything had changed. I was pregnant and living with a man I didn't love. And he was the father of the child growing within me.

When I arrived at our duplex I sat down and thought about how I'd tell Steve.

Suddenly the phone rang. It was my sister, Darlene, who was a registered nurse. When my symptoms worsened I'd called her about my condition. She'd suggested I make an appointment with my doctor. I suspected she already knew what was wrong, but was still anxiously awaiting solid answers. "So what did the doctor say?" she asked. I took a deep, trembling breath but, before I could answer, she went on. "You're pregnant," she said joyfully.

"*Yeeeessss,*" I wailed.

"That's wonderful!"

"But, Darlene, Steve and I aren't married. I can't afford this right now. We are struggling as it is, just to make ends meet."

"Kathleen, if you wait until you can afford a baby, you'll never have one. But all of that doesn't matter anyway—one is on the way, and there isn't anything you can do about it but be happy. Look, if need be, I'll raise your child, or you can move home, and we'll all help. You know how much Mama loves babies. She'll flip when you tell her. Of course, you'll have to wait until she gets out of the hospital. Maybe this will be the very news that sets her straight."

"I haven't told Steve yet."

"Listen, before you make any rash decisions, come home and talk to Mama and Daddy. You might be surprised at their reaction."

We chatted a bit more and then hung up shortly before Steve came home from work. "Well, 'sickie,' what's wrong with you?" he asked.

"I'm pregnant," I quietly answered.

"What? We can't afford a baby right now. We can barely pay our bills the way it is."

"Under no circumstances will I consider having an abortion." With that, I turned away and ran upstairs, barricaded myself in the extra room, and refused to say another word to him about it.

The next day I arranged with my employer to go home for a while. I left without telling Steve where I was going, or if I'd ever be back. I was angry and disappointed with the way my life had turned out. Just a few years before I'd envisioned a far different future. Now I was out of control, away from God, and sliding downhill toward a dark abyss.

As I made the two-hour drive home, I thought of my father. How would he receive the fact I was pregnant? I was scared that Daddy, for the first time in my life, would turn me away, forcing me to deal with my mistakes on my own. I knew he would be disappointed with me, which was hard enough, but the thought of him turning me out was even more painful.

My heart raced as I reached home. I stepped out of the car, and Daddy greeted me with a warm hug. I asked how Mama was doing. He said she was improving but it would be a while before the doctors could stabilize her medications.

I swallowed hard. "Daddy, I'm pregnant." I threw myself into his arms and wept. He held me tight as I babbled out the story. I told him I knew he was disappointed, but I didn't know what else to do. I stood there in his arms and let my father's love envelop me once again.

"You'll always have a home here. Somehow we'll make it work. We'll just go to Tulsa right now and pack your things. You come back home, so I can take care of you."

"But I can't leave my job. I have so many responsibilities and bills. I can't ask you to take all this on, especially now that Mama is so sick."

"Don't worry about that; we'll work it all out. Maybe you can help when Mama returns from the hospital. You can find yourself a job here and work until the baby arrives. Just come home. Everything will turn out fine."

For the first time I completely understood the biblical story of the prodigal son, and how that young man must have felt when his father so graciously welcomed him home. I couldn't believe it. Daddy's response gave me the courage I needed to take control of my life. I could face whatever came my way now that I knew my family would stand behind me.

That weekend we went to visit Mama in the hospital. I was afraid of what I might see: locks on the doors and bars on the windows. Surely through the eyes of a worried daughter such a place would appear more like a prison than a place of healing. I shivered when I thought of patients wandering around, flashing strange, vacant eyes. But I was relieved to find out, this time Mama was in a regular hospital. Her doctor simply wanted to stabilize her medications.

As we walked into her room, Mama smiled at me. "Who are you?" she asked.

I looked at Daddy. He just shook his head. "Patricia, this is your youngest daughter, Kathleen," he said.

"I only have one daughter," she replied. "Are you sure she isn't one of my granddaughters? Is this Candy or Crystal?"

Although I knew she was ill, her words wounded me deeply. She began to babble in broken sentences and engage in nonsensical conversation. It was heart-wrenching to see her that way. Her wrists and ankles bore the marks of restraining straps. Her hair was in disarray, and some of her clothing was torn. I couldn't take any more. I excused myself and went into the lobby. It was the first time I'd actually seen Mama sick. I knew about her illness, but facing it head-on was a tremendous shock.

Those last few roller-coaster days had sorely taxed my strength. When we got home I crawled into bed, fell into a deep sleep, and began to dream. There, in my mind's eye, was my mama. She smiled proudly while holding my child in her arms. Her expression revealed no sign of disappointment regarding the circumstances of the birth. She was simply a grandmother loving an innocent child. When I woke up the next day, I knew what I had to do.

On Sunday I drove back to Tulsa. Steve met me at the door. "Where have you been?" he asked.

"I went home for the weekend," I said, walking inside.

"Well . . .," he said meaningfully.

I hesitated for a moment, then went on. "The way I see it, Steve, you have two choices. You can either stand beside me, and help me raise this child, or I will pack my bags and be on my own. Whatever you choose, it will be final."

With that I went upstairs. I lay down on the bed in the spare room and fell asleep. When I awoke it was dark outside. I was hungry but a bit nauseated. I started down the hall to get something to eat.

Steve met me. "Please don't leave. I don't want to live without you." There were tears in his eyes. Although I was relieved he wanted me to stay, I wondered if it was really the right thing to do. But because I was glad the baby would know its father, I reluctantly agreed to stay.

Time seemed to fly by. Soon Steve took off for management training in Dallas, and I was left at home to plan for the baby. I began having spasmodic cramps in my back and side. At work, when I bent ever so slightly I'd double over in pain. Because I was about six months pregnant by then, I attributed it to muscle strain or false labor.

Finally one night the pain was so bad I couldn't sleep. I knew I was running a fever, and the spasms had intensified. So first thing in the morning, I called my doctor, and she told me to come to her office right away. I began to fear I was going into labor. I was scared that, after all I'd been through, I'd lose the baby or, worse yet, it would be born dangerously premature.

By the time I arrived at her office, my fever was 104 degrees, and I was shaking violently. I was taken in immediately for lab work. It turned out I had a severe kidney infection. I was also dehydrated. The cramps I was experiencing were indeed preterm labor.

"Do not go home; go directly to the hospital," my doctor firmly instructed me. "We have to get you rehydrated and monitor your infection closely until we get these contractions to stop. Either go to the hospital now or you'll lose your baby."

I went straight across the street and checked myself in. Soon they began administering medications, and I called Steve to tell him what was going on. He told me since he was at corporate headquarters he'd talk to his supervisor and have someone fax over the necessary insurance documents. However, he would not be home for a few more days.

Alone in the hospital, I turned to my best friend from college, Tina, who had recently moved across town. We had barely hung up the phone when she arrived. Tina had always stuck by me, despite my failings. I considered her a sister more than a friend. I smiled when I recalled gathering around the dorm piano while Tina played and we sang old hymns from our childhood. An elegant woman, over six feet tall, Tina was often referred to as Tigna, the Amazon Woman by her old college buddies. Although at times she didn't appreciate our humor, she tried to play along. I often relied on her shoulder to lean on when things got tough. Having her in Tulsa made all the difference in the world.

We chatted a bit, then she asked if I'd chosen a name for the baby. We hadn't. "Well, I've been thinking about it a lot. Have you thought about Ashley?" she asked. It was the first time I'd considered that name.

"Ashley? You mean like the *Gone With the Wind* Ashley? Seems a little feminine if it's a boy."

"Sure," she said, "but if it's a boy, you can shorten it to Ash. It's a nice name either way."

"I'm not sure," I told her, but I promised to give it serious thought.

After I'd recovered fully my mind raced once again toward our rapidly depleting finances. I tried to conserve economically in any way I could.

Finally the news arrived. Mama had been released from the hospital. So on Mother's Day, Steve and I went home for a visit. My sister had a small dinner at her house, just Mama, Daddy, her girls, Steve, and me. It was good to be home. Mama was a little more like herself, but I could tell she was drugged to the hilt. No matter what the circumstance, she wore a drunken grin permanently affixed to her face.

Daddy looked old and haggard. It was the worst I'd ever seen him. Since Mama came home he'd been responsible for her care. He was visibly exhausted. I asked him if he was getting enough rest. He told me Mama was up and down all night and he had to get up constantly to check on her. If I could come and stay with him for a while, then maybe I could watch Mama and he could get some rest. I would be home soon. I gave him my word.

Daddy went back into the kitchen to help Darlene. Mama immediately came over to the sofa where I was halfway napping. She patted my tummy, then felt all around to see if she could feel the baby move. Finally she leaned over and whispered, "I can hardly wait to hold you, my little grandbaby." She had a mischievous look on her face, but when she glanced at me, her expression became somber. "You need to come home, so I can take care of you and the baby."

"Soon, Mama," I promised, "just a little while longer."

"No, you need to come now," she stated firmly. "As a matter of fact, you're just going to come home with me today."

"No, Mama, I have to get my things gathered up. I need the baby bed and my clothes and stuff. I just have a few more things to tidy up before I return. Be patient just a little while longer. Your new grandbaby will be here in about a month."

Mama frowned but continued to rub my tummy and hum to herself.

"Have you picked out a name yet?" my thirteen-year-old niece, Kristen, asked.

"Well, not really. We just can't come to an agreement. For a boy, I like Connor Sean, but Steve likes Phillip Don. If the baby is a girl, we'll name her Ashley Megan," I told her.

"I like the name Zachary. That's what I want to name my little boy someday," Kristen said proudly.

Steve and I looked at each other. "I really like that," I said.

"Me too," Steve said. "Okay, let's get the book and see what it means." I pulled out our baby name book and looked it up. "Zachary: Strong of character." I glanced at Kristen. "Would it be all right, if the baby's a boy, if I named him Zachary?"

"Sure!" she said brightly. "That would be neat! I can say I named my baby cousin."

It was the first name Steve and I agreed on, but then Daddy piped in. "Well, if you're going to name him that, then his middle name needs to be something simple, like Billy or Tommy, something easy to remember."

"I like Tommy, or rather Thomas. That settles it. If the baby is a boy, his name will be Zachary Thomas. If it's a girl, she will be Ashley Megan."

With baby names decided upon, and a promise to Mama that I'd return soon, Steve and I went back to Tulsa. Our plan was simple. I'd go home and stay with my parents while Steve took a job in Long Beach, California. He'd be working with his old boss and friend at a large hotel right on the ocean. Steve reasoned this was our best option. We'd have to sell most of our things to afford his trip to the coast. We had garage sales and packed whenever time allowed. However, being only a month away from delivery, I found packing a major feat. I was weak and ill, but I refused to believe it.

One afternoon my boss, Ray Kassim, pulled me aside. "Have you seen your doctor lately?" he asked. There was genuine concern in his warm, brown eyes. Ray was like an adoptive father to me. He was Lebanese and had a wonderful, exotic accent. He wore a cheerful smile and I always looked forward to his visits.

"I see her every two weeks," I told him.

"Kathleen, I want you to understand, I am a father. I have watched my wife give birth to my children, and when she's pregnant she is more radiant and beautiful than you can imagine. Please don't take this the wrong way, but you look terrible. Your hands and feet are swollen, and there are dark circles under your eyes. Your skin looks dull and blotchy. Believe me, you are not well, and you should go to see your doctor right away. In fact, I insist."

"Oh, Ray, I'm all right. I'm just tired. That's all."

He waved aside my protest. "I think you should honestly think about taking a leave of absence, Kathleen. You must get well before you have your baby."

Now I was really scared. "I can't, Ray. I can't afford to be off from work, even for a day."

He nodded understandingly but insisted, "Go see your doctor, and find out what she has to say. I really think she'll agree with me."

Reluctantly I gave in. "Okay, I'm off tomorrow. I'll call now and see if I can get in for a checkup."

"Good!" He flashed me one of his smiles. We went on to discuss the restaurant and how it could be managed in my absence.

The next day after some lab work, I went to see my doctor. When she walked in I knew by the expression on her face there was trouble. "You're a very sick lady," she said. "You have an elevated protein count, and you're showing signs of preeclampsia. This is a very serious condition that, if it gets out of control, can cause death for both you and your baby. I'm prescribing bed rest, and you'll need to be checked constantly. In fact, I'm considering admitting you into the hospital."

I gasped. "I can't do that. I can't quit my job. I can hardly pay my bills now. Besides, I don't have any insurance, and I can't possibly afford an extended hospital stay. Please, is there something else I can do?"

She sighed. "I'm reluctant, but if you could be placed on limited hours, and promise you'll get some rest, maybe your condition will stabilize. Honestly, though, unless you can stay off your feet, your condition will only get dangerously worse."

"Listen, I'll try anything. I can come here each morning, and you can test me to see how I'm doing. But I need to work as long as I can. Besides, I'll need to transfer soon. I have to move home to live with my parents until after I have the baby and can get back on my feet. If I can just make it through the next few days, I'll be all right—my family will be able to look after me."

She relented. "Okay. We'll try this, but you need to prepare for the worst."

When I got home I immediately called my boss.

"That's what I thought," he said. "You are very sick. You need to be home resting."

"Ray, if I can just work a few more weeks, it would be a big help." I began to beg. "Maybe I can be a roving supervisor and go to various locations to give other managers a break. That way, if I'm ill, it won't hurt your stores."

"Let me see what I can do," he reluctantly agreed.

Ray made arrangements for me to work lunch hours at one of his other stores. I was given strict instructions not to lift anything, not to overwork myself, but simply to run the cash register and handle the books. I could have kissed him. It wasn't fulltime work, but at least I'd have some income until the baby arrived.

Less than a week later, when Steve and I were packing our belongings for the big move, the phone rang. It was my sister. "Kathleen, are you alone?"

"No, Steve's here."

"Okay, I want you to sit down right now." I could tell she was upset. Her voice was trembling. I sat down in the doorway to the garage.

"What is it?" My mind turned back to Mother's Day and how bad Daddy had looked. My first thought was he'd suffered a heart attack.

"You're sitting down, right, Kathleen?"

"Yes, I'm down. Now what is it, for God's sake?"

"Kathleen, Mama is dead."

The world started to spin out of control. "What?"

"She killed herself, Kathleen. She hung herself from the tree in the backyard. Daddy found her this afternoon. He fell asleep on the couch, and Mama went outside. He knew when he woke up something was wrong, so he went looking for her. He said he walked down the driveway a short distance, but she wasn't there. Then he saw her in the tree on the way back. Oh my God, Kathleen, it was just awful. Daddy called me, and I came right away, but there was no doubt, she was dead."

I listened to her, trying to take it in as the words continued to spill from the phone. Mama was dead. The reality slowly echoed through my mind. Wave after wave of shock and disbelief washed over me like a hurricane.

I struggled to find my breath. "I'm on my way home. I'll be there in a few hours."

"Let me talk to Steve." I handed over the phone, methodically walked to my room, and hastily packed my bag. Darlene's words repeated over and over in my head . . . Suicide . . . Dead . . . Hanging in the tree. I couldn't believe it. It wasn't true. It was a cruel joke. Just a few more days and Mama would have been able to hold her new grandbaby. I recalled our last phone conversation. Mama had begged me to come home right then. Just like she had on Mother's Day. I'd put her off and assured her I'd be home soon. I remembered the desperation in her voice, and I remembered how she said, "Good-bye, I love you. No matter what, don't forget that."

Now I knew. Mama had been saying good-bye forever. Slowly her words came back with crystal clarity. Mama had been planning this all along. Then it occurred to me, if I'd gone home when she asked, she might still be alive. It was my fault. If I'd only come home, I could have helped Daddy. Mama wouldn't have been left alone. I'd been selfish, and now my mother had paid with her life.

The rest of the night was a complete blur. I headed home to bury Mama while Steve stayed behind to finish packing. During my drive back to Guthrie, guilt raced through my head. It was dark when I arrived, and I began to slip into a dreamlike state of shock.

The next couple of days were filled with preparations for the funeral. Darlene monitored my condition, which deteriorated daily. I could only function on a physical level for two or three hours a day. Mentally, I was limited to minutes.

I stayed with Daddy as he grieved. I'd rarely seen my father cry. Now he was sobbing uncontrollably. Of course he blamed himself, the same way the rest of us did.

Together, my brothers, sister, and I learned Mama had called each of us to say good-bye before she took her life. We all had opportunities to step in and rescue her, but none of us recognized what she was capable of.

Over the next few weeks I discovered things about my family that were hard to bear. I learned about the pain my mother had lived with from the time she was a child, how she'd been sexually abused. And I learned how my father had chosen to stay with her all those years despite her mental problems. It was a lot to digest—the loss of my mother, a funeral, frightening family secrets, and the impending birth of my first child.

Over the next couple of weeks Darlene took care of me. Steve drove out to California to begin his new job, and I waited, and waited some more. Finally, on June 9, at 3:30 A.M., I went into labor. I got up and began milling around the house.

Daddy heard me and got up too. "Is it time?" he asked nervously.

"Too early yet," I said, "but it'll be today." Daddy looked relieved but still as nervous as a june bug in a henhouse. I think he managed to put away two packs of cigarettes that morning. Darlene, who'd spent the night with us, was elated. She watched me closely. I called Steve in California and told him the news. He spent the rest of the day trying to get a flight home.

We finally went to the hospital about ten that morning, and I checked in. Because of my lack of insurance, an epidural was out of the question. The only medication I could receive would be general pain relievers. Only if they had to do a cesarean would I get anything more. A few hours into labor, I cursed our lack of insurance. I would have killed for an epidural.

Everything was going relatively well up until that final few minutes. I was almost ready to push when both the baby's heart rate and mine suddenly dropped. The nurses rushed in and immediately called the doctor. Unfortunately, my regular physician was away on a business trip. Her partner, Dr. John Hamilton, came immediately. It was a rushed delivery, but after it was over everyone was all right. I looked over to the table where they were cleaning the baby and asked, "Zachary or Ashley?"

Darlene smiled as she said, "It's Zachary."

"If only Mama were here," I said, and passed out from exhaustion.

Two

Transplanting

*Plants of great vigor will almost always struggle into blossom,
despite impediments. But there should be encouragement, and a
free genial atmosphere for those of more timid sort,
fair play for each in its own kind.*

MARGARET FULLER

Once again we were on the move. Only this time our little family was
headed for the "greener pastures" of California. For a while we lived in a
Long Beach hotel, where Steve found another job. I wasn't particularly
happy about moving so far from my family, especially with a brand-new
baby, but I couldn't help but look forward to the adventure California
promised. Since I was a child the Golden State had tempted my imagination. After all, that's where the movie stars, as well as the rich and
famous, live.

Yet, despite my hopes, I became depressed and withdrawn. I had no
one in California I could turn to. Even with a newborn baby by my side,
my days were filled with sorrow. I clung to Zachary as the only person
who loved me unconditionally. I knew my dependence on him was

unhealthy, but he was all I had. Eventually we settled into a lovely rental home, and I decided my best option was to stay home with Zachary and care for a few other children while Steve worked at the hotel. It kept me busy, and working from home seemed like the logical choice.

However, no sooner had things settled down than Steve lost his job. We'd already moved four times in two years, but this one seemed the worst of all. How on earth were we ever going to make this one fly?

While we counted pennies and scrimped to survive, Steve hunted for another job. Two months later the hotel offered him another position. This time he'd be the general manager of a small hotel near Hollywood. So once again we packed up our things and moved.

From the day we arrived I knew there'd be trouble. The hotel, even though it was straight across from Children's Hospital, was in a somewhat trashy neighborhood. Granted, it was near the famous Sunset Strip, but I still hated it. Our apartment inside the hotel was large, but it was dark and had the distinct odor of cigarette smoke. No matter how hard I tried, I couldn't get rid of that smell. To make matters worse, almost every night I heard gunshots. Homeless people were everywhere, there were prostitutes standing on the corner, and I could see used hypodermic needles in the gutters and on the ground in the nearby parks. I felt I'd moved smack-dab into the center of hell. I often thought about the safe and sheltered farm in Oklahoma where I grew up. What ever possessed me to move away?

Feeling the need to contribute more to our family budget, I found work at a local bank. Although I made a few friends, I still hated Los Angeles. When I'd finally had enough, I told Steve. I didn't want to put up with the lifestyle, and I wasn't going to raise my child that way. He reluctantly agreed and attempted to get a transfer.

Shortly afterward, I found out I was pregnant again. At least this time, we were both employed and had good insurance.

Then we received more good news. A branch of the hotel in Jacksonville, Florida, had an opening for Steve. After some thorough questioning about the location, we decided to make the move. I was so relieved to get out of L.A., I packed our things in record time. We had two weeks to drive the nearly 2,500 miles across the United States. It was late winter, and we were going to start all over again in a new state. Even though I was grateful to escape California, I was weary of moving. I'd grown up in the same house all my life and was unaccustomed to the upheaval that comes with so much change. I was trying to raise my child in a safe and secure environment but couldn't seem to get settled in one place long enough to put down any roots.

We took separate vehicles to Florida, and I used the time away from Steve to do a bit of thinking. Zack sat with me in the car while Steve drove a Ryder truck full of our things. The drive across the mountains was treacherous. We were nearly snowbound near Flagstaff, Arizona. Had we stopped for the evening, we'd probably still be stuck there. The highways were closing down, and visibility was less than twenty feet. It was all I could do to see the taillights of the huge truck in front of me. My hands were frozen to the wheel, but somehow we made it through. We finally stopped in Gallup, New Mexico, for the night. It took me a while to pry my nervous hands from the steering wheel.

We made it into Oklahoma the next day and stopped for a visit with Darlene and my dad. We decided we'd leave Zachary, and my car, with my sister for a short time while Steve and I got settled in Florida. Once we had a place to live, I'd come back for them.

Within days I'd planted my feet firmly on Florida soil and tried to settle in for the long ride. I even landed a managerial job at the hotel where Steve worked, and we found a lovely home to rent. Things were finally looking up.

Feeling more comfortable, I was able to concentrate on my pregnancy. I discovered if I chose to deliver in a birthing center instead of a hospital my insurance would pay 100 percent of the cost. I quickly found one in St. Augustine, just a short trip from Jacksonville.

Not long afterward I made the decision to have my tubes tied directly after birth, since the cost would be wrapped up in the delivery. My doctor tried to talk me out of it, saying I was too young for such a procedure, but I was adamant.

This time my pregnancy was relatively routine, with no unexpected illnesses or catastrophes. Feeling strong and well, just a few weeks before my due date, I decided to sit down at my computer and design a birth announcement.

We'd gotten an ultrasound a few days before and learned the baby would be a girl. I was overjoyed; now I had my perfect little family, one boy and one girl. I mulled over the name we'd chosen for our daughter, the one inspired by Tina, my old college buddy—Ashley Megan Eckles. It sounded like such a lovely name for a little girl. But then I began to wonder. Would it suit her later? Would Ashley still be a lovely name when she was no longer a child in pigtails but a sophisticated adult?

Out of the blue, and for the first time in ages, that still, small voice within spoke to me. "You won't need to worry about her name. She will not grow to adulthood."

I was shaken. Not only by the finality of the statement but by the fact that it had been so long since I'd heard the voice of God. Even though my convictions were still strong, I hadn't been to church since my mother's funeral. I wondered what it meant. What was God trying to tell me? Why would my child die before she reached adulthood? Surely she'd be healthy. There were no problems with the ultrasounds. If she were anything like Zack, she'd be as strong as a horse.

But what about violent crime? At that very moment a news report flashed across my television. "One out of nine children in the United States will fall victim to violent crime." It was a staggering statistic. Would Ashley be one of them? I adamantly shook off the feelings of terror that threatened to overwhelm me. No, this wouldn't happen to my family, not to my child. I'd simply make sure she always had the finest care. We'd always live in good, safe neighborhoods. I'd do everything in my power to see that such a horrible fate didn't befall Ashley. This shadow of impending doom wouldn't cloud the birth of my beloved daughter. With sheer determination I shook off the ominous feelings and continued writing her announcements.

Florida is hot in the summer, and I was very pregnant. I was thankful for air-conditioning, but even the shortest trips to and from the car were almost more than I could handle. Gatorade became my mainstay. Regardless of the discomfort, I gleefully awaited my little one's birth.

Finally the day arrived. I was awakened early in the morning by the telltale signs of labor. I called the birthing center and told them I'd be in shortly. I packed my bag and roused Steve.

We made it with plenty of time to spare, and the nurse quickly got me settled into a private room. The space was bright, cheerful, and painted a lovely, delicate yellow. One window overlooked the small parking lot, where I could see the marquee out front announcing the births of the day. Soon Ashley's name will be there too, I thought.

Before long the doctor entered the room, did a quick exam, and told me if all continued to go well we should have a baby by noon. And, fortunately, everything went just as planned. My beautiful daughter, Ashley, was born at 12:35—the perfect gift from God.

That evening Zachary was brought to the hospital to meet the newest member of our family. As Zack's smiling face came around the corner, I was overwhelmed by his innocence. He was just over two years old, but he was so bright, talking in complete sentences and already potty trained. I hugged him and introduced him to our adorable bundle. "This is Ashley," I said. "She's your new baby sister. It's your job now, as her big brother, to watch over her and make sure she doesn't get hurt. She's just a little baby and needs you to teach her all the things you've already learned."

He nodded and proudly said, "'K!" He tenderly reached out and held his sister's hand, then looked up at me expectantly.

As I read his heart's desire by the look in his eyes, I asked, "Do you want to hold her?" He nodded. He quickly clamored into the chair, ready to receive his sister. Steve gently placed her in his chubby little arms. "Now be very careful not to drop her. It will hurt her, and you don't want that to happen." He nodded. I watched carefully as he held Ashley and looked into her face for the first time. Tears immediately welled up in his eyes. "What's wrong, Zackie? Why are you crying?" I asked.

"I'm just so happy to have a baby sister." It was a sweet and tender moment that will remain with me forever.

Later that evening I prepared for my surgery by trying not to think about the finality of it all. I loved kids, and if I could afford it, I would have had ten, but I knew that wasn't possible. I asked Steve one more time if he'd consider having a vasectomy instead, but the issue was closed.

I was alone when they wheeled me into the operating room, and I watched as the anesthesiologist and the doctor prepared for surgery. My heart was racing, and the nurse noticed I was fearful. "Just relax. We'll take good care of you," she said. I simply nodded.

The doctor came and asked me once more, "Are you still sure you want to do this? We can call this off right now."

"No, I'm ready." I thought back to his previous warning. I was only twenty-six years old. Would I want more babies later? Would things change that drastically for me in the future? I couldn't see that far down the road. I just knew I was at the breaking point financially with the two children I already had. I had to go through with it.

As the anesthesia entered my veins, I wanted to scream "*Stop!*" But instead I bit my lip and succumbed to sleep. When I awoke the deed was done. I shed a few tears for lost possibilities, then went on with the business of living.

I took Ashley home and tried to make a go of our little family. But stability was short-lived. When Ashley was nearly one, it was time to move again. Steve's mother was ill and financially unable to keep her home. She'd sign the deed over to Steve if he'd move back to Oklahoma. Although I loved my home state, I agreed reluctantly, wondering how we'd ever find jobs in that remote corner of the world. Sure, it was closer to my roots, but his mother's house was twenty miles from any significant town, and at least forty from anywhere we might find work. Even though we wouldn't have to pay rent, we still had car payments and credit card bills that were astronomical. It was truly a leap of faith.

Also, for the first time in ages, I actually loved my job and could see a future with this company. My boss urged me to reconsider. He even offered me a general manager position at another location if I'd stay. I think he could tell I wasn't happy with the move, or perhaps he just didn't want to lose two of his managers at once. Whatever it was, it made me rethink my whole relationship with Steve, and even consider seriously the possibility of leaving.

In the end it was Zachary, almost three, and Ashley that kept us together. The thought that they would be without their father prompted me to pack up our things one more time and move halfway across the country to a future filled with even more uncertainty.

Back in Oklahoma, I tried to look on the bright side. I was happy the kids would get to know their paternal grandmother. It was obvious she cared for our children and was always good to them. But less then a year after we returned to Oklahoma, my mother-in-law died. Although we were not close, I felt sorry for Steve.

Not long afterward, I seriously considered leaving again. I'd known for a long time I was unhappy. I had known from the beginning I was not in love with this man. What I didn't realize was I had sacrificed everything that made me who I was. I no longer drew or painted. I no longer sang. I never went to art shows, musicals, or plays, all the things I'd so dearly loved before Steve and I got involved.

Our credit was maxed out, and it took everything we could do to keep our heads above water. I began stashing away money, a little at a time. I was preparing to leave. After all, I reasoned, I'd emotionally walked out the door long before.

Finally the time came. We went to my sister's wedding on May 2, 1993. At the reception I took my sister aside and asked, if the kids and I needed a place to stay for a while, could we depend on her? Without a moment's hesitation she agreed. Thank God for sisters.

After several surreptitious trips to Oklahoma City, I broke the news to Steve. It was over. I was going home to my family. All I wanted was the things I'd brought into the relationship, and my children. He could keep everything else, if he'd just let me go. In retrospect, I see that I gave up far too much, but at least I was out of a loveless relationship. All that mattered was coming back to people who loved me for who I was. I'd be home, where my heart had always been. Steve never saw it coming. He tearfully begged me to stay. "Please don't take my kids away from me. We really can't afford this."

Despite his objections, I shed the remnants of my past with relish. For the first time in ages, I looked forward to each passing day. Michael, who'd been divorced for years, and I picked things up almost where we'd left off twelve years before. While I was moving back and forth across the country, he'd been quietly living in Oklahoma raising his son, David. We quickly discovered each of us had been pining away for the other. Neither of us had been happy without the other. We both loved our children, and were both thankful for a second chance at happiness. It wasn't long before we decided to blend our families.

Michael's dad, always the practical man, asked his son, "Are you sure she isn't just looking for someone to raise her kids?"

Michael reassured him. "No, Dad, we really do love each other. It's the real thing this time."

Before long we went back to church—in fact, the very same church where we'd grown up, been baptized, and dated as teens. It was close to home, and besides, Michael's parents, Luther and LaRue, were both charter members there. Mike's brother Brad also attended, and sometimes his other siblings, Debbie and Mark, came by. It was a wonderful family atmosphere. There was no doubt; this was where we'd marry.

Soon wedding preparations were under way. Just a few months before the special day, Ashley and I made the short trip to the mall and purchased the prettiest little dress for her. She was going to be the flower girl, and she needed to be almost as fancy as her mom.

While I sewed my gown, we talked about every detail of the wedding, what she'd do as flower girl, and just how she'd look. Ashley was very feminine and loved to play dress-up. She'd take the remnants of my sewing and pin them on her Barbie dolls, or fashion them into delicate scarves. We had a great time preparing for the wedding. The moment we got home, carrying her dress with ruffles on the sleeves and skirt, she insisted on putting it on. "Oh my," I said. "You're just so pretty. We'll need to have your portrait made." And we did, just a few days before the wedding. To this day those pictures are some of my most priceless possessions.

Michael and I had decided Zack would carry the ring, and since his son, David, was older, he'd be the head usher. Michael's brother Mark would be the best man, and Darlene would be the matron of honor. It was a simple wedding, with only close family and friends in attendance. However, reciting our vows was extremely important to me, representing our public commitment to each other. The wedding didn't need to be spectacular or fancy, but it was crucial it be held in a church.

I asked my father to walk me down the isle. At first he said he wasn't up to it, he didn't feel well. He was afraid his ongoing breathing problems would make him start coughing in the middle of the ceremony. I was disappointed but reluctantly agreed. But my sister wasn't having any of it and, in the way only a sister can, she convinced my dad to fulfill my dream.

Finally the day arrived. On June 16, 1994, Michael and I were married. It was truly the happiest day of my life. The handiwork of our loved ones was everywhere. LaRue made some of her melt-in-your-mouth cookies, prepared a beautiful, fresh fruit tray, and used her craft expertise in decorating the church and the reception hall, where my sister and nieces joined in for good measure.

I was so proud walking down the aisle that day, holding my father's arm as we went to meet the love of my life, to be joined with my last chance at happiness. I kissed my daddy, then he handed me off to Michael, and I took his hand.

We stood before Reverend Rex Haymaker. As we recited our vows, great tears rolled down both our cheeks. Never before had either of us been so happy. It had taken us twelve years to get it right, but we'd finally made it.

At the reception LaRue hugged me as she whispered in my ear, "You are the daughter-in-law I always wanted for Michael. I love you, and welcome you to my family." It was the finest gift she could have offered. Her acceptance was so important to me.

We left the church in a horse-drawn surrey, provided by my sister and her husband. It wasn't a long ride, just four miles to our home, but it was romantic. The following morning we took off for a honeymoon with my dad's sailboat to one of the many nearby lakes. We'd planned on staying a full week, but I'd never been away from my children that long, and I missed them terribly. So we cut the romantic getaway short and came home to enjoy a little time with the kids before we went back to work.

Soon Mike and I were thoroughly involved in building a life together. It's hard work melding two families into one. Our house was small for five people, and with all my stuff, and all of Mike's things, we were cramped to the ceilings. We worked like mad every evening, and on weekends, clearing trees from around the house, with the intention of either building a new home or adding on to the one we already had.

Mike's dad had allotted him a corner of the family's 160-acre farm when he married the first time. After his divorce was final, Mike borrowed money from his father and purchased a small modular home. Even though Michael didn't actually own the land, it was never an issue. He knew, if worse came to worst, he could buy a plot from his dad later.

In our spare time we alternated between running kids to football and baseball practice. Since we both volunteered as Cub Scout leaders, we enrolled Zachary and David in that program as well. It was a real challenge trying to discover things the boys could learn that would earn them merit Scout badges, but we were having so much fun it didn't seem like work. I've always said Mike is just an overgrown Boy Scout anyway. He was able to draw upon his military and police training to help teach the boys camping skills and good citizenship.

One day we took the entire den of eight little Cubbies, along with Ashley, for a tour of the police station. We had a real hoot locking the boys in the jail cell. We let Ashley have the key. When it was time to let them out, she was too small to turn it, so I jumped in to help her.

Within moments the kids ganged up on Mike. Delighted, he let them put on the handcuffs and throw him in jail. Mike showed them the process of an arrest, and even made fingerprint cards for everyone. The trip taught them to respect the police and know them as friends. Many things we did offered hidden rewards. But most of the time just being together was enough.

Mike and I were looking forward to our first Christmas as a married couple. I'd started a new job in the insurance industry, trying to have a Monday through Friday position so I could be home with my children on the weekends. I'd just gotten home one evening when Michael met me at the door. "I have something terrible to tell you, honey. Your sister called and said your daddy passed away." The news hit me like a brick. I crumbled into a heap of tears as Michael held me.

"Mom is coming over to watch the kids, and I'll drive you down to the hospital where your family is gathering."

"What happened?" I asked. "He seemed to be improving and was actually getting out more lately. I just don't understand." My dad regularly needed the assistance of oxygen and was on constant medical care. He'd smoked nearly all his life, and his lungs just couldn't take it anymore. Despite the fact he tried to quit, he relied heavily on the stress relief the nicotine afforded him. Apparently he'd gotten into a coughing spasm and was unable to get to his medicine in time to stabilize himself. He was found dead in his easy chair on December 19, 1994, in front of his television watching football. I like to think that's how he wanted to go.

As hard as his death was, he'd prepared us for it for many years. We'd groan as he'd preface many statements with "After I die . . ." It was just Daddy's way, and we all understood. We also knew, very well, how Daddy wanted his affairs handled after he passed on.

As we went through the process of distributing and disposing of his worldly goods, we found ourselves mourning the loss of our mother all over again. So many of their years were wrapped around each other. Everywhere we looked we found remnants of her memory. It was apparent to us that Daddy still loved her and was still grieving her death, even after six years. We thought he'd gotten on with his life. He had a lady friend he'd dated steadily and went on long trips with, but he never remarried. Going through old photographs and personal items helped us finally come to peace with our mom's suicide. Daddy's funeral was a somber occasion but marked by the fitting tribute of him being laid to rest next to Mama. Side by side, just as they'd lived their lives.

The next few months were filled with discussions among my siblings about the distribution of the estate. The first thing we did was agree not to fight, because we knew Daddy would want it that way. If there was an issue, the item would simply be sold, or we'd do sealed bids to determine who took it.

My first selection was the sailboat. I had so many years of fond memories with Daddy on it and, most recently, our honeymoon. I just couldn't let it go. The rest was simply stuff, so we all managed to get through it without any hard feelings. Everything remained remarkably civil. I kept hearing my daddy's voice playing over and over in my head. "I don't want you all to fight over my things; it just isn't worth it. Try to get along."

As winter turned into spring we were wrapping up the estate, and I was ready to get back outside, put my hands in the soil, and nurture the outdoor foliage from seed to blossom. The previous summer my sister-in-law, Debbie, had added a water garden to her yard. It was so beautiful, I thought I'd give it a try too.

One afternoon as I was browsing through our local store, Ashley pointed out a little kit, complete with pump and liner, for a small water garden. I grabbed it and placed it in my cart, thinking how lucky I was to get the last one. Even though it was still far too cold to get serious about its construction, I'd have it ready for the first warm rays of sunshine. Ashley wanted to get started immediately and insisted we open the box as soon as we got home. Together we went through the kit, joyfully planning for the day we'd watch the water lilies blossom.

One crisp Sunday morning Rex preached a powerful sermon on spiritual gifts. I listened intently. "God has equipped you for service in his kingdom. It is up to you to use your gifts for his glory. Find your gift and use it." That morning I went forward to the altar and rededicated my life to Christ. It had been fourteen years since my baptism, but I was just now coming full circle, ready to start anew.

I prayed a simple prayer: "God give me a powerful message, with the opportunity to share it with a hurting world, and I will do your work."

I'd always wanted to get more involved with the church but never seemed to find my niche, a ministry that fit my personality or my busy lifestyle. But what message could I share with others? I knew my family had many crosses to bear. I knew my experiences with my mother's sickness, as well as my mistakes with Steve, could be a part of it. But I needed God to show me.

I left the altar with a newfound sense of hope. I'd started my life over, cleaned up my act, and was trying my best to make a difference in my family, my community, and my world. God would hear my prayer, of this I was certain. He would grant me a healing message to share with a hurting world. But in my calm assurance, little did I know just how my prayer would be answered, or how my quiet, happy life would be changed forever.

Three

Clouds on the Horizon

They are not long, the days of wine and roses:
Out of a misty dream,
Our path emerges for a while, then closes
Within a dream.

ERNEST DOWSON

Monday, April 17, 1995, approximately 5:30 P.M.

"Mommy, would you be sad if I died?"

I looked over at the seat next to mine and studied the face of my four-year-old daughter. We were on our way to soccer practice and, as usual, were in a hurry. There never seemed to be enough time.

In the morning I hurried to get everyone ready, then rushed over to Nana's, where I'd leave Ashley for the day. Then I'd rush to work, rush all day long, just to get in rush-hour traffic for my final rush home. But, as most parents have experienced, it didn't stop there.

We were running through life at a feverish pace. David, nine, and Zack, six, were Cub Scouts. Then there was soccer and football practice filling almost every waking hour. I had very little time to just be a mommy. Ashley asked, on several occasions, if she could play soccer or learn to dance, but I never enrolled her. I just couldn't imagine how I'd have time to take her somewhere too. But we did have special moments.

Ashley was always singing. I'd often find her performing for her dolls and stuffed animals. If she didn't know the song, she'd simply make one up. Perhaps her love for music came from my singing while she was still in the womb. Without a doubt music was a part of her life, her sense of joyous expression. But mostly I believe it was a reflection of her gentle, happy spirit.

Just the month before Ashley and I had gone to the Oklahoma Opry to see my niece Kristen perform. Ashley asked me why she couldn't go onstage and sing too. I tried to explain that she was too little. But when a young girl sang, Ashley became more determined. Finally I promised her, we'd look for a song to practice so she could perform later. For a moment that did the trick, but then, being the strong-minded child she was, she turned to me and said, "But, Mama, I already know lots of songs. I want to go now." I smiled when I thought back on her joyful determination. Could this be the same child now asking such a poignant question?

Studying her face intently, I searched for a reason, any reason, why she'd ask such a thing. Maybe she was thinking about Grandpa. My father's recent passing had been a highly emotional and traumatic time for the whole family. That must be it, I decided.

"Would you be sad if I died?" she asked again.

"Oh yes, honey," I said. "It would break my heart. I'd miss you so much. You know, you're my only baby girl."

"But, Mommy, I'd be in heaven with Jesus. I'd be an angel."

"I know that, honey, but I wouldn't be able to hold you and kiss you. I'd be so sad missing you, I wouldn't know what to do. Besides, you're already my little angel."

"I wouldn't want you to be sad."

"I couldn't help but be sad; I'd miss you so much."

She thought for a moment, and then everything seemed to change again. A brilliant smile lit up her face. "I love you, Mommy!"

"I love you too, baby."

Tuesday, April 18: I was rushing, as usual. Another day, another opportunity to do it all in record time. I'd started a new job the day before, and it was much more challenging than my previous temporary position as a receptionist. I was anxious to prove what I could do. This time I'd be working for Producers Co-op, a large cotton gin close to downtown. The country atmosphere suited me just fine; it was sort of like coming home. The drive was farther, but the extra pay made it worthwhile.

The offices were small yet comfortable. My boss, Dan, was a great man. Everyone was so helpful, I felt I'd be happy there.

After a full day at the office, I was headed for home. Exhausted, I was thankful for the few moments alone in the car. Tonight was Cub Scouts. Did I have the energy? Oh well, I'd muddle through somehow.

That evening after baths it was time for bed. As usual, Ashley called to me from her room, "A kiss and a hug for Mommy!" That was our routine, and she had it down pat. So, I hurried to her side, tucked her in, then took the lead while we recited prayers, her small voice echoing right behind mine. Although she knew them by heart, it was a game to her, a special time just with Mommy.

"Now I lay me down to sleep. I pray the Lord, my soul to keep. If I should die, before I wake, I pray the Lord, my soul to take." She threw her arms around my neck and gave me a fierce hug and kiss. "Mommy, I don't want to go to Nana's tomorrow," she said, a frown forming on her mouth.

"Why?" I asked.

"Because I want you to stay home and play with me," she said.

I gazed at her sadly. "Honey, you know Mommy has to work tomorrow. I want to, but I can't stay home."

Tears filled her eyes, and her lips started to tremble. "But, Mommy, I want you to stay home and play with me," she wailed. "I need you to stay and snuggle with me."

I took her in my arms and squeezed her tight. How I longed to grant her wish. But there were bills to pay, and they weren't going to go away by magic. "You love making necklaces, right? Maybe Nana will let you string some beads tomorrow."

She immediately brightened. "Ya think?"

"Well, yeah, if you ask her with your sweetest voice, and look at her with those big blue eyes, how could she say no?"

"Okay. I guess I will go to Nana's then." She smiled sweetly, giving me another hug.

"A kiss and a hug for Daddy," she called. That was it—my evening dismissal. I passed Mike in the hallway on his way to Ashley's bedroom. What a great stepfather he'd become. He'd been with the boys when he was summoned. We paused for just a moment, and quickly kissed.

"Don't forget to turn on her light," I reminded him. Ashley liked her small horse lamp left on. Like many children her age, She was afraid of the dark.

He rolled his eyes. "How could I forget?"

We chuckled, going our separate ways. Across the hall the boys were arguing as usual. I gently chastised them, kissed them good night, then shut the door behind me.

I took one last peek at Ashley. I found her snuggled deep in her bed, already asleep. As I paused to gaze at her beautiful porcelain face, with dark eyelashes swept across her cheeks, I felt, if only for a moment, I was beholding an angel.

Four

Thunderstorms

My eyes are red with weeping;

darkness covers my eyes.

Yet I am innocent,

and my prayer is pure.

O earth, do not conceal my blood.

Let it cry out on my behalf.

Even now, my witness is in heaven.

My advocate is there on high.

JOB 16:16–19 THE LIVING BIBLE (LIV)

A loud, annoying buzzer jolted me from my sleep. I hastily looked at the clock. It was 5:30 A.M. Turning off the alarm, I climbed out of bed and staggered to the bathroom. After my early routine I made a dash to the kitchen and started a pot of coffee. I glanced at Mike's face. He looked as worn-out as I did. There was no doubt about it, we just weren't morning people.

We watched the news on Channel 4, hardly mumbling a word. At 6:30, Mike dutifully rose, kissed me good-bye, and left for work. As soon as he shut the door, I hustled to the boys' room to get them going. It wasn't easy.

When I finally succeeded I headed toward Ashley's. Normally she was the first one up. She'd typically jump out of bed with a bounce in her step the minute she heard my voice. But that morning she was curled into a tight ball and had pulled a pillow firmly over her head.

"Come on, Ashley. It's time to get up."

"*Don't want to,*" she wailed, pulling the covers tighter around her.

"Come on! I don't have time to argue with you. Now here are some blue jeans and a T-shirt. Put these on while I look for your socks and tennis shoes." I glanced back and was surprised to find her scooted deeper under the blankets. I went to the bed and threw down the linens. "*Come on,*" I yelled.

"*Noooooooo,*" she wailed, snatching the covers back up like a protective cloak.

I couldn't understand it. Ashley was always the easiest one to wake. Unlike the rest of us, she was a morning person.

I began begging. "Ashley, you have to get up. You'll make Mommy late for work."

"Please, Mommy, stay home with me today." Fat tears poured down her cheeks.

Oh, how my heart ached. Given the choice, there was nothing I'd rather do. In fact, if I hadn't just started my job, I would have considered it. "Ashley, we went through this last night," I explained while helping her into her clothes. "You know I have to go to work. So you don't have a choice. You need to stay with Nana. Besides, why on earth are you acting like this today?"

"Because!"

"Because why?"

"Because I miss you so much!" She threw herself into my arms, and I held her close.

"I miss you too, and I'm sorry, but you know I have to go. Now what can Mommy do to make it better?"

"I don't know." She wept miserably as she wiped her nose with the back of her hand.

"Remember, you need to ask Nana if you can make string bead necklaces today."

Ashley nodded sadly and slid off her bed. She grabbed my hand as we walked to the kitchen together. In a moment the boys were trailing behind us.

"What's for breakfast, Mom?" David asked.

"Cereal. What else?" I said.

"Not again," Zachary moaned. "I hate cereal. Why do we have to eat that all the time?"

"You will need to get up a lot earlier if you plan on having something else. And if you get up earlier, then you'll have to go to bed earlier too. It's your choice." Zachary looked at me in frustration.

Ashley came closer while I poured the cereal into bowls. "Can I have mine in a bag?" she asked.

"Sure," I said, putting her cereal in a little zipper-lock container.

Satisfied, Ashley smiled, then scampered off to her room. She returned moments later with her hairbrush and a bow. We'd bought it the weekend before, and she'd proudly proclaimed it her new favorite accessory. I studied it closely. It was pink with "confetti," ribbons and sparkles. "Would you fix my hair, Mommy?" she asked sweetly.

"Sure," I said, as I began brushing her honey-colored hair back into a ponytail. I wondered how any child of mine had managed to have such straight hair. I shook my head and giggled as I carefully attached the bow in place.

She turned and gazed up at me. "Am I beautiful?" she asked, striking the pose of a fashion model.

"Absolutely gorgeous! Are you ready to go?" Ashley nodded.

"Boys, go get in the car. Ashley, you too."

I turned to collect my purse and keys, then headed for the door. I saw Ashley rounding the corner, clutching her stuffed cat. "Can I bring Kitty-Kitty to Nana's?" she asked, rolling her baby blues up in an imploring gaze.

"Oh no, honey. Put him away. He'll get dirty, and then he can't sleep with you anymore. Besides, you have so many toys there now." She looked disappointed but ran to her room and placed him back on her bed. When

Uncle Mark had given her Kitty-Kitty for Christmas, Ashley had immediately declared it her new "special friend."

She loved her dolls and stuffed pets. I'd often find her in her room
brushing Barbie's hair and talking to her animals as if they could answer.
Each one had a specific place on her bookshelf. But as special as these dolls
were, Kitty-Kitty was her favorite. He shared her bed at night and warmed
her pillow during the day. Each evening before she fell asleep, she'd hug
him tightly, drape her little arm across his sleek body and pull him as close
as she could.

Ashley ran through the house toward the car while I locked the door
and followed. We drove the short distance to Nana's house.

The minute we arrived everyone piled out of the car. The boys ran
ahead, but Ashley quietly walked with me, holding my hand.

As we stepped up into the house, I made an observation: Mike and I
needed to fix Mom's back stoop. Her house was old but comfortable, like
a cozy, favorite shirt. Mom had patched the historic site together for years.
Little by little it was getting done. She and Luther had moved in when
Mike was just eight years old. Debbie, Mike's little sister, had been born
there. When my in-laws bought the place, they were told the house should
be condemned. For a while Mom thought about it, but soon she came to
love the old home for all its country charm and history. As the years passed
a deeper affection began to grow. Sheetrock in this room, wallpaper in that
room, a little fix for the roof, and before she knew it the house became liv-
able. Mom was proud of her home and loved restoring it bit by bit, sav-
ing every nickel and dime for each phase. She was a homemaker in every
sense of the word, and this house was her warm and safe nest. Lately,
though, she'd become discouraged with its progress. Ever since she suffered
a back injury at work, things had taken much longer to finish. Some days
she couldn't even straighten up. Although she was only fifty-five, sometimes the pain made her look much older.

"Good morning," she sang out. No matter how tired she was, or how
much pain she endured, Mom was always glad to see us and was always
up for a hug from her grandchildren. That morning she was still in her
nightgown and bathrobe. Her long, silver-gray hair hung in a disheveled
braid across her shoulder. She sat in her rocking chair, watching the news

and drinking coffee. The stove was slightly lit, just enough to take the chill off the morning. She stretched her slippered feet next to the heat. Jasper, Debbie's little golden cocker spaniel, lay close by.

"Are you boys ready for school?" she asked.

"Well, I'd rather stay home," David said.

"Me too," Zack chimed in.

"So you want to stay here and torment me?" she said. "I don't think so."

The boys giggled, then changed the channel to cartoons. They quickly found their favorite spot on the floor while they waited for the bus.

Nana was a wonderful baby-sitter. Mike's sister and brother also entrusted their little ones to her. Since she'd hurt her back, she was mostly confined to her house. But because she and Dad had a limited income, she really needed the extra money, and we needed a loving, reliable baby-sitter. So she watched the grandchildren while we worked. And the children loved her. She'd bake cookies and cinnamon rolls almost daily and she always had ample crafts supplies—beads and scraps of cloth.

LaRue was the happiest person I knew. Content with her marriage and how her children had been raised, she always had something cheerful to say. LaRue was gifted with creative talents. She was constantly cooking, sewing, or working in her garden. She'd gently caress her projects as if they were her offspring. And the satisfaction I saw on her face when she completed each one was priceless. I loved to watch her hands. Her motions were so expressive; it was almost like watching a ballerina. She had long, graceful fingers and carefully groomed nails. She usually wore her long hair in a tight bun on her neck, or a French braid down her back. But the best thing was when she freed it. I loved to watch the interplay of her hands and hair as she brushed and braided the delicate, silver strands. LaRue was a beautiful woman from the inside out.

I sat on the piano bench, and Ashley climbed into my lap. She was absently playing with a small toy she'd found. Mom and I chatted for a few minutes. Then I rose to go. As usual, I hugged and kissed the kids and admonished them to behave. As I moved forward Ashley ran ahead of me and threw her back against the door. She stretched her arms out wide, blocking my way, bracing her feet and smiling mischievously.

"What are you doing?" I laughed.

"You can't go." She giggled.

"Oh, yes I can. I'll just pick you up and move you. Now will you let me go?"

"Not until you give me a big hug and kiss." She giggled again.

"But I already gave you a hug and a kiss." We were both enjoying the game.

"But, Mommy, I need another one!"

I crouched low, and Ashley ran toward me. I scooped her up, and she immediately threw her arms around my neck and offered me a tight bear hug. Then she leaned back, smiled, and pressed her lips to mine as hard as she could. We finished by rubbing noses. I held her for a minute and whispered, "Mommy's got to go, baby." I smiled as I watched Ashley's golden ponytail swish from side to side while she slid from my arms and ran to the living room to play, giggling all the way. What a lucky mom I am, I thought.

I stepped outside to a cloudless Oklahoma sky. There was a slight nip in the early spring air. LaRue's forsythia bush was in full bloom, and the fragrance filled my senses. I started my car, turned up the radio, and backed out of the drive. How I loved to watch the Oklahoma sky. I'd never lived anywhere with sunrises and sunsets as breathtaking as ours. Sure I'd enjoyed aspects of Florida and California, but at heart I was just like Dorothy—for me there was no place like home. As I drove past fields of ripening wheat into the city, I hummed and sang along to my favorite taped show tune, "Oh, What a Beautiful Mornin'," from *Oklahoma*. Yes, it was a beautiful morning and a glorious day. Everything seemed right with the world. No doubt about it, I was blessed.

I arrived at the office at 8:00 and immediately dove into my work. Even though I was still new, and hadn't yet developed a routine, I was determined to do well and work independently. It was relatively quiet, just a few calls and a few pickups at the silos.

April 19, 1995, 9:02 A.M.

In the still of the morning my concentration was broken by an enormous blast. Everything on my desk shifted to one side. Gary, one of the salesmen who shared my office, and I ran to the windows to see what was wrong. "Is it the grain elevator?" I asked. We looked toward the compound first, but everything appeared all right. Then Gary pointed to a cloud of dust rising over the city skyline. We watched in amazement as the dust cloud turned into thick, black smoke.

"That's downtown," he exclaimed. "Whatever it is, it's big!"

"I wonder if there was a building being demolished this morning?"

He looked at me. "Not that I know of, Kathleen. Besides, those things are usually publicized."

Just then my boss, Dan, and our office administrative assistant, Cindy, joined us at the window. "Maybe we should turn on the TV and see if there's something on the news," she said.

I walked to the cubicle next to mine and switched on the TV. I flipped through the channels till I came across a station with a view of downtown. It was the Channel 9 TowerCam. In all the confusion the report said there'd been an explosion at the federal courthouse. "Police and Fire in the vicinity have all been activated. Helicopters are being sent in. Please stand by," the reporter implored.

We clustered tightly around the TV, shocked and horrified as the first pictures came across our screen. There was a large building; it seemed at least ten stories. A huge chunk of the structure was gone, exposing the interior. Large slabs of concrete were hanging like sheets inside the crater. Paper streamed like confetti from the open wound of the building. Nearby cars were on fire, and sirens were going off everywhere. "Look at that," Dan shouted. "At least a third of the building is gone."

"Which building is it?" I asked.

"I can't tell yet," he said.

Soon the reporters had more information. It was the federal building, not the courthouse. Hundreds had been injured or killed. Traffic was blocked; ambulances couldn't get through. A desperate call went out for doctors, nurses, off-duty police officers, firefighters, anyone who had first aid training, anyone who could offer help.

Then came the footage that made me shudder. Terrified, injured people were pouring out of the area. We all stood transfixed. Suddenly Dan turned around. "I have to go and see if I can help," he said as he grabbed his jacket and cellular phone. We didn't watch him leave. We were far too involved with the news. Tears welled up in my eyes as I watched the injured carried on stretchers and the walking wounded staggering out.

I mumbled, "It would be nothing short of a miracle if anyone else makes it out alive." Everyone nodded in agreement. My eyes fixated on a young woman in obvious panic. I could read her lips as she screamed, "My baby, my baby!" Oh my God, I thought. There is a child in that building!

I felt helpless, ashamed I had not paid more attention to my first aid training so I could help. I was the only female child in my family who'd decided against nursing as a career. Sighing, I returned to my desk. I could still see the TV screen from a distance, and I knew there was nothing I could do. I felt I should go back to work.

Then the reporter offered more horrible information. There was a day-care center in the building. The children! My tears started coming hard as pictures of bloodied and burned little ones were released, some being rescued from across the street at the YMCA. Again I saw a young mom in a panic trying to find her missing child. She had fragments of glass and concrete covering her shirt and hair. She'd been very near. What if they were my children? Helplessly I sat there trying to work with tears rolling down my cheeks. I silently prayed for their protection. Thank God no one I knew could possibly be in that building. My boys were safe at school, and Ashley was at home with Nana.

Suddenly Cindy's voice came over the intercom. "Kathleen, you have a telephone call. It's your sister."

"Hello, Darlene."

"Kathleen?"

"Yes."

"Oh thank God!" My sister burst into tears. "I didn't know if you'd been hurt. I've been trying to call you for about an hour. I was so worried. I want you to come home."

"No," I said. "You know I just started this job. I need to stay here. Maybe I can think of some way to help."

"Please come home," she begged me.

"I can't, Darlene. I need to stay until they tell me to go. Do me a favor, though. Call Mom and tell her I'm all right." I gave her the number, quickly hung up, and immediately resumed my TV vigil. Within ten minutes the phone rang again. This time, since Cindy was away from her desk, I picked it up.

"Producers Co-op."

"Kathleen?" It was my sister again.

"Yes."

She took a deep, trembling breath. "Where is Ashley?"

"What do you mean? She's with Nana, of course."

There was a long pause. Darlene took another long breath, then slowly went on. "Didn't you know she and Luther had an appointment with Social Security this morning?"

"Well, yes."

"Kathleen, the Social Security office is in the federal building. It's in that building that's on the news."

"No it's not," I argued. "Social Security is at the Capital Complex across town."

"No," she said flatly. "Remember I worked at the VA? Social Security is in that building, the one on TV. I just talked to your brother-in-law, Brad, and he said his parents had an early appointment, but he didn't know what time it was supposed to be."

Suddenly her words hit home. "Oh my God, Ashley! She can't be in that building!" I burst into tears. "I have to go down there and find her."

"Kathleen, they won't let you near the place. Why don't you start by calling the hospitals?"

"I have to go. I've got to find my baby!" My hands were trembling, and I began to shake violently.

By that time everyone in the office had heard my cries and gathered around me. I looked up to see their worried expressions. "My baby," I cried. "My baby is in that horrible place!" Gasps circled the room.

"Kathleen, they have a number for the Red Cross," Dan said. "Let me get it for you."

Cindy added, "I'll get the numbers for the hospitals and help you start calling."

Panicked, I snatched up the phone and called Mom's house. Brad answered.

"Brad?"

"Yes."

"What's going on? Where are Mom and Dad?" I almost begged.

"You don't know?" he asked.

"No. They were home when I left this morning. Dad was in the bathroom getting dressed."

He took another breath. "They told me yesterday they had an early appointment with Social Security. I guess that's where they went. Where's Ashley?" His voice cracked as he asked the question. He already knew the answer, but, as I, had refused to believe it.

"She's with Mom and Dad." A new flood of tears assailed me. Dear God, I thought, not my Ashley.

"Look," he said, "I'm going downtown to see if I can find them."

"I need to call all the hospitals and see if she's there," I said frantically. "Then I have to call the Red Cross, and I still need to contact Mike."

"Okay," he said. "I have your office number, and I'll call you if I find them. Here's my pager number. If you find them first, please page me."

We hung up, and I immediately dialed the Red Cross. It took almost ten minutes before the phone rang. Finally I had someone on the line. "Hello, is this the Red Cross?" I asked.

"Yes," said the female on the other end. "How can I help you?"

"I'm looking for my little girl." A fresh onslaught of tears hit me.

"Can you tell me what she looked like?" she asked solemnly. "How old is she? What is she wearing?"

I took a deep breath. "She's four and a half. She has blond hair, blue eyes, and is about three feet, six inches tall. She has a chubby, round face with a dimple in her left cheek. She was wearing Lee blue jeans, a gray T-shirt with red and white writing, a baseball team or something, and she had a long-sleeved denim shirt jacket on over that. She had on pink and white tennis shoes with white socks."

"Just a minute." The woman laid the phone down, and I heard her inquiring in the background. Moments later she returned. "I'm sorry, ma'am," she said. "There aren't any children here that fit that description. Have you called Children's Hospital or St. Anthony's yet? Some of the kids have been transported to those facilities. You might try there."

"Thank you," I sobbed.

"Ma'am, I'm sorry she wasn't here. I really hope you find her."

After that every call was the same. I dialed each hospital, checking to see if any new children had been brought in.

Then I called Mike at work. Because he's a welder in a machine shop, I couldn't speak to him directly, so I asked to leave a message. The receptionist transferred me to Sherri McCall, the assistant personnel director and a high school classmate of mine.

"This is Sherri."

"Sherri, this is Kathleen Treanor. I have to get in touch with Michael immediately. We're not sure, but we think his mom, dad, and Ashley were involved in the bombing."

"Oh God!"

"I know he's at lunch right now, but he usually sits in the parking lot outside. Could you or someone else give him the message to call right away?"

"Yes. I will make absolutely sure this is taken to him immediately."

"Thank you, Sherri."

I knew Sherri was good for her word. I hung up the phone, then rested my head on my desk while I tried to collect my thoughts. Dear God, what do I need to do next? I have to find my baby, but how? The police aren't letting anyone downtown. How can I get to her? I have to do something.

The phone rang again. It was Mike. "Kathleen? What's up?"

I was so thankful to hear his voice, I began sobbing uncontrollably. We'd been married for less than a year, but Mike was my soul mate. He was the perfect husband—always romantic, attentive, and caring. He looked upon my children as his own and loved them unconditionally. So many times he'd thanked me for giving him a little girl. "Looking at Ashley is like looking at you when you were small. I can just imagine you at that age," he'd tell me. Mike was a strong, practical man. I never saw anyone, or anything, get the better of him. He was a reserve police officer in our little town, and a first sergeant in the Oklahoma National Guard— the youngest "Top" in the Guard. Mike's always been proud to serve his country, and I was proud of him. When my dad died, he was there to comfort me. He cried with me and we held each other, but mostly he held me together. There was no doubt about it; this was the voice I needed to hear. Mike was my hero.

"Did you know there's been a bombing downtown?" I asked him.

"Yes, one of the guys back in power assembly told me. He said they were activating the National Guard and expected me to get a call soon to go down and work."

I tried to get control of myself. "Honey, I just talked to Brad. He was at your mom and dad's house when I called a few minutes ago. As far as the two of us can figure, Mom, Dad, and Ashley are in that building. We aren't sure when their appointment was, but we do know they had one scheduled for this morning at the Social Security office. Brad has gone downtown to look for them."

"Naaww, their appointment was at the Jim Thorpe Building over by the Capitol," he insisted. "No, wait a minute, Social Security is a federal agency; it would have been in that building." There was a huge pause as he digested the truth of what he had just said. "Oh God."

I went on. "Do you know if Mom was going with Dad or not?"

"I'm not sure," he said. "They were talking about it a bit last night, but I was only half listening. I think they were planning on going together, but I'm not sure."

"Brad couldn't find their appointment card. Do you remember what time they were supposed to be there?"

"No, but I do remember it was in the morning."

"Listen, I just heard on TV they're setting up an information area down at St. Anthony's Hospital. Let's go and check the lists for their names. I need you," I almost begged.

"Do you want me to come and pick you up?" he asked.

"Yes, oh yes, I need you here. Please hurry."

"Okay, honey, hold on, I'm on my way."

I replaced the receiver, then immediately jerked it out of its cradle and started calling the hospitals again. At that moment Dan came in. "Kathleen, they have more information at St. Anthony's—names, or descriptions, of wounded being channeled to other hospitals. Come on, I'll take you there."

"I can't leave yet. My husband is on the way. We're going to go there when he arrives."

Cindy came in and handed me my purse. "Look," she said, "when he gets here, I'll tell him where you've gone. Now go, see if you can find your Ashley." I looked into her large brown eyes and saw genuine compassion. She hugged me. "You just be sure to call and tell us what's happenin'," she said in her southern drawl. "You let us know how we can help. Okay?" She pushed me after Dan.

I hurried outside to Dan's red Ford truck and climbed into the cab. I have vague images of streets and buildings passing by, but I cannot remember much else. I simply sat, staring blankly out the window, whispering prayers the entire way. "Dear God, not my sweet baby. What did she do to deserve this? This can't be happening to my family, my happy family. She's still alive. There is still hope. I'm going to find her. Please, dear God, I have to find her."

Suddenly the truck came to a stop. We were as close as we could get. We parked in someone's yard about two blocks away and raced on foot the rest of the way. When we reached the hospital several people met us outside. I asked a young man where the lists of names were. "My daughter, my baby, I've got to find my baby."

"Follow me," he said. He led us through the hospital and downstairs, where many families of missing persons were gathered. There were two large tables set up with four women seated behind them. Papers were scattered everywhere. Each woman had a phone. All of them rang incessantly. I got in a line of desperate people, all with horror written across their faces, and tried to regain my composure while I waited my turn.

Finally I was next. "My name is Kathleen Treanor. My daughter, my mother-in-law, and father-in-law may have been in that building. They had an appointment with Social Security . . ." I trailed off miserably. "Please tell me you've found them."

"I'm not showing their names, but you're welcome to look on the wall and see if anyone new has been posted." She pointed through the open doorway and picked up the nearest ringing phone. I ran to the wall where the names were posted on huge sheets of paper. I pored over the lists carefully, searching for a sign of any of them. But I found nothing. When I came to the end of the list, a heart-wrenching sob burst from my lips. I sat down in the nearest chair, put my head in my hands, and wept uncontrollably. Dan stood behind me and gently squeezed my shoulder.

One by one nurses, pastors, and volunteers came to me offering words of hope and comfort. "I just talked with two people who were in the Social Security office," one said "and they came out all right. There is still hope." Her promise helped me regain some control.

During the entire ordeal a wonderful woman, Roberta Donaldson, sat with me. She was a nursing home administrator and didn't know how to help except to sit, listen, and cry. She told me over and over, "Whatever you need, I'll see to it you get it." That seemed to be the consensus of people everywhere. But in reality none of them would be able to give me what I truly needed. This kind woman continued to hold my hand, following me wherever I went, offering me tissues and trying, in the only way she knew how, to comfort me simply by listening. As long as I live I will never forget Roberta.

Dan stayed about thirty minutes, until Mike arrived. I was so glad to see him, I threw my arms around his neck and sobbed on his shoulder. Dan took that opportunity to hand me his cellular phone. "Here, take this," he said. "Use it however you need and as much as you need. I don't know how much battery is left, but I hope it holds out." With that he shook Mike's hand, squeezed my shoulder, and turned and left.

Mike and I waited the remainder of the day. We were joined by 150 to 200 others, all seeking news about loved ones, and all in various stages of shock. Every time a new name was posted, we'd run, to the wall to see if anything had changed in our world. But for Mike and me, it was always the same. Each time we'd come away miserably disappointed.

During the middle of the afternoon I looked up and saw our friend John Mobley, the hospital administrator. John's son Benjamin was a sweet little neighbor boy who came home from school every day with my sons. Mom would watch them for about fifteen to twenty minutes until Mike got there around four. Then all the children would come to our house until I got home. Zachary and Benjamin were best friends. Over the course of the school year Ben's mom and dad, and Mike and I, had started a great friendship. When we explained why we were waiting, his face fell.

He seemed to know what we didn't; there was little hope. "Is there anything I can do?" he asked. I shook my head.

"Mike," I said, "my car. The co-op will close soon, and the compound will be locked."

John hesitantly asked, "Would you like me to move it to the parking garage across the street?"

"Oh no, that would be too much to ask," Mike said.

"No, really, it's no trouble at all. After all, it's the least I can do."

Soon we relented. "We are lucky to have such nice friends," I said. Mike nodded in agreement.

A few moments later I saw an acquaintance, Jeff Welch, manager of Little Caesars, carrying an armload of pizza boxes. When he came back I grabbed his arm. He looked shocked to see me. "Kathleen, what are you doing here?"

"It's Ashley. We think she's in there with Mom and Dad."

"Oh God. Is there anything we can do for you? Have you eaten yet? Can I get you some pizza?"

"No thanks, Jeff. I'm not really hungry."

He nodded in understanding. "Just let me know if there's anything we can do for you. Okay?" With that he squeezed my arm and walked purposefully away. Jeff and Little Caesars had set up an impromptu restaurant near the coordination site. Food was being funneled in free of charge to keep rescue personnel fueled for the enormous job.

Everyone was genuinely concerned and trying to help. No one knew just how to respond, but each person in their own way did the best they knew how. Each shed a little light, trying desperately to overcome the darkness. I watched with both pride and horror as people rose to the occasion. Early on one reporter asked, "Can they handle this? How could they possibly be prepared to handle this in Oklahoma?" But the people of my state responded with dignity and compassion. It wasn't the first time we'd had to deal with devastation. Our state was often rocked with floods and tornadoes. We had overcome the destruction of the Dust Bowl. Now we had this.

Periodically we'd call Debbie. She'd decided to stay by the phone in case Mom, or someone else, called with news. And she was there for the boys when they came home from school. She was having a rough time too. Mom was her best friend. They were so close that when Debbie was pregnant with her daughter, Nikki, Mom had a dream about it before Debbie even mentioned her pregnancy. Debbie was still hoping for a miracle. So were we.

Later that evening an announcement came over the intercom. The First Christian Church at Thirty-sixth and Walker had opened its doors as a place of refuge to anyone who wanted to come. There was food, pillows, and blankets to make us comfortable. All future news would be directed there.

We prepared to move to the church by calling home. The battery on the cellular had given out, so we searched for a pay phone. First we called Debbie. We told her where we were headed and asked if she'd talked to Brad.

"No," she said, "and I've paged him several times. I just wish he'd call and tell me something. I spoke with Mark, though. He was on his way to an interview in Dallas but is coming home now. He should be here later tonight."

"Well," Mike said, "there's nothing you can do except wait. We'll try to keep you as informed as we are. So far, they're not telling us much."

After we hung up I immediately called Darlene. We related our plan to move and told her there was still no news. She'd been busy calling all our family. She said our cousin Earl and aunt Macy were on their way. I explained that their coming might not be a wise idea, since we might not know anything for days.

"You're probably right," she offered. "I'll call them back and tell them to wait until we know something. I also got through to Steve. Kathleen, do you want me to come down to the church to be with you?"

"No, that won't be necessary. That is, unless you want to come . . ." Darlene got my message loud and clear and promised to join us soon.

Hanging up the phones, we hugged Bobbie good-bye and thanked her for her kindness. Then Mike and I ran to our truck. We were afraid of missing important updates.

Before we knew it we were in the church parking lot. It looked as if the entire city's news stations had converged on the sanctuary. When we walked inside we were asked our names. A volunteer told us we'd be called shortly and pointed to where we should wait. Again we dutifully complied. We scanned the room for familiar faces from the hospital. We saw a few, but mostly these seemed to be different people. Across the room food was being piled on large tables, and volunteers were offering plates with gentle smiles. However, few partook of the donated bounty.

Before we knew it our name was called. Mike and I looked at each other, then hurried over to the table, pushing our way through the crowd.

"We are the Treanors," Mike said.

"Come with me over here," replied one of the male volunteers. We were led to the opposite side of the room, where we sat down at a table. What they hadn't explained at St. Anthony's was this was where the medical examiner was getting physical descriptions of victims. I was shocked when asked to describe Ashley so she could be "identified through forensics." The phrase brought on visions of utter destruction. How could it have come to this? How could my little girl need identification through birthmarks or dental records?

During this interview I looked up and saw at least two or three TV stations setting up. As far as I could tell they hadn't talked with any family members. The Channel 4 news reporter was crying. She passed me, offering sympathetic glances as she dabbed her eyes with a tissue and tried to steady herself for her report. None of that mattered. I didn't care for sympathy. I just wanted Ashley. I wanted someone, anyone, to bring me my baby! And if that meant talking to every reporter, every rescue worker, everyone, then that was exactly what I'd do.

Through waves of tears I described everything Ashley was wearing that day, right down to her little panties and socks. The examiner asked me if she had any scars or marks that would help identify her. I looked at him, horrified he'd ask such a thing. He apologized and explained that he needed to be thorough. I nodded and thought for a minute. Her dental records—she'd had a crown on one of her back molars. That was all I could think of, that was just all.

Then he moved on to Luther and LaRue. What were they wearing? I didn't know, because Mom had still been in her nightgown and bathrobe when I saw her that morning. I crumbled, and Mike took over. With each of the examiner's questions hopelessness washed over me. I tried desperately to hold back a scream.

Enough! I had to go down there and find them! Luther and LaRue were such wonderful people. Perhaps they'd just stayed, trying in their own way to help with the rescue. They were just in shock and hadn't thought to call. Or maybe if we checked the morgue ourselves, at least we'd know if they were there. Then the waiting would be over. I explained my plan to Mike.

The volunteer just shook his head. "That wouldn't be a good idea," he said. "If she's out there, she is being well cared for. Besides, they're not letting anyone in the perimeter unless they're police, fire, or medical."

Now I was furious! This was my little girl. She would be scared and hungry. I gazed outside. The sun would be going down soon. Once it did the temperature would drop drastically. Ashley would be cold. It had been too warm that morning for a coat, and I'd dropped her off in only a light shirt jacket. Waves of protective instinct hit me. The thought of my baby girl suffering when I couldn't help was too much to handle. I was being bombarded with mental pictures of the horrible footage of burned and bloodied children. Every image became Ashley. Reports of a child's hand found in the street became Ashley's. People in body bags all became Ashley. I started to rock, moan, and cry. People came and went, but I paid them no notice.

At one point my cries got so out of hand we were led to a private room in the back of the church. There two young counselors from Tulsa sat with us and "validated" our feelings. I was angry with them. Who were they to tell me how I should or shouldn't feel? I said nothing and quietly succumbed to the darkness.

Suddenly Darlene burst into the room. We held each other and cried. She'd just spoken to our brother Ralph. Years before Ralph had been in Vietnam and was still dealing with horrible memories. She wasn't sure he could handle the news. But when she told him he began to relay the last conversation he'd had with Ashley. The kids and I had gone out to his farm to dig up and transplant some of my mama's flowers. Ashley had followed him around trying to get his attention. Ralph said he'd been ignoring her, so she tackled him. She threw herself into a bear hug around his legs and wouldn't let go until he picked her up, talked to her, and let her kiss him. I smiled when I thought of my big, tough, thick-skinned brother melting under Ashley's touch. The image of David and Goliath took shape. My daughter knew no strangers and loved everyone. So I wasn't surprised by the story a bit. It was just her way.

Our pastor, Rex Haymaker; Wayne Russell, the Sunday School director; and Barbara Murray, one of the ladies from our church, all filed in. I was glad to see each of them. Rex embraced me in a fierce hug while I wept. I pulled back and asked him, "What kind of animal does things like this to innocent children?"

"It is evil, and evil does not protect anyone to reach its means," he answered. "Always remember, this was an act of evil. God did not do this."

I nodded and once again slipped into a semiconscious state. I vaguely heard Mike and Darlene filling them in but couldn't bring myself to participate in the conversation.

"Here, drink this," my sister said. I shook my head and turned away.

"Kathleen, if Ashley is alive, she's probably hurt, and if that's the case, she'll need you to be strong. If you make yourself sick, you won't be able to do that. So come on, drink something."

I took the drink. She was right. I had to be strong, for Ashley, for the boys, and for Mike. I could not allow any more hurt for my family.

The boys! No one had told the boys! But how do you tell a six- and a nine-year-old that not only their nana and granddad but their baby sister were involved in this horrible explosion? I thought of how David would take the news. Nana was the one he went to when he needed a hug. She was always there.

Then there was Zachary. He'd cried the day Ashley was born, because he was so happy to have a sister. They'd been constant companions since he was two. As much as they fought, as brothers and sisters will, it was obvious Zack loved Ashley. He was her big brother, and he took his protective job seriously.

A volunteer interrupted my thoughts. She wanted to know if we'd be staying at the church all night. Mike and I looked at each other.

"Don't you think you'd be more comfortable at home?" Darlene asked.

"No, Darlene. I want to be here, if they find her."

"Kathleen, you need to understand"—she hesitated for a moment, then went on—"it's been too long. They probably won't find her alive."

I shook my head. "She can't be dead. Don't say that!"

"Look," she said tenderly. "I've been a nurse a long time. With trauma like this, there's very little hope she's still alive. Go home, Kathleen, where you are comfortable, and get some sleep. I'll stay here and call you the minute I hear anything."

"So you'll be staying through the night," one of the counselors asked.

"I will," Darlene said.

I turned to Mike. "Take me home."

Once again I slipped into oblivion. I heard background voices, almost a whirlwind sound, but couldn't make out what anyone was saying. How could my sister have given up so soon? Until we knew there was still hope. I tried desperately to believe God wouldn't allow anything to happen to them. They were good Christians. The Lord would protect them; everyone would see. God would send a legion of angels to keep them from harm. Thoughts of Mom and Dad, and how devoted they were to their church, flooded my mind. If anyone belonged to God, they did.

All the way home I thought about when Mike and I were teenagers. I remembered how instrumental Mike's parents were in getting us involved in the church. How readily they'd accepted me as part of their family. And when I went away, how fiercely LaRue had protected her son. Then finally, after eleven years of being separated and making our own share of mistakes, how quickly they once again accepted me into their family. That kind of love is rare.

During the thirty-minute drive to pick up the boys, I lay my head in Mike's lap as he gently caressed my hair. When we pulled into Debbie's driveway I sat up and tried to prepare myself. Soon we'd have to tell them. They'd need me to be strong.

"What in the world are we going to say?" Mike asked.

"The truth," I whispered. Whatever that is, I thought.

We got out of the car and walked to Debbie and Buddy's door. Debbie was clutching Nikki tightly, and her eyes were rimmed in red. Instantly we were enfolded in a fierce clutch and sobbed into each other's shoulders. "Do you know anything about my parents and Ashley?" she asked.

"No, nothing," I said, staring meaningfully into her eyes. "Where are the boys?"

"In the bedroom playing," she said.

"Do they know?"

"No. I didn't know what to tell them. They kept asking me what was wrong, and why wasn't Nana at home today, but I couldn't tell them." She looked down at the floor, and her lips trembled. Buddy paced in the background next to Mike.

"Honey," I said, "we have to do this."

"I know," he said, "let's get it over with."

We called the boys into the room. As their bright, happy faces rounded the corner, I dreaded taking their innocence away. I motioned Zack to me, and David went to Mike. We faced each other with the boys on our laps.

"Do you know about the bombing?" I asked.

Zack said, "They were talking about it at school."

David added, "They said on the news a lot of people had been hurt and some were killed."

I nodded. "Yes, honey, but that's not the really bad part." I took a deep, trembling breath. "This morning Nana, Granddad, and Ashley were all in that building."

"Were they hurt?" David blurted out, tears filling his eyes.

Again I took a deep breath. "We're not sure yet, baby. No one's been able to find them. That's where we've been all day, looking for them."

"Is Ashley all right?" Zack asked, staring intently into my eyes.

I had never lied to him before. I couldn't start now. I pulled him into a tight hug. "I don't know for sure yet, but the reports say everyone who got out alive has already been found. I've been calling and calling, and no one has seen Ashley, Nana, or Granddad." I let this sink in. "We might not ever get to see them again, but we cannot give up hope just yet. They haven't been found, but maybe a miracle will happen for us, if we pray our special prayers tonight. We have to pray they're not hurting somewhere."

"All right." He nodded as he laid his head on my shoulder.

"Let's go home now and try to get some rest." With that we stood up to leave. We looked over at Debbie and Buddy. They were still talking to their sons, Tyler and Chris.

We stumbled to the truck. My mind wandered to Luther and LaRue. When I was young I'd prayed I'd find the kind of love they shared. Luther and LaRue went everywhere together. It was obvious, by their words and actions, they were still in love. When Mom and Dad went somewhere in the truck, she'd scoot over as close to him as she could get, and they'd hold hands just like teenagers.

Only two Christmases ago Dad had bought her a diamond wedding ring to symbolize their unending love and stashed it in a box of chocolates. I saw the mischief in his eyes as he urged LaRue to open it and sample the candy. She was so ecstatic when she discovered what was inside. At times I almost sensed electricity pass between them. Without a doubt they had a love most people only dream of. Yet, they always said, without God in their life their marriage might not have lasted. Luther and LaRue knew where to place their gratitude.

I tossed my head from side to side. I couldn't believe this was happening again. I was still mourning my own mother's death, I grieved for the knowledge she'd never know my children. Of course LaRue could never take Mama's place, but she filled a need in me that no one else could. I guess, even at my age, I still desired a mother—if nothing more than someone to advise me and to offer mature answers to some of life's questions. LaRue had a way of offering heartfelt wisdom completely born from love.

Over time we'd grown to count on Mike's parents' strength. How could we possibly make it through this crisis without their wise counsel? If only I could talk with them. But that was impossible, because they were lost, along with Ashley, somewhere in the rubble.

Five

Eye of the Storm

Deeper and deeper, I sink into the mire;
I can't find a foothold to stand on.
I am in deep water,
and the floods overwhelm me.
I am exhausted from crying for help;
my throat is parched and dry.
My eyes are swollen with weeping,
waiting for my God to help me.

PSALMS 69:2–3 REVISED STANDARD VERSION (RSV)

I'd been staggering around in an incoherent daze for far too long. Mike led me to our room and gently helped me undress. I collapsed into bed, clutching only the faintest shreds of hope. I was inundated with unsettling thoughts of my daughter. First, her smile filled with sweet and gentle laughter, immediately followed by horrifying images as she lay, bloodied, broken, and alone. While I tried unsuccessfully to sleep, I continued to pray, "Please God, not my baby girl." I repeated it over and over while staring at her picture and clutching Kitty-Kitty to my chest. Minutes turned into hours.

I finally dozed off in the early morning, only to be awakened by the phone at 5:00 A.M. I was filled with expectation. *Maybe they've found my baby,* I hoped.

"Hello." My voice wavered.

"Kathleen?" It was my sister, Darlene.

"Have you heard anything?" I asked, as tears once again poured down my face.

"No. I'm sorry, Kathleen, nothing." She hesitated as I sobbed uncontrollably. "Kathleen, I know this is hard for you to hear, and I don't want to be the one to say this, but I'm afraid it's been too long. If Ashley were alive, we'd know something by now." Darlene wanted desperately to be the voice of reason. She wanted to help me face the inevitable.

"Don't say that. How could you give up on Ashley like that?"

"Kathleen, I'm just trying to prepare you for the worst. I'm just trying to help. You have to get a grip on reality."

"I'll get a grip when I darn well please!" I was furious. God wouldn't let this happen to my little girl. Everyone had to have faith!

The phone was silent for a few minutes; then Darlene cleared her throat.

"Listen, I need to tell you something. Oprah Winfrey wants to interview you. I've been here visiting with her assistant producer Natalie for most of the night, and she promises to be very sensitive to you and Mike." Darlene paused. "I watch Oprah regularly, and, Kathleen, she seems so spiritual. I know she won't ask anything that might hurt you. Do you think you can do it?"

"Oprah?" I asked incredulously.

"Yes, Oprah. Do you think you can regain some of your composure to talk with her? I need to give her producer an answer."

"I don't know. . . . Oprah wants to talk to me," I asked again, not really comprehending it. "Why . . . I don't know if I can. The only thing I know is, I want to hold my daughter."

"Do you think Mike could do it if you can't?"

"I guess so. He's been so strong."

"I'll tell her if you can't do it maybe Mike can, okay?"

"All right, I'll ask him in a minute. We need to get up anyway. It's going to be a long day."

"Yes, I know. I'll see you in a little while. I love you."

As I said good-bye, my eyes fixed on a picture of Ashley hanging on the wall. It had been taken the year before, but she hadn't changed much. Maybe, I thought, I should bring it with me today.

I looked at Mike. He had dark circles under his eyes. He stared back at me. It was obvious he wanted to say something to help, but nothing would come. Instead he reached across the bed and gathered me into his arms while we cried together.

Finally, exhausted, I pulled away. "We should go to Mom and Dad's and find some of their pictures. We could show their photographs around in case someone has seen them."

Mike nodded, then rose to get dressed. "Give me a few minutes to pull myself together." With that he slowly walked into the bathroom and turned on the shower while I went into the kitchen to make a pot of coffee. Soon Mike emerged looking somewhat better.

"Your turn," he said. I shook my head, refusing any creature comforts until Ashley was found. "Look, it's going to be a long day. You'll need everything in your favor; otherwise this will be harder than it has to be." He grabbed my hand and pulled me toward the bathroom. He started the shower, handed me a washcloth, and gently shoved me in. I stood almost motionless as warm water ran down my back. The soothing flow seemed to help, but within an instant guilty thoughts overwhelmed me. Ashley couldn't feel better, why should I?

I stepped out of the shower to dry off. As I looked into the mirror, a stranger seemed to be looking back. Could that old, tortured woman be me? There were dark rings around my eyes, and my skin was pale, almost translucent. My hair hung sloppily in wet rings down my face. Why was God punishing me so? Was I too happy? Did I have too much?

I tried to choose what I should wear. It was a little cold—a light sweater and pants would be best. I knew I needed to wear something comfortable. I didn't want anything to take away from my search for Ashley.

I walked over to the wall and took down her picture. As I turned I saw Kitty-Kitty on the bed. I reached down to pick him up. I had to bring Kitty-Kitty along. Ashley would need him when I found her.

I walked through the house noticing every toy she'd left lying around—a pink dinosaur on the floor, a hair bow on the table, and Barbie sitting on the couch. I went into her room and sat heavily on her bed. My daughter's presence seemed to surround me. I buried my face in her pillow and succumbed to the grief. The next thing I knew, Mike was beside me rubbing my back. "It's time to go," he whispered.

"Okay. But, Mike, we need to go over to Mom and Dad's to get their pictures."

"Yeah, and we still have to drop the boys off for the day."

I nodded.

We made the short trip over to Luther and LaRue's. I saw Mike's lips tremble as we pulled into the driveway. I watched my strong husband as he turned off the ignition and stared at the old house. His hands turned white as he gripped the steering wheel. He sighed, opened his door, and got out. He reached for my hand. "Please come with me. I need you." His voice broke as he looked toward the house once more.

I came around the truck and grasped his hand. Mom's flowers were in full bloom, and the smell of lilacs almost assaulted us on the short walk to the door. Mike hesitated just inside the entrance.

For the first time I could remember, the house was cold, silent, and lifeless. I looked at Mike and realized he was thinking the same thing. He'd spent so many years in this house, and for the first time no one was home to greet him.

In an almost surreal moment we became keenly aware that everything was just as Luther and LaRue had left it. Yesterday's cold coffee was still in the pot, and the remains of the breakfast dishes were in the sink. Dad's work boots waited by the door to be pulled on as he did every night to check his beloved cattle. Toys were strewn about, evidence of the much-loved children who played there.

We headed for the study. Mom's chair was empty, and her mending was waiting. As we stepped into the room, the photo of Dad nearly leapt out at us. Even though it had been taken nearly ten years earlier, he still looked the same. Mike reached up and pulled it off the wall. "This is old," he said, "but it will do."

Mom's picture would be harder to find. As far as we knew she'd never had a portrait made. She was not a vain woman and saw no need for photographs.

We headed upstairs. Michael went straight for the large box of family pictures Mom kept beside her bed. We opened it and sifted through decades of memories. We found only one snapshot, but it was old and blurry. Disappointed, we went downstairs.

"Why don't you call Debbie to see if she might have some recent pictures of Mom?" I suggested. "She can look for them while we're at the church. I'll go wait with the boys outside."

As I walked to the truck, I was captivated by the rows of flowers. Mom had tenderly planted each one. Who would tend to them now? I wondered, as I climbed into the truck and waited for Mike.

"Where are we going, Mama?" Zack asked.

"You'll be going over to Danny and Karen's house today. Karen is going to watch you guys while Dad and I look for Nana, Granddad, and Ashley."

"Will Jeremy and Jeanette be there?" he asked hopefully.

"I don't know, baby. We'll just have to wait and see."

Danny and Karen were old friends of my husband. Danny and Mike were both welders at Autoquip, and they shared an interest in building and refurbishing cars. Danny was the closest thing to a car expert Mike knew, and Mike thought very highly of his opinions. When they heard what had happened to our family, they immediately offered their help. I was thankful to have a safe place for the boys while we continued our search.

Soon Mike returned, and we headed to Danny and Karen's place. The boys were quiet in the backseat. There was no sign of their usual bickering. I turned to look at them. Zack and David were staring out the side windows. My heart ached for them both. How could we offer comfort to our boys when we were hurting so much ourselves? I hoped Karen would be able to distract them, even if for just a while.

Karen met us at the door with red-rimmed eyes and pulled me into a tight embrace. "Oh, honey, I am so sorry. You know I'm here for you and will do whatever you need me to."

I nodded as the tears rolled down my cheeks. "Just take care of my boys, Karen. That's enough for now."

She smiled. "You know I'll love doing just that." She gave me one more squeeze as we turned for the door. "Just call if you need anything."

We hugged Zack and David, got back in the truck, and headed toward the city. I held Mike's hand tightly, as if he could somehow save me from what was to come. I felt my sanity slipping away. I squeezed Kitty-Kitty close to my chest and started rocking back and forth.

When we reached the church, it looked as if an army had mobilized. Several Guardsmen were stationed around the building, and the entrance was sealed off. The press had been assigned a waiting area roped off with bright yellow police tape. They were not allowed outside its perimeter, nor were they allowed to "harass" the families. Volunteers were waiting to unload supplies from a multitude of trucks at the entrance.

Before we parked we spotted Rex and Wayne. They were a welcome sight. It was almost as if they'd lost a family member too. Luther and LaRue were charter members of our little church. Luther had been on the committee who hired Rex to be our preacher. Wayne was Luther's best friend and had been a deacon for many years. Luther was an usher. It was a job he enjoyed tremendously because of his great love for people. LaRue often kept the nursery, sometimes taught Sunday School, and sang soprano in the choir. But mostly she provided the much-loved cinnamon rolls for the parishioners. She and Luther were greatly respected and loved by the members.

Because of Rex's immense size, I often thought he'd be a formidable opponent. He stood well over six and a half feet and was stoutly built. Some described him as a towering mountain of a man. But I knew him as a tenderhearted friend who saw to the needs of his flock with a vengeance. I was thankful to have him on my side. I knew he'd make sure people would do right by us, and by Ashley, Luther, and LaRue.

Wayne was no small man himself. Second in height only to Rex, he stood over six feet tall. Ashley called him Santa Claus Man because of his white beard and hair, as well as his round tummy. In many ways he took on Santa's benevolent characteristics. He loved children. He always had treats for them and would tweak their cheeks every chance he got. He fascinated Ashley. The first time she saw him she stared him down. I think she was expecting he would whip out his bag full of goodies and distribute them accompanied by jolly salutations. When she realized Wayne was just like everyone else, she adopted him into her ring of admirers. I'd often catch Ashley with her arms flung tightly around his knees.

I hugged them both, and together we walked to the entrance. We were ushered into the fellowship hall with other waiting family members and were offered food. But I still couldn't eat. Not yet, not until Ashley had been found.

Darlene spotted us from across the room and quickly approached. I must have looked terrible, because the first thing she did was touch my forehead. "How do you feel?"

"How am I supposed to feel? I'm numb." I sighed. "I can't sense her presence anymore."

She simply nodded and turned to the tall, black woman behind her. "I don't think she's up for this, Natalie."

Natalie stepped up and introduced herself. "Hi, I'm Natalie Jason, associate producer of the *Oprah* show. I'm sorry about what's happened to your family." She held out her hand. Mike and I mechanically shook it. "We were hoping one of you would be able to talk to Oprah via satellite."

Mike said, "Honey, do you think you're up for it?" He looked deeply into my eyes. By then, I was shaking uncontrollably. I could only shake my head no.

"Do you think you could do it, Mike?" Natalie asked.

"I think so. Where do we have to go?"

"We'll have to go down to the site; that's where our cameras are."

Mike turned to look at me. "I can't leave her this way."

I looked up and grabbed his arm. "You have to do this for Ashley, as well as Mom and Dad. I need the world to know how special they are. I need the world to be looking for them. I'll be all right. Everyone will take care of me. You have to do this."

He looked deeply into my eyes. I looked back, willing him to see my determination. He drew me into his arms and held me tightly. "Okay. Are you sure you'll be all right?"

I nodded. Natalie motioned to someone across the room. "Great," she said, "We'd better hurry."

I watched them retreat, then sat down to wait. Darlene came and sat beside me. "Kathleen, will you be all right if I go home and get some sleep?"

I nodded. "Rex and Wayne are here. I'll be fine."

Darlene hugged me tightly. "If you need me, I'll be right back. I'll return as soon as I get some rest."

Rex, Wayne, and I waited, sometimes watching the small television in the room, other times simply lost in our thoughts. At one point they joined other ministers to discuss how to handle the tragedy. They came to an agreement. This was not to be an evangelical opportunity; they were there simply to minister God's love to hurting people.

I filled my time praying for a miracle—that Ashley would be found and returned to me unharmed. But as more time went by miracles seemed to grow further from my reach. The closer I came to admitting she was gone forever, the deeper my mind slipped into despondency. I just couldn't imagine my daughter dead. What mother could? It was unthinkable that my bright, loving, happy little girl could be taken away. This was something that happened to other people, not me. I clutched Kitty-Kitty and rocked back and forth, trying to come to terms with reality.

A Red Cross worker brought me a bottle of water and a box of tissues. She knelt in front of me and held my hands. "I just want you to know, you're in our hearts and prayers." I nodded, looking at her through tear-soaked eyes. She squeezed my shoulders and sat beside me for a minute. "Do you need anything?" she asked. I shook my head no. "Okay," she said. "I'll check on you occasionally, just in case you do." Then she gently moved on to the next family.

Moments later I looked up from my fog to see a pretty young woman standing in front of me. She was dressed in a smart business suit, with the biggest brown eyes I'd ever seen. She clutched my arm and started to speak. "I saw you with that stuffed animal, and I just had to talk to you," she said. Another woman stood beside her. I looked from one to the other; they were as different as night and day. The second woman, with long, raven black hair, was dressed in black leather, a miniskirt and heeled boots. She reached out to embrace me.

The first woman spoke again. "Did you lose a child?" she asked bluntly.

I nodded. "Yes, my four-year-old daughter."

"Oh! Was she in the day care?"

"No." I shook my head vehemently, everyone had it all wrong. "She was there with her grandparents, and they were going to the Social Security office."

Her face registered shock. "Listen, I represent Feed the Children and *The Geraldo Rivera Show.* Larry Jones and Geraldo are getting together and putting on a telethon to help raise money for the rescue effort. Would you consider helping us?"

"What do you want me to do?"

"Could you come down to the site and do an interview with Geraldo and Larry Jones?"

"I don't know. I'm waiting for my husband to come back from there. He just did a live interview with Oprah. I won't leave until he comes back." The brown-eyed woman protectively put her arm around me.

Just then Mike came up. "Are you okay?" he asked.

I nodded, then turned to introduce him to the women in front of me. Suddenly I realized I didn't know their names. "These ladies . . . are with Feed the Children, and they are doing a telethon and want us to help." With that the two stepped forward and introduced themselves. The first woman was Cindy Jones; the other, I believe, was Dawn. They asked Mike if he would mind coming down to the site. He looked concerned. "Could you give us a minute?" he asked.

"Sure," Dawn said. "I'll go find my friend and be right back." Dawn walked away, and Cindy Jones took a step back to give us some privacy.

"Honey, are you sure this is what you want?"

"We have to," I said adamantly. "The world needs to know how terrible this is. Besides, Feed the Children was one of my mama's favorite charities. I want everyone to know how beautiful and precious Ashley was. No—is! I want everyone to look for her. Besides, this waiting and doing nothing is killing me."

"Okay, babe, whatever you want."

After we agreed to the interviews Michael and I gathered our things to go. They were having transportation problems, so we all piled into the truck and headed for the First Baptist Church, near the downtown area. As we pulled up, we could see the explosion had struck the house of worship. It was becoming clearer in my mind—for anyone to survive a bombing that could damage structures blocks away would be nothing short of a miracle.

Silently we walked from the parking lot across the street to the church. Dawn explained she wasn't sure where they were going to be setting up and asked if we could give her a minute to find everyone. We roamed the halls of the church looking for her crew. Finally, she found a phone and called her producer. She made arrangements for a van to pick us up in thirty minutes. We went downstairs and sat on some sofas in the hall. She produced a pad of paper and asked me to tell her everything from the beginning. Slowly I recounted the whole story again, trying not to leave out any details. Periodically she'd prompt me with questions to keep me going.

Suddenly I looked up and found a photographer snapping photos. He tried to be unobtrusive, and it was clear by the tears on his face he was moved by my story. After Dawn and I finished he stepped forward and asked if he could make a copy of Ashley's photograph. He just needed to get it near some light. I cautiously handed it to him. He explained he was a reporter from Kansas, then thanked us for sharing our story.

Before long the van arrived, and we all piled in. While we were en route to the bomb site, we heard the perimeter was sealed off and they weren't letting just anyone through. Fortunately, there was a doctor riding with us, so by using his credentials, we were allowed to cross the lines to get to Sixth and Harvey, one block northwest of the bombing.

As we drove downtown I observed the buildings firsthand. Every window was shattered or missing completely. Many buildings had obvious structural damage. One had a steel I-beam sticking out of its brick exterior. It felt like a war zone, and I was being transported to the front lines.

Then the federal building came into view. I gasped as the tears flowed even harder than before. If Ashley had been in there, there was no way she could have survived. It looked as if a giant wedge had been carved out of it. I could not see the "pancake" area, but I could see giant slabs of concrete hanging from their rebar all along the edge of the destruction. Up close it was much more devastating than what I'd seen on television. I lay my head in Mike's lap and sobbed. He gently rubbed my shoulders and tried to calm me as we pulled into the lot where the media were allowed.

The minute we stepped out Geraldo greeted us, hugged us, and expressed his sympathy to each of us. Tears streamed down his face as he looked at the photograph of Ashley. He quietly shook his head, then ushered us to an RV, where we waited with other victims' loved ones.

We sat next to Greg Leisure and his wife. Greg's only sister had worked in the federal building. He showed us her picture, and we cried together.

Frances Jones, Larry Jones's wife, came in. She knelt beside the sofa and prayed Ashley would be found. Then she draped her arm across my shoulder and whispered, "God is always with us, just as He's also with Ashley." I clung to her words as if they were a lifeline.

Eventually we were ushered out of the RV for taping. I stared hard at the pavement, thinking how unjust it was for the authorities to forbid me to go inside the building to search for my daughter. I got angry. What kind of an animal would do this to innocent people, innocent children? If I could only get a hold of him, I would rip him to shreds with my bare hands.

Geraldo started his show, zooming in on the building. He described the scenes of appalling destruction. I continued to stare at the pavement, surrounded by broken glass. I looked up at the nearby buildings. It was obvious; Ashley had not survived. It was inconceivable anyone could make it out alive.

Geraldo started down the line. He began by interviewing a fireman. Next were Greg Leisure and his wife. I listened to their story. His sister had two children and a husband. She'd spent her life working for HUD, helping other people get homes of their own. Now she'd never be coming home again.

Next was Narilyn. Her adult daughter had been working in the day-care center. When she heard the news she'd jumped in her car in search of her loved one. Her two stepdaughters, whom she had raised, sat beside her sobbing.

I was trembling, and with each story of loss I got worse. How could I expect my baby girl to make it out when adults could not? I clutched Kitty-Kitty to my chest and rocked.

"One of the most heinous and horrific aspects of this is how many innocent American children were targeted by these bastards," he said. He gently approached Mike and I then went on to explain how Ashley had been with her grandparents at the Social Security office on that fateful day. He held up my baby's picture. "This is Ashley, four-year-old Ashley. This was an appropriate target by terrorists. . . " Geraldo broke off as I began sobbing again. "Oh, Kathleen." He squeezed my shoulder and pointed to Kitty-Kitty. "Was this Ashley's?"

"Yes," I sobbed, "it was Ashley's. She wanted to take it with her this morning—yesterday morning—and I wouldn't let her. Now she doesn't have anything to hold on to." I paused, gulped back more sobs, and tried to regain some of my composure. "I know that Mom and Dad would take care of her, if they were able, but I don't know, they were on the first floor . . ." I could say no more.

Geraldo turned to my husband. "Mike, did you know immediately?"

Michael was a little more in control. "No, it was about an hour later. I had called home to see about them, and my little brother told me they'd left. It wasn't until that evening we found their 9:00 A.M. appointment card."

Geraldo took a deep breath. "We'll talk much more with them later." Then he went to John Cole, who'd lost his two godsons, Aaron and Elijah Coverdale, in the bombing. I remember John holding it together pretty well, but his words were a blur.

Edye Smith sat just to my left. She'd lost her two sons, Chase and Colton. Because of where she worked she'd been able to watch some of the rescue. Her brother had recovered the bodies of the two little boys. At least she knew.

The entire show was a tearful account of what so many were going through. The audience was crying, Geraldo was crying, even some of his crew members were crying.

Larry Jones came in and spoke to the audience. They were trying to raise money to "bury the children." I knew him to be very sensitive to the needs of kids everywhere. Now he was trying to raise money to help bury those he could not help in any other way.

This was all a nightmare. I no longer heard what was going on around me. Mentally, I was searching the building for my beautiful baby girl. I didn't care what others wanted. I just wanted my daughter.

Finally the taping was over. They asked us to stay for a later interview, but we were determined to get back to the church. That was where our family was waiting. Suddenly I began to panic. "How will we get back?" I asked Mike.

Cindy Jones stepped forward and took my arm. "We're not far away. We'd love to take you," she said, leading me in the direction of their van. John Cole and his family came with us. They drove us back to where Mike had left his truck. We thanked them and said our good-byes.

When we arrived at the church, we were nearly assaulted by our family with news. Brad grabbed my arm. "Your ex wants to take Zachary. I told him he couldn't have him until you came back."

I looked at him in disbelief. "What? With all that's going on? Where is a phone? I have to get this straightened out, right now." Volunteers pointed to a room with several telephones. I found an available one. Mike was right behind me. I dialed the number and Karen picked up.

"Karen?"

"Yes."

"What exactly is going on?" I asked.

"Well, from what I can tell, Steve's on his way over here to get Zack."

"Karen, did you talk to him?"

"Yeah, he was pretty upset."

"Oh hell, this is all I need right now."

"Kathleen, he's just pulled up."

"Wait, Karen. Is there anyone with him?"

"Yeah, a blond woman."

"That's probably our old friend Sylvia," I said. "Let me talk to Steve." There was a pause, then his voice came over the phone. "Hello?"

"Steve, what are you doing?"

"I'm getting my son. I have joint custody, you know."

"Look, I don't need this right now. If you have some 'beef' with me, we can deal with that later. We have other things to worry about now."

"I just want to see my son," he said. "Don't take my son away from me too."

"What do you mean by that?" I bristled at his implication.

"Take it however you like."

I simply sighed. "Let me talk to Sylvia." I listened as he handed over the phone.

"Kathy?"

"Sylvia, what's going on?"

"Kathy, he just wants to be with his little boy for a while. Zack needs to be with his family, and you're looking for Ashley. Just let Steve have him. They'll be at my house, and you know where that is. You can call or come over any time. I promise. Steve was upset before and said some things he didn't mean. He's okay now and has calmed down. He just wants to see Zack."

I took a deep breath. "Sylvia, I'm depending on you to make sure my son comes back home."

"I know, Kathy."

"Let me talk to Karen." Karen came to the phone. "It's okay, Karen. Zack can go with his daddy."

"Kathleen, are you sure?"

"I just have to have faith. Thanks for looking after the kids today."

"That's okay, we were happy to help," she whispered.

"Mike and I will come and get David as soon as we can."

"Take care." I heard the tremble in her voice as we hung up the phone.

Mike was talking with Natalie in the hall. When they noticed I'd hung up they motioned me over. She asked how I was doing. I shrugged my shoulders.

"Listen," she said. "Oprah wants to meet you. She's coming here to talk with you and Mike. Would that be all right?"

I glanced at Michael. He looked a little rough around the edges. But he nodded; if it was okay with me, he'd comply.

"You'll have a problem getting into the church," I said. Rex was standing nearby. He told us about a prayer service organized for that evening. Natalie assured us we'd be done in plenty of time. We asked if the rest of our family, and our minister, could wait with us. We needed them nearby. She agreed.

We waited in a quiet office. Before we knew it Oprah arrived. Everyone was introduced, and she expressed her sympathy. She spoke with us while her crew set up, getting details about what we knew and how we felt.

Then she began taping. I explained it had been like a nightmare, a terrible, terrible nightmare. I told her I wanted to believe I'd simply wake up and Ashley would be in her little bed with that precious smile on her face, singing, "Good morning, Mommy." We were still holding out hope she was alive. I wanted to go and look for her, but they wouldn't let me. I knew approximately where she was, but they wouldn't let me try. An intense mother's instinct overwhelmed me. All I could think of was she was still in there, hurt, scared, and hungry, and I couldn't do anything about it. I wept.

When we finished taping we asked Oprah to join us at the prayer service. She jokingly replied, "I'll look like a raisin in a rice paddy." Then she glanced at Rex and Wayne. "With these two on either end, I'm certain I'll be all right. I don't think anyone would try anything with these two around." She looked at Rex. "How tall are you anyway?" He smiled and gently laughed.

We entered the sanctuary through the back door and sat in the second row. The press was lined up along the wall. Oprah sat between Wayne and me. She cried with us. She prayed with us. And she prayed for us. She hugged me after the service and told me to let her know if there was anything more she could do. I thanked her and asked her for only one favor— to never forget.

As we left the prayer service I looked at Mike. "You know, we've done all these national interviews, but what about the local ones? If anyone knows where Ashley is, it's someone right here in town. We need to reach out to the locals too."

Even though I was taxed well beyond my limitations, I was willing to do anything to reunite with my child. I felt driven by panic. What if Ashley never came home? She was such a pretty and sweet little girl, someone just had her and was reluctant to bring her back. The more people knew we were looking for her, the more would be helping us search.

As providence would have it, just as we stepped outside I saw Robin Marsh, a local news reporter, walking across the parking lot. Mike and I watched her every morning as we ate breakfast. Seeing Robin was like seeing a trusted family friend. I ran over to her. "Robin, Robin, please, you have to help me find my baby. She was in the bombing . . ." I started crying again.

She grabbed my hand. "Okay," she said, "tell me what happened." Quickly the camera came on. Suddenly several National Guardsmen approached to stop the interview. They thought Robin had assaulted us. Mike explained it was our desire to get Ashley's picture out to the public, and Robin repeated over and over, "She came to me, she asked to talk to me." She was firm with them as her hand continued to grip my arm. Once they understood the situation they explained that other members of the press would like to talk with us too, if we were comfortable doing so. We nodded in agreement and, with the blessing of the guard, went on with our interview.

When I could say no more, Robin hugged me, then handed me her card. "Look," she said, "if you need anything, anything at all, don't hesitate to call. Thank you for sharing your story. I promise to put your little girl's picture on the six o'clock news. Maybe someone will call to say they've found her. God bless you." She hugged me again while we said a tearful good-bye.

Mike and I slowly walked to the other members of the press. They were starved for a story, any story. At first questions were being fired from all directions. I was so overwhelmed by the microphones and cameras, I couldn't think and started to turn away. But my anguish stopped me. I had to press on, for Ashley.

As I turned Mike looked deeply into my eyes. "You don't have to do this anymore, honey."

I shook my head. "No, Mike, I have to. Everyone has to know how special Ashley is."

When it was obvious we were overwhelmed, someone in the press apologized and promised they'd slow down, asking only one question at a time. I showed them Ashley's picture and told our story once more—three of our family members were missing, one was my little girl. We had to find them. They had to help us find them.

Finally, I had to stop. I wanted to be near my family. I turned to Mike and said, "Take me home." He nodded and led me to the truck.

The minute we arrived home I staggered to bed. I tried to escape reality through sleep, but it was no use. I knew it, now more than ever—my precious, loving little girl wasn't coming home. I lay there in fits of grief, reliving Ashley's life—her day of birth, all the birthdays, Christmas, Easters, memories of snuggling together, singing little nonsense songs, and her funny, ornery little smile.

Why would God do this to my family? Was He punishing me for being too happy? I mentally shook my fist toward heaven. "Whatever I've done to offend you, God, this punishment is too harsh. Why my baby girl? Things like this happen to other people, not me." I tossed and turned, alternating between accusing God and blaming myself. It was another night of hell.

Six

April Showers

How frail is humanity! How short is life, and how full of trouble!
Like a flower, we blossom for a moment and then wither.
Like the shadow of a passing cloud, we quickly disappear.

JOB 14:1–2 LIV

At 5:00 A.M., I stopped struggling with insomnia, got up, and made a pot of coffee. Then I wandered to the couch, where I rocked repetitively back and forth, staring at Ashley's picture.

The house was silent. Zack was with his father, David was asleep in his bed and Mike in ours. I'd never felt so alone. I'd never felt so empty. She wasn't coming home. The tears had temporarily stopped. I felt as if my mind had separated, with two distinct thoughts at conflict. One was anger that wanted to rage against God and man. The other was sadness and hurt that made me want to crawl off somewhere and die.

I rose and started mundane chores. I mechanically tried to arrange platters of food church members had brought by, stacking dishes in the refrigerator and along the counter. I couldn't remember when I'd last had food or water. My body was dehydrated, pushed beyond its limits. I felt empty, drained of my soul, my heart.

I looked down at my hand. I'd accidentally cut it on a knife in the sink. I was bleeding, and I hadn't even known it. I stared as the red, sticky fluid flowed down my fingers. It was a small cut, nothing serious, but it made me think of the blood my daughter had shed. My innocent, loving daughter, her blood spilt, alone in the cold, dark rubble of that building.

Michael quietly approached me. He picked up a towel and stanched the flow of blood from my wound. "What are you doing?" he asked. I looked at him, unable to respond. He cleaned the wound and applied a bandage. Then he looked into my eyes. "Are you all right now?" he asked. I shrugged stiffly, saying nothing. Part of me wanted to die. I turned back to the sink, refusing to think about what was happening.

I heard someone pull up and glanced out the window. There were two cars. One was my sister's; I didn't recognize the other. I walked outside. An older man jumped out of his vehicle. "Are you Mrs. Treanor?" he quickly asked.

"Yes," I said.

"My name is Bennett. I represent a nationally syndicated newspaper. This is my photographer. I understand your family was affected by the OKC bombing."

"Yes, my daughter and my in-laws were in there."

"I thought that's what I'd been told. We sure had a time tracking you down. It just so happened we ran into the Prices at Hardee's in town, and they were able to tell us how to get to your home. You wouldn't mind talking to us, would you?"

"I guess not, I've talked to everyone else. Would you like to come in and have some coffee?"

"That would be great," he responded as they moved toward my door.

While I prepared another pot of coffee, Bennett began firing questions. His photographer stood quietly behind him, hardly speaking and refusing any refreshments.

I mechanically went through the story again. No, Ashley was not in the day care. She just happened to be with her grandparents. No, I had not yet been notified of her whereabouts. Of course we assumed the worst.

Yes, she was only four, going on five in July. No, she'd never been in that building before.

"I'm sorry, what paper did you say you were from?" I asked.

"Here's my card. I am a freelance writer for the *National Enquirer*. I do stories all over the United States."

I stopped cold. The *National Enquirer*! I began to regret asking him inside. That tabloid had a reputation for embellishing stories. I feared they would exploit the situation. "Look, sir, this situation is sensational enough. Please don't turn it into a circus. I loved my daughter, and this is very painful. Please, don't make it worse."

"Oh, no, no, I wouldn't do such a thing—not at all. I'll even send you a color plaque with the story engraved on it. We did that for another article I wrote, and it turned out really nice. Would that be all right?"

I cautiously nodded in agreement. Encouraged, he continued with his questioning. The photographer, who'd been quiet until then, asked if he could take some pictures. I looked at him and nodded. I saw silent tears running down his face. I will always remember, and cherish, the look of heart-wrenching compassion in his eyes. My initial assumption had been wrong. He was a real person too, with real feelings. He seemed to understand.

"I have a three-year-old son at home," the photographer explained. "When you tell me these things, it makes me want to drop everything, go home, and hug him. Being away from him right now is horrible. I almost understand how you feel."

I lowered my head and acknowledged his sympathy, not knowing what else to say.

"Follow me, I have something to show you." I led the photographer into Ashley's bedroom. There, on the wall, were little handprint drawings she'd made at church. All her Barbie dolls were lined up waiting for her, and Kitty-Kitty sat in his place of honor, atop Ashley's pillow. Everything was just as she'd left it. He sobbed and shook his head.

Then he photographed the room. It was heartbreaking to watch. Finally, I rose from her bed, apologized, and left the room.

I began sobbing. My baby wasn't coming home. There wouldn't be a first day at school. She so looked forward to going to kindergarten. There wouldn't be any best friends. There wouldn't be a first boyfriend, no dance classes, no music lessons, no taffeta prom dresses or a delicate, lacy wedding gown. I wouldn't be able to teach her to cook, or sew, or all the things my mom had taught me. All my plans and dreams had been mercilessly ripped away. All the joy I'd found in the last two years, with Michael and our new family, was gone. My heart and soul had been left raw and bleeding. Why had God allowed this to happen? I had to find some answers. I had to find some meaning.

When I returned to the living room, Bennett was talking to my sister. Within moments he sat down next to me and continued his questioning. He seemed confused by our blended family. I had to explain the marriage over and over again. Finally, he had everything he needed and left.

I sat by the phone, staring at it, hoping for news from the recovery team. Shortly afterward, when it did ring, I grabbed it with all my might. But it was not the message I'd been waiting for. Each time it rang my hopes rose, only to come crashing back down. Instead of news about Ashley, it was either a reporter requesting an interview or kind people from all over the nation calling to tell us they were praying. Although my head told me there was no hope of finding Ashley, my heart would not let me give up. I just had to see her one more time.

I cut each conversation short with the thought that whoever had Ashley would need to get through on the line. We had only basic service. I called the phone company and requested call waiting as well as caller ID. The Bell employee told me it would be at least forty-eight hours before they could initiate the service. I started weeping into the phone, knowing that would be too late. She promised to put a rush order on it. But without any explanation from me, she seemed to know I was involved in the bombing. That kind young girl must have moved mountains, because within a few hours the service was activated. If I had known who she was, I would have kissed her. I was grateful for each and every small miracle.

In the afternoon the medical examiner's office called to ask if they could come out and dust the house for Ashley's fingerprints. I asked why. They explained they needed to identify the children. I hesitated, caught my breath, and said, "It won't be necessary for you to do that. I had all of my children fingerprinted just a few months ago. I have Ashley's fingerprint card here, and you can come and get it, or I will bring it to you." The caller seemed surprised. "You have your children's fingerprints?" he asked.

"Yes, my husband is a reserve cop here in Guthrie, and we are also Cub Scout leaders. We did this as a community learning session with our den last fall, and Ashley went with us."

"Ma'am," he said, "you are the only parent I've called who had anything like that."

"I never thought I would have to use them," I said. "She has dental records too. Will you need those?"

"Yes. That would be helpful. Most children that young don't have dental records either."

"I know, but Ashley had some problems with her teeth when she was a baby. She has crowns on three molars. I don't have the records here, but I'll call her dentist in Tulsa and ask him to send them to you if that would help."

"Yes, that would be most helpful. We can be there in just a few minutes. Can you give us directions?"

After giving him the instructions to find my house, I hung up the phone. A weak smile crossed my face when I recalled the trip to the police station with the Cub Scouts. Ashley went everywhere with the boys and did everything they did. I remembered her standing on the step stool and giggling uncontrollably as Mike made her fingerprint card. When we'd finished that evening, the boys were all quoting bad TV lines and playing cops and robbers, with Ashley right in the middle of everything.

The ringing of my doorbell brought me back to reality. Marsha Matthews, my Sunday School teacher and friend, was standing on the porch. I stepped outside, and she tearfully embraced me. Then she held me away for a second and looked into my eyes.

"I have something I have to tell you—a confession of sorts," she said.

I looked at her quizzically.

"LaRue and I recently talked about how it's sometimes harder to take care of one child than several. I knew on Wednesdays LaRue sat for Ashley without the other grandchildren. I realized I needed to come and get her some Wednesdays so she and Megan could play."

I managed a small smile. Ashley and Marsha's five-year-old daughter, Megan, were friends. They often played together at church.

She went on. "Well, Tuesday, all day, I kept thinking I should call LaRue and see if Ashley could come over to play the next morning, but I kept putting it off and putting it off. All day I had this urge to call, but I ignored it, because I had so much to do. It just seemed every time I thought about it, something would come up, and I procrastinated."

I watched silently as the tears fell down her cheeks.

"Kathleen, I knew the Holy Spirit was speaking to me, yet I ignored it. The bomb went off on Wednesday morning, the very day Ashley should have been playing safely at my home. I didn't listen, and now Ashley has paid the price."

We hugged each other and wept.

"Marsha, you didn't do this. God didn't do this. This was an act of pure evil. How could you have known what was going to happen? You can't shoulder the responsibility for Ashley's death. It wasn't your fault."

Marsha sighed. "I think God is using this to teach me what can happen when we don't do as He tells us. Not obeying His voice is serious, and He is showing me the consequences."

"Marsha, if that's what you've learned, then Ashley's death wasn't meaningless. If you learned something, if someone is saved from future suffering, there is meaning here. We have to find some meaning." My voice began to trail off. "Remember, Marsha, this wasn't your fault."

We visited for a short while, then she excused herself, hugged me, and got into her vehicle. Suddenly I remembered a song for the funerals. I reached into my car and pulled out a demo tape of the Christian single "Why," by 4Him. It was a song I'd been planning to sing at church. The words were particularly poignant now. I leaned through the open window and pressed it into the palm of her hand. "Marsha, please give this to Dennis, so he can perform it at the funerals." Dennis Rigdon was our church's music director and had a beautiful, rich baritone voice. I knew he'd sing it with grace. With the promise she would take it directly to him, Marsha drove away.

I breathed a heavy sigh and looked over the blooming flowers in my garden, flowers Ashley and I had planted together. I needed to find meaning. I needed to understand why God had let this tragedy befall my family. I knew being a Christian didn't guarantee a perfect life, free from tragedy, but I'd never expected anything like this.

I don't think parents can possibly prepare themselves to bury their children. It's unnatural. And the fact that Ashley was murdered just made things harder. I felt angry, hurt, heartbroken, and isolated. Even though I had my loving family around me, I still felt alone.

Would I ever experience happiness again? Would I ever be able to laugh? I couldn't imagine how. Without my "heart," how could I go on? I closed my eyes and whispered a prayer. "Please, God, you know how I hurt. You know how much I love Ashley. Why? Please tell me why you took her away. What terrible sin did I commit to have earned such punishment? Please, help me understand. Please, help me go on. And please, help me to change, if that's your will."

The tears started again. I got up, went into the house, and threw myself on my bed. Mike came in and held me.

Later that evening Michael's uncle Andy and aunt Lanita, along with their daughter, Terry, and grandson, Ryan, arrived. Michael hadn't seen them in years, since Andy was in the Air Force and transferred frequently around the world. Mike's brother Mark had called them in Alabama with the news that LaRue, Andy's older sister, might have been involved in the bombing. We invited them to stay with us. It was a godsend. Lanita quickly helped with all the household chores.

Then, finally, the call we'd been waiting for arrived. Around 4:00 P.M. the medical examiner's office telephoned and asked us to come to the church right away.

"Is it about Ashley?" I gasped.

"I don't know, ma'am, I was just told to call your family and have them come down."

"All right, we're on our way."

I hung up the phone and immediately began shouting orders at everyone. We had to call our family and get them down there. We had to hurry.

Within fifteen minutes we were all on our way. I clutched Mike's arm in the truck. Debbie and Buddy held each other tightly in the backseat.

Mark didn't say a word. The drive was filled with apprehension. What would they tell us?

We pulled up to the church and rushed to the entrance. The National Guard greeted us. The minute we identified ourselves, we were ushered in.

Volunteers took our names and brought us to another room where Steve was already waiting. In a flash a tall man approached us and introduced himself. He was one of the medical examiner's assistants as well as a chaplain.

"Are you Ashley's mother?" he asked.

"Yes," I practically shouted. My heart began pounding even harder than before.

"Please come and sit down." He ushered me to the seat by the desk, which was littered with papers, documentation on death and funerals. My breath was ragged.

"What is it? Is this about Ashley? Have you found her? Tell me where she is, so I can go to her!"

He sighed heavily, then spoke as gently as he could. "Mrs. Treanor, I'm sorry to inform you, your daughter was found among the dead." That was all I heard. The rest is a complete and total blank. I crumpled into a helpless, sobbing heap. I heard a distinct buzzing in my ears as the room swirled wildly around me. I vaguely remember screaming for my baby over and over again. People surrounded me. I felt Rex behind me, attempting to shelter me from harm. But it was no use. I slipped into oblivion.

Then, as suddenly as I collapsed, I came to attention, demanding to be taken to her immediately. I needed to hold my daughter. When I was told I couldn't, I started screaming again, ranting that she was my baby and I had the right to see her. I needed to see her. She wasn't dead. They were all lying to me. This couldn't be happening, not to my little girl.

The room was racked with grief-stricken sobs. Brad began rocking and crying loudly, and Debbie broke down as well. One of the counselors went to her side. When Debbie saw the woman, she screamed hysterically and fell to the floor in a faint. The second she was revived, she screamed, "My mama, I thought she was my mama! Get her out of here! She isn't her!" The counselor left the room in a rush as Rex tried to explain. The woman's hair was the same length, color, and texture as LaRue's. It was a cruel trick of circumstances, more than Debbie could bear.

We gathered our things and staggered out of the office. As we were leaving, I heard Mike ask about Ashley's time of death.

The medical examiner said it was 9:04 A.M. Mike was shocked. All the news reports had indicated the bomb went off at 9:02; surely she wasn't alive for two minutes after the explosion. The examiner clarified; there really wasn't any forensic science that could pinpoint the time of death that accurately; 9:04 was when the police thought the bomb actually exploded. The 9:02 indicator they had come to rely on was based on a clock in the building that had stopped at that moment. He assured us Ashley had not suffered. Then Michael asked if they'd wait until they found both Luther and LaRue before they called us back. We could only bear to do this one more time.

My ears fixated on the examiner's last words: "She didn't suffer."

"How do you know? Were you there for her? How can you claim to know if my daughter suffered?" At the time I thought I'd screamed these words with all my might, but Mike tells me now I didn't speak at all. My "shouts" were nothing more than accusations raging in my mind.

I wanted to die. Why hadn't it been me in that building? Ashley didn't deserve this. I begged Mike to bring me my baby. I knew if anyone could do it, he could. But all Mike could do was shake his head and stroke my face. I never saw him look so helpless. I felt as if my heart had been wrenched from my chest. I was simply living on, feeling my life's blood flowing out of me, yet somehow unable to die. Everything became fragmented, surreal, as if I were on the outside looking in through broken glass.

Mike half walked, half carried me to the truck. I laid my head in his lap for the entire trip home. I was completely numb.

When we arrived home Mike gently helped me inside. I went to Ashley's room and lay down on her bed. I pulled all her stuffed animals around me and held them tight. I could do nothing but cry. I remained there for hours, with Mike sitting beside me, tenderly stroking my face and back. There was nothing to say. He knew now they weren't coming home. There was nothing to do except plan their funerals.

A couple of hours later he got up, made the boys dinner, and got them ready for bed. Then he came back, practically carried me to our room, undressed me, and put me to bed. Still, I felt nothing. In what was almost an out-of-body experience, I seemed to be observing a complete stranger, a woman in absolute pain. Could that really be me? No, this had to be an evil, horrid nightmare. Surely I'd wake up and the person lying there would be gone. This kind of thing doesn't happen to people like us. We've always protected our family from harm. That's why we lived in the country, in a small town. There was no possibility of danger here. But I was wrong—dead wrong.

When I awoke the next morning I realized it was me in that bed. This was reality—my reality. I had to bury my little girl. The thought of making funeral arrangements for Ashley sickened me, and I ran to the bathroom and vomited.

I returned to my bed and lay there, staring at Ashley's picture on the wall. How could she be dead? I'd just kissed her good-bye a few hours ago. She was smiling and happy, everything was all right. How could this be so? She wasn't dead. The examiner had found someone else's child. She wasn't really gone.

The ringing of the phone interrupted my thoughts. Mike answered and brought the receiver to me. It was Darlene. "Kathleen, how are you feeling?"

"How am I supposed to feel?"

"I don't know, Kathleen. I'm so sorry. I know this is hard, but you are going to need to pull yourself together and make Ashley's funeral arrangements. I'm down here with Bobby Smith at the funeral home, and I think you should come and do this now."

"I can't," I said flatly.

"Yes, you can, and you must," she insisted. "She needs to be buried right away."

"Okay." I quietly complied. "We'll be there in a few minutes." I told Mike what we needed to do, stood up, and got dressed.

When we arrived at the funeral home, Bobby Smith met us at the door. It seemed as if I'd just seen him. He'd handled my father's funeral just a few months before, and I was impressed with his thoughtfulness as well as his attention to details. He led us into his office, and no sooner were we seated than Steve and our friend Sylvia arrived. I looked at them blankly. I was kind of glad they were there but couldn't comprehend how they knew where to be. That's when Darlene told me she'd called them.

Bobby told us not to worry about any expenses. A local company had offered to donate a casket, custom-made from their factory. Woodcrest Baptist Church had made arrangements for payment of funeral costs, and Marna Gay had called from Furrow's flower shop to say she'd donate the flowers. All we needed to do was pick out what we wanted.

I nodded as Bobby passed me a book filled with pictures of children's coffins. He said he didn't keep any on display because they upset people too much to see, but that Central Caskets could make anything in the book we liked. I picked the first white with pink trim casket I saw. It was only a box, I thought. She wasn't really going to be in there, but she'd like the satin pink lining anyway. Steve and I chose a spray of pink baby roses and daisies. How she'd love to see the flowers, her own precious, eternal garden. There were a few details to wrap up, then we rose to leave.

"I want to see her," Steve said quietly.

Bobby shook his head. "I don't think you really understand what you're asking. She's not in any shape to view."

"She is my child, and I want to see her," he repeated firmly.

Darlene hurried over and grabbed my arm. "You can't let him, Kathleen, you can't let him see our Ashley. You don't understand how bad it is, you mustn't let him."

I just stood there and shook my head, listening to all the voices around me. Darlene kept repeating, "Don't let him do it, Kathleen."

Steve whispered, "She was my child too, Kathy."

I looked to Mike for guidance. He wasn't looking at me; he was staring at the ground. I looked at Steve. He had that deer in the headlights look in his eyes. And Darlene was furious.

"Stop it! Stop it! Everyone, please be quiet and let me think."

A hush came over the room. "Bobby," I said, "will it cause you any undue problems to let him look at her?"

He answered me with a concerned look in his eyes. "He will have to stay back where I tell him to, due to the chemicals and such. I can't put him at risk. There are the OSHA rules I have to contend with. But if he doesn't mind seeing her from afar, then I guess if he just has to, well then, I can let him."

Why was Bobby so hesitant? What did he know that I didn't? What horror had he seen? "In that case, I don't have a problem with Steve viewing her body."

Darlene screamed, "You can't! He can't. Don't you understand, Kathleen, you can't let him in there!"

"Darlene, it's his nightmare. I can't deal with this right now. If he needs to do this, it is his prerogative, and I can't stop him any more than he could stop me. So please stay out of this."

Darlene began fuming and talking animatedly but quietly with her husband across the room. I asked Bobby to take care of everything. I was on the verge of collapse. The room started spinning, and I began to hear a high-pitched whirling sound. Mike grabbed my arm, led me out to the truck, and took me home.

The rest of the day I lay on the bed, staring at Ashley's picture, tracing the outlines of her pretty face, holding on to Kitty-Kitty, and weeping the tears of a mother who's lost her child.

I've often heard people say they've cried a river of tears, and I thought it was only a phrase. But I cried so much that day my pillow was drenched. My body was racked with pain, as if I'd been beaten from head to toe with a baseball bat. I wanted to die. I wanted to be with my Ashley. My arms ached with the pain of wanting to hold her tender, warm little body just once more.

I moved mechanically through the next few days, answering phone calls, making phone calls, nodding my head yes, and shaking my head no. Whatever was required of me, somehow I managed to do it.

I dug out Ashley's flower girl dress for her burial. We'd picked it out less than one year ago in preparation for Michael's and my wedding. It was frilly and lacy and had little bows in all the right places. It had a delicate, white straw hat, with a tiny pink rose on the front. I polished her small white shoes and found her little lacy socks. I laid out some clean panties. Each item I pulled from her dresser was carefully caressed and meticulously inspected.

I gathered up everything and took it to Bobby. He looked at the clothes. "Those won't be necessary," he said. I stared at him blankly. Then he took a deep breath and told me, "I can't put her in these. . . . I . . . I could put them in with her if you want." He was trying very hard not to say anything that would cause me more pain. Then I realized what he was trying not to say—that she was so destroyed he simply couldn't put her in clothing. It had been two days, and she'd been in an explosion.

I handed him my bundle of delicate, lacy items and said, "Do what you think is best. I just can't see these anymore."

I turned around, walked through the door, and drove immediately home. For many months to come my house would become my haven, my refuge, and in some sense my prison.

Seven

Drought and Devastation

You have allowed me to suffer much hardship,
but you will restore me to life again,
and lift me up from the depths of the earth.
You will restore me to even greater honor
and comfort me once again.

PSALMS 71:20–21 LIV

I fought my way through a cold, distant fog. Nothing seemed real. I was an actress playing a role, living someone else's existence. Just a few days earlier I'd been living a life of great joy, and now, without warning, I'd been flung into a reality of utmost despair.

That Sunday, we reached out for a lifeline and attended services at our church. I sat in the pew, as frozen as a statue, staring into space and not really hearing the sermon. Rex was struggling, but I couldn't see beyond my own pain. I was angry with God. Although I was able to reason the Lord had not done this horrible thing, I had to wrestle with something almost as difficult—He had allowed it to happen.

After the sermon Rex's daughter, Abby, wept as she hugged me tightly.

There were no answers for this horror, no scripture to magically recite and make it all go away.

Monday morning arrived, and I methodically dressed for the funeral. I had only one black dress, and it happened to be one Ashley had helped me make. She'd participated with enthusiasm, little hands assisting as we pinned the fabric to the pattern and cut it out with care. I'd given her the scraps, and she'd fashioned some primitive clothes for her dolls. She sat next to me while I stitched the material and mimicked my moves precisely. When she caught me watching she'd wrinkle her nose and giggle. Yes, this was a special dress. I wasn't the greatest seamstress, and the outfit was far from perfect, but because Ashley and I had shared those tender moments, there was no doubt about what I'd wear.

When I finished dressing I went to my daughter's room and snuggled up on her bed. I pulled all her stuffed animals around me, trying desperately to feel her presence. The telephone rang in the background, but I ignored it. I needed to be alone with my grief.

Mike walked in holding the wireless phone. "Kathleen, it's Bobby at the funeral home. Steve is down there with a lawyer. He wants to have Ashley's coffin opened."

I sat up and looked at him in shock. "Tell Bobby we're on our way." I grabbed my shoes. Frustration and rage flared up in me like I'd never known before. "Honey, get your badge and your gun. Let's go."

I headed for the door while Mike called the police. I sat in the truck seething. This was the last straw, and his timing was impeccable! All my anger about the bombing was suddenly heaped upon him.

When Mike came to the truck, I saw worry in his eyes. We drove to the funeral home in silence. As we pulled up I reached for Mike's gun, took it out of the holster, and cocked it. "This is it. I'm going to kill him!"

Mike reached over and took the weapon away. "Kathleen, you know how much I love you. I couldn't stand losing you right now. If you kill Steve, they will take you away from me. Why don't we let the authorities handle this?" I knew he was right, but it took every ounce of my will to agree.

I stormed from the truck to the door. As I flung it open I saw a man I didn't recognize. He approached me and identified himself as Steve's lawyer. "Listen," I said, "I don't care who you are, you'd better get out of my way before I knock you down." I pushed past him and went to the room where Ashley was. Steve was there with a police officer. "Why can't you just leave us alone?" I screamed. Steve tried to talk to me, but I was so blinded by rage I couldn't hear a word he said.

The officer pushed me out of the room and into Mike's arms. Mike spoke calmly to the policeman while I continued to scream at Steve. Then my husband pulled me into Bobby's office, sat me down, and gave me a stern look. Bobby followed us into the room. "Do you have a lawyer?" he asked.

I shook my head. "I've never needed one—until now. The only one I know is Ralph Hood. He's handling Daddy's estate."

Bobby shook his head. "That's fine. I think I'd better call him. We need him over here immediately." While Bobby dialed the phone, Mike sat silently holding my hand.

It wasn't long before Mr. Hood arrived, sat down, and assessed the situation. All the information came pouring out. Yes, it was true, Steve wanted Ashley's casket to be open for viewing. Because of the state she was in, that was absolutely impossible. Ralph went back and forth between Steve's lawyer and us. It was finally agreed, Steve could view the body alone one last time, but the funeral would go on as planned.

I apologized to Bobby, and Mr. Hood, for all the trouble we'd caused and thanked them for their help. Mike and I left the funeral home. Never in my life had I felt so emotionally drained. I dreaded having to face people at the funeral, but I knew it had to be done. I needed to put this behind me.

We went home, gathered up our family, and prepared to leave. When we arrived at the church, the press was already there. They were setting up in the southeast corner of the churchyard. Wayne Russell had stationed himself at the front door. "I wasn't lettin' any of those vultures in here without talking to ya'll first."

"Thank you, Wayne. If they want to come in as people, and not as reporters, I think that will be okay. We have allowed the photographer from *Newsweek,* and one German TV station, to come in and film the funeral. They promised they would honor Ashley and not be obtrusive."

He nodded and put his arm protectively around my shoulders. "Don't you give it a second thought. We'll take care of everything."

We went into the fellowship hall, where there were probably thirty to fifty people already gathered. I sat down in the first chair I came to. My cousin Nancy sat beside me. "Kathleen, my church in Texas has taken up an offering to help with the expense of the funeral and all, but I understand those costs have already been covered. Is there something else the money can be used for?" My mind was empty. I just shrugged my shoulders.

Darlene tried to help. "You know, Ashley sure would have liked some playground equipment. Do you think your church would allow the donation to be used for that?"

Again I shrugged. It just didn't matter. Ashley would never play there, or enjoy anything that was given in her memory. "That might be nice," I said vacantly.

My aunt Macy sat down on my other side. She put her arm around me. "Are you all right?" I didn't answer. Of course I wasn't all right. Nothing would ever be right again. She reached into her pocket and pulled out a small, shiny angel pin. "I thought you might like this," she quietly said, pinning it to my collar. "I have one for Zack and David too."

I glanced around the room. There were so many people. Many I didn't recognize. Mike tried to introduce me to some relatives, but to this day I'm not sure who they were. I was still in a surreal dreamlike state.

When we were finally ushered into the packed-to-capacity sanctuary, I didn't understand why everyone was looking at me. Then, at the center of the altar, I saw the little white box, surrounded by mountains of flowers and stuffed animals. Ashley would have loved all the flowers, I thought. I sat in the front row and looked over to my left. Steve and his family were there. I turned back around and stared at the box. There was no way Ashley was in there. Someone has taken her, and I wanted her back. "It's just a box, not my daughter," I almost chanted to myself.

I listened carefully to Rex's eulogy. It was racked with pain. "Ashley's ministry continues," he said. "It continues in the hearts of those who love her. We may never understand why she was taken from us. All we know is, we love her, and God must be our comfort now."

Dennis Rigdon sang "Why." Then my precious friends Janice and John Mobley and their son, Benjamin, began their presentation. The quiet strains of "Amazing Grace," sang by Willie Nelson, filled the sanctuary while slides of Ashley as a baby and as she grew began flashing on the wall next to the wooden cross. I sobbed openly. My mind raced. Oh my God, she really isn't coming home. Is this all I have left of my daughter—photographs?

Rex invited anyone to come forward to share memories of Ashley with the congregation. My sister and Aunt Bettysue walked up. "If anyone is in heaven, Ashley is."

Next were Benjamin and John. John picked up his six-year-old son and held him to the microphone. In childlike innocence he spoke. "She was my good friend, and I'll miss her."

Sandra Fosche, the mother of one of the Cub Scouts, came forward and shared the last time she saw Ashley. It was at a scout meeting. I'd caught Ashley rummaging through Sandra's purse looking for candy, and I'd scolded her. Sandra said, "I just want you to know, she was welcome to look for candy anytime she wanted to."

Waynett Martin, Zachary's den mother, came forward. "I have a very special memory of Ashley," she said. "We had a campfire at our farm just a few weeks back, and Ashley came with her brother. We had an Easter egg hunt, and she was right in the middle of everything. At one point, one of the children found a rope, and Ashley had organized all the other little sisters to tie the boys up. She was not letting any of those fellows push her around. She was in charge and lovin' it."

Never again, I thought.

Rex rose and said a prayer, inviting everyone to come by and express love to the family. A huge line formed. One by one those in the sanctuary hugged Mike and me. Mike's fellow Guardsmen were there, dressed in full uniform. The Cub Scout leaders came in formal scout attire. Teachers, friends, acquaintances all proceeded by, one by one, offering a hug, a handshake, a kind word.

I looked over at the small, white coffin. Doug Haymaker, Rex's fifteen-year-old son, walked up to the little box and carefully placed a hand-held kiss on the top, right where Ashley's face should have been. It broke my heart. I knew how much Ashley loved him. I just didn't realize how much Doug was hurting too.

When the procession ended the four pallbearers walked somberly to the casket, picked it up, and moved it to the hearse. As we were escorted to the limousine, I heard the click of cameras in the distance. Many reporters hurried to their cars to get to the cemetery. I watched as the flowers were gathered and the hearse was closed.

I leaned my head on Mike's shoulder. I looked into his eyes and saw streams of tears on his cheeks. We held each other as tightly as we could. I turned to look behind us. There must have been a mile-long procession of cars. In front was the entire Guthrie police department. At each stop one officer would leave the procession and guard the intersection, saluting as the cars passed by. I was bewildered beyond comprehension.

It took almost fifteen minutes for everyone to arrive at the cemetery. I watched them take the white box out of the hearse and place it over the hole in the ground. Bobby and Rex came to the door of the limousine and escorted us to a place reserved in front. I didn't want to be there.

Zack sat beside me, and I put my arm around him. He'd cried during the eulogy and now looked so worn, so tired, and so very sad. He stared into my eyes, searching for understanding. It hurt to see his confusion. How could I explain something I didn't comprehend myself? He was too young to have to face such difficulty. My heart ached for him.

After everyone was seated Rex read the Twenty-third Psalm, offered a prayer, then excused the crowd. He announced the family would be returning to the church for a time of reflection and asked the press to respect our grief. We were escorted to the waiting limousine.

The ladies of our church had prepared a banquet. There was enough to feed a small army, but I wasn't hungry. Although I hadn't eaten anything since April 19, I just couldn't start now. Darlene fixed a plate and put it in front of me. "You have to eat," she said. I absently pushed the morsels around the dish, managing only to consume a few bites. I knew we were only half done. We still had to do this all over again for Luther and LaRue.

I got up and went to the sanctuary. I needed to be alone. Cindy Duffle, one of the ladies of the church, sat beside me, placing her arm across my shoulder. "I have something to tell you," she said. "Ya know, for years, LaRue asked us to pray for Michael. It broke her heart to see him away from church. Then you showed up, Kathleen. Before long, you and Michael were coming to services, and LaRue stopped worrying about her son. Then you were married, and she had the most peaceful expression on her face. You, my dear, were an answer to prayer."

"Thank you, Cindy. LaRue gave me a precious gift." I shared what she'd whispered in my ear at our wedding, that I was the daughter-in-law she'd always wanted.

Tears streamed down my face as we sat quietly looking at the array of flowers. I got up, went to each one, and opened the cards. Some came from people we knew and others from those we didn't. I didn't grasp why complete strangers would send flowers to Ashley's funeral. It would be many days before I understood the life that was now mine.

I heard Mike in Rex's office. I walked in and stood behind him. He was retrieving our messages from the answering machine at home. "There are eleven messages," he said. I watched as he wrote down each one. Most were calls from reporters, but the third one was from the medical examiner's office, as were the seventh, eighth, and eleventh, each emphatically saying they had information and needed us to call them back immediately.

Mike dialed the number. They requested we come to the First Christian Church. For the second time in less than a week, we gathered up the family and headed toward bad news.

When we arrived we were ushered upstairs to a large room—the same place they took us for Ashley. The examiner asked for Mike, and he stepped forward. "We regret to inform you, both your mother and father were found among the dead." Debbie and Brad began sobbing loudly. Brad was rocking in his chair. Although we knew when Ashley was found Mom and Dad would be too, the words were still difficult to hear. Reality once again hit us square in the face. Mike signed the appropriate paperwork and gave them Bobby Smith's phone number. We filtered out of the church, agreeing to meet Bobby at 10:00 the next morning. God help us. We had another funeral to arrange.

The next day we repeated the process of choosing caskets, flowers, and tributes for Mom and Dad. Mike's brothers and sister agreed they should be buried as they lived, side by side, at one funeral. They chose a black coffin for Dad and a white coffin for Mom, because those were the colors they were married in. Debbie decided on the flowers. Bobby gave Michael an envelope with Dad's wallet and Mom's gold cross.

"If you want," Bobby explained, "you can open your dad's casket. His injuries are not that bad. He has a few burn marks on his face, but that's all."

"What about Mom? Can we do that for Mom too?" He sadly shook his head no.

When everyone left Michael asked for a lock of LaRue's hair to give to Debbie. Bobby looked at us sadly. "I can't," he said.

"I don't understand," Mike whispered, his face registering confusion.

"I . . . She . . . It just won't be possible." The look on Bobby's face spoke volumes. There was no need for further explanation.

"We will bring you their clothes tomorrow," Mike said as we turned to go home.

I woke up the morning of their funeral with the flu. It seemed the days of stress and starvation had finally taken their toll. I called our family doctor for an appointment. When I told the nurse who I was, she expressed her condolences and asked me to come right in.

Dr. Dixson had been our family physician for years. When he came in to perform the examination, he looked at me carefully. "How are you holding up?" he asked.

I shrugged my shoulders. "About as well as can be expected," I answered.

"Are you sleeping?"

"Not a lot."

He nodded, then proceeded with the examination. "Well, it's a viral infection. I'll write you a prescription for some antibiotics, and I'm also going to write you something to help relieve the stress. You can take it if you want, but I think some rest would do you good. You take care now. There are a lot of people praying for you and your family."

I filled the prescriptions and took the penicillin immediately, as well as one of the pills to calm my nerves. But instead of relaxing me, it seemed to put me into a stupor. I was already a zombie. This didn't help. Michael had to lead me around like a dog on a leash. I didn't know, or care, where I was going.

When I arrived at the funeral, I noticed how much it resembled Ashley's. Janice and John provided another slide presentation. Dennis Rigdon sang, as did my niece Kristen. Rex gave another beautiful eulogy.

When it was time for people to come forward and share memories of Mom and Dad, Mike was the first one to the podium. Wearing his dress blue uniform, he barely contained his tears as he looked at the black and white coffins in front of him. I thought of how proud Luther and LaRue were of Mike and his military service.

I can't remember his exact words, but I do recall the pain in his voice. As the service ended Michael led me to the waiting limousine.

I'd become detached from myself. It was as if I were floating above my body, watching the whole thing from afar. Michael had arranged for the bagpipes to be played by the son of one of his fellow Guardsmen. "Dad always loved hymns played on the pipes," he said as the sound of "Amazing Grace" filled the spring air. It was a beautiful tribute to a man and woman who had lived their entire lives resting peacefully under the wings of God's grace.

The next morning dawned sunny and warm. The house was strangely silent. I wandered into Ashley's room. I caressed all her little things as I started packing them into boxes. I took the sheets off the bed and put them in the washer. Michael followed me back into the bedroom. "What are you doing?" he asked.

"Our house is too small to make this room a shrine," I said. "I have to do this now, or I'll never be able to."

Tenderly he helped me go through all of Ashley's things. There was one little dress I'd made for her that I just couldn't give away, and a handful of toys that were too special to let go, but most everything else was packed up and removed. I put Ashley's garment with my wedding dress. It was almost a year since our wedding, and my gown still hadn't been cleaned and stored. Now would be a good time to do that. I put a few playthings in a small box and labeled it "Ashley's Special Toys."

Ashley's bed was the bottom portion of a bunk. The top was what Zack slept on in David's room. Mike and I put the beds together and moved Zack into Ashley's room. It took nearly all day to change things around. By the time I was done, I had several boxes of clothes and toys to donate to Goodwill.

A few days after the funeral, Doug Haymaker sent me a long letter:

It was Easter Sunday, and she was wearing her blue Easter dress and a straw hat. It was the last time I'd see "my Little Friend." She was in my mom's classroom, and my mom asked her what was wrong. She said, "The Easter Bunny didn't visit my house." So Mom said, "You know what, the Easter Bunny didn't visit my house either."

After that, she smiled, and I saw love in her blue eyes. Ashley was standing next to my mom, so I took her hat off, picked her up, and kissed her. I told her I loved her. She said, "I love you too!" Then I played with her blond hair.

After church I gave her another hug and kiss, then told her I loved her once again. She said, "I love you too!" I promised to see her next week. Those were the last words I ever said to Ashley Megan Eckles, "my Little Friend."

When she played with the boys after church, they'd always pick on her, and she'd scream, "Bodyguard, get over here and help me." I can no longer be her bodyguard, because on April 19th, "my Little Friend" died.

On April 24th, we held "my Little Friend's" funeral. That was the saddest day of my life, because I knew I'd never see her again until I die and go to heaven. On the day of her funeral, it was rainy and gloomy.

As I was waiting to hug the family, I kissed my hand and touched her casket. I will never forget that rainy and gloomy day as long as I live. I also will never forget April 19, the day so many loved ones, and "my Little Friend," died.

It has been hard for me to move on. All I think about is that day and "my Little Friend." Without Kathleen, I wouldn't know what to do. I love her very, very, very much! She's like a big sister, or even a mother. Her whole family is very kind and loving. I love them all. I know I will never get over that dreadful day, but I can move on. It's going to be a long time, but I can do it. I'm still having a hard time dealing with it.

Lately, I've had nightmares about the day everybody remembers. It was the worst day of my life. It's the scariest thing I've ever gone *through. All I dream about is being there with Ashley and trying to help her.*

I want to thank all the rescue workers who helped find "my Little Friend." Not only Ashley, but everybody. I also want to thank Kathleen for being there when I was hurting and whenever I need to talk to somebody. That means a lot to me, and I appreciate that. I love her a lot, and I thank her for always being there for me.

I miss you, Ashley.

Love, your friend,

Doug

I began studying the Book of Job. I tried to understand why God let these horrible things happen to His servants. I asked the same questions over and over again. Somehow, I had to make sense of it all. Why would God separate me from my baby? Then I began hearing from friends, family, and strangers.

"God loves her even more than you do. You must know, she is well cared for in heaven." But that didn't make my arms ache any less.

"She's in heaven now. No one else can hurt her." True, but I can't experience her love anymore.

"You must be thankful, you still have your other children." Ashley was my only daughter, and my relationship with each child is unique. My opportunity to pass the legacy I received from my mother and grandmother died with her.

"Someday you will thank God for this." Oh yes, for God's sake, hurt me some more.

"I know how you must feel." Come on! No one could possibly know how I feel.

In the years to come there'd be many more hurtful platitudes. But I have chosen to forget them simply because I realize most people were just trying to help. They didn't have the vaguest idea what to say. How could they? How could anyone be prepared for such heartache?

As the days went on I began to wonder. How could I ever look at life the same way? Since the bombing I approached people differently, and I spoke differently. I felt different. I wasn't as trusting. I realized people were often too involved in their own problems to notice how the careless words they spoke grated on my broken heart.

But despite the darkness surrounding me, my nightmare had only begun. The days, weeks, and months to follow would present unimaginable challenges and the ultimate test of my last lifeline—my faith.

Eight

Flowers of Compassion

Little things seem nothing, but they give peace, like those meadow flowers which individually seem odorless but all together perfume the air.

GEORGES BERNANOS

People from around the world reached out with loving arms, offering whatever they could—a shoulder to cry on, a kind word, a prayer. Even the U.S. Postal Service went substantially above and beyond their call of duty. One envelope arrived safely from Ireland with only the following address: "To the Parents of Ashley Eckles who was killed in the bombing."

I opened each letter and read every word.

Dear Kathleen and Mike:

We, who are strangers to you, are taking the liberty of writing to let you know how deeply saddened we feel about the carnage in Oklahoma City. We have watched our television screens, and read our newspapers, with mounting horror and anger since Wednesday the 19th. On Sunday morning, we opened our newspaper to see a picture of a happy, smiling Ashley Treanor, missing with her grandparents

Luther and LaRue Treanor. The fact we bear the same surname rein-
forced our anger and disgust at this obscene bombing.

We want you to know, we are praying for all the victims and
their despairing relatives, but particularly for you and your family.
We are sure you will get many letters from strangers such as us. Please
don't feel you have to reply.

With our prayers,
Luala and Vincent
Greentrees Park, Dublin, Ireland

There were other letters from individuals bearing our last name. We
may never know if we're related, but the similarity caused them to connect
with our plight and to reach out with compassion.

The following letters arrived addressed to Mike and Kathleen Treanor,
Oklahoma City, OK:

Dear Mike and Kathleen:

I saw a photograph of your daughter, Ashley, in one of our
National newspapers, and I was filled with anger to think a heinous
act of terrorism would claim such an innocent life.

When I read the accompanying story, and realized the full extent
of your loss, and that we share the same name, I felt compelled to
write to you.

My wife and I have two daughters, aged 23 and 25, and we know
how much we love and care for them. But we cannot begin to under-
stand the depth of anxiety, sorrow and disbelief you must be suffering.

We live in a violent world and such acts of terrorism are occur-
ring all too often. It's only those whose lives, and families, have been
devastated who fully understand the futility of such anger.

I hope this letter will convey, people thousands of miles away are
thinking of you, and in some small way, this will help give you
strength and resilience for the future.

Yours Sincerely,
Mike
Abergavenny, Gwent UK

And

Dear Mrs. Treanor:

I was reading in my weekly Catholic New York *about the tragedy in Oklahoma City when your name caught my eye—Kathleen Treanor, the same spelling as my maiden name. I want to offer you my sincerest condolences on the loss of your little girl and her grandparents. I've been remembering you in prayer, that God will give you consolation in this terrible time. God doesn't abandon us.*

I hope you'll be able to get grief counseling and group help. It will give you something to hold on to. Please take care of yourself.

It's likely we're related somewhere back through the generations. My dad's family came from County Monaghan, Ireland. Treanor is a popular name in Monaghan town as we saw when we visited. God be with you.

Sincerely,
Kay
Bronxville, NY

The letters from children were the most heart-wrenching. They brought up the same question I'd asked myself so many times before—Why?

Each one tried to offer comfort, each allowed me to let go of a little more pain. I didn't understand why these people were writing to me, but I was thankful for their words.

May 8, 1995

My name is Bobbie, and I'm a Senior in High School. I'm from Colorado Spgs, CO. I'm writing to you, and letting you know, I'm here to cheer you up. I am always here to be leaned on. Fear from the bombing has been a big deal here in Colorado Spgs. Even though miles apart, we share our hearts.

The loss of people is something we'll never understand. There must be faith in the hearts of all. The strength in your heart will ease your pain. Remembering the happy times will bring a smile to your

face instead of the bombing bringing a tear. Everyone is curious why,
or how, someone can do this. I hope to hear from you. I'd like to know
how things are going. I sincerely hope things go well.
    Your True friend,
    Bobbie

The most helpful letters I received were from mothers, and grand-
mothers, who'd also lost a child. They tried to prepare me for the road
ahead:

Dear Kathleen:
    The magnitude of your tragedy is overwhelming to me. I wish I
could put my arms around you, and your sons, because I know the
positive power of a hug.
    On December 30th, my future daughter-in-law, Shannon, was
struck down by a maniac's bullet in the Planned Parenthood facility
in Brookline, MA. She was simply doing her job as a receptionist.
    The senseless loss of this beautiful, caring woman is something
none of us can comprehend . . . especially my son, David. Shannon
was a truly loving, compassionate human being, who loved children.
We have often joked my daughter gave us two grandsons, and it
would be Shannon's and David's Duty to give us granddaughters.
Now due to a terrorist's gun, that's not possible.
    Remember, all Christians believe, we'll be reunited with our lost
loved ones on that reckoning day. I believe, when you see Ashley, she'll
tell you Shannon has been holding her hand.
    My heart is with you,
    Gayle
    Andover, MA

Here is another one that spoke to my heart.

Dear Kathleen:
    I am so sorry for your loss, but I know little Ashley is a beauti-
ful angel with Jesus. The pain and hurt is terrible.

I lost a 30-year-old son with cancer a few months ago. Although he was ready to meet Jesus, it leaves such a void in me and his 6 brothers and sisters.

For little Ashley, there is no words that can make it easier. I have a 5 year old Ashleigh, granddaughter, and I know what it would do to us if something happened to her.

I want you to know my family, and I, will think of you every day, and you, and your family, will be in our daily prayers.

May God love and Comfort you Always.

Respectfully,

Ruth

This letter came from a woman I worked with briefly shortly before the bombing.

Dear Kathleen:

You've been in our thoughts every day here at Farley. We miss your smiling face! I know the coming weeks, and months, will be hard to bear, but I think you are strong enough to survive this heartache.

As one who also lost a child suddenly, I know that terrible pain. You will carry this loss forever, but one day, your thoughts will not be about the death, but about Ashley's life. When that happens, life is bearable again.

One day soon, it will seem everyone else's life is back to normal, and you are the only one still grieving. That is natural, and only a mother who has lost a child understands that isolation. We think the world should stop, but it won't. If that happens, and you need to talk to someone who understands, please call me.

You, and your family, are in my prayers,

Judy

The letters kept coming. Each one helped me to realize how much people cared.

Dear Kathleen, Mike and family,

I hope this note doesn't make you feel worse at this time. I know, many years ago, I lost a little 5 year old girl to leukemia. There isn't much that can make you feel better.

I do hope you read this note. I'm not a professional mourner; I'm a grandmother now and felt such grief over the tragedy that struck your family and the others in Oklahoma City.

The pictures I saw of your precious little Ashley came home to me. She could have been one of mine. If you don't mind, I'd like to add her to my list of extended grandchildren and keep her memory in my heart and prayers.

I enclosed some dimes. Our little Laurie loved the penny gum machine, so we take pennies to the cemetery when we go. Now there are dime machines, but our little Laurie would have wanted us to give some to your little Ashley when you go to the cemetery.

We'll probably never meet, and you needn't feel obligated to return a letter. If you ever want to talk though, please feel free. You and your family are in my prayers, and I will not forget, you and your sweet little girl. You aren't alone.

I'm so sorry about your loss, little Ashley and your parents.
Sincerely,
Janice
Carrollton, TX

And

Dear Kathleen:

I realize, we've never officially met; however, we do have a mutual common bond. Like you, I kissed my child good-bye one morning and my nice normal life ended there. My baby was injured in a tragic accident and my life changed forever. Like you, I have experienced the ultimate grief, the loss of a baby, and like you, I wondered why God had taken away this precious gift from my arms.

There is little I can say to make you feel any better—therefore, I won't even try. Your memories, your friends, and your faith will be the only things that will carry you through the next few weeks. Please know, time is a great healer. Eventually you will be able to talk about Ashley without a knot forming in your throat, and without tears, but also know every day for the rest of your life, you will think of her.

After the loss of our son, we did find some strength in a support group. Please know that I am always available if you would like to talk. However, if you feel the need for more structure where both you and your husband, and even your other children, might find some strength, I have enclosed a listing that was published in the paper.

I work with Cindy, she provided me with your name and address. Cindy is a valued friend and dear person. You are fortunate to have church friends like her. Hold tight to these friends, the winds will blow strong some days—strong enough to knock you off your feet—when this happens, reach out and hang on tight—the winds will subside.

Please know, there are people all over this state that are thinking and praying for you. As Oklahomans, we must band together and never let the people forget the tragedy that has happened in our state. We are here to help you keep Ashley's spirit alive.

In Christ's Love,
Denise
Edmond, OK

More letters poured in, touching my heart and offering salve for my wounded soul.

To the family of Ashley Eckols:
I was going to send a card to you, but cards are filled with other people's words, and I wanted these words to be mine.

As a parent, who also lost a child due to the deeds of an evil hearted person, my heart aches for you. It is difficult to understand the death of a child always, but under circumstances such as these, it is totally incomprehensible. I won't ever pretend to understand or explain it.

There are things I do understand and believe. I believe our children are with God. We, as parents, love our children to the best of our ability, but He is the ultimate of love and caring, and we can be secure, they are safe now. I also believe, we will be reunited with our children, as this is His promise to us, and it is one promise, we can depend on.

I'm sure, there are many well meaning people giving you advice as to what you should do right now. May I make a few suggestions to you from experience? Please feel the feelings, as painful as they may be. Take your prayers, and tears, to the Lord, as He is full of compassion, and He hears your pleas. Reach out and accept all the love your friends and family have to offer, and someday the skies will appear blue again, the sun brighter, the flowers filled with beautiful color, and smelling sweeter than ever before, and you will find peace.

I know, Californians are believed to be very selfish and self-indulgent, but please know that this tragedy has touched all our hearts deeply.

The Lord has His arms wrapped tightly around you and will help you through this. People tend to forget about your pain and get on with their lives, but you will be in my prayers and thoughts always. I will contact you again in the weeks and months to come in hopes I might lift your spirits. May God bless you and bring you peace.

Your friend in Christ,
Patti
Chico, CA

This one was received just before Ashley's birthday, July 25, 1995.

Dear Kathleen:

Just want you to know, I will be thinking of you all in a special way this Saturday and remembering cute little Ashley. It doesn't matter how many days, months, or years go by—the city, the nation, the world will never forget what happened.

I know you have a million memories of Ashley and all the fun things she did. I'll be thinking of you and remembering her the way she was in her happy, sweet picture. What a special, adorable child.
Fondly,
Susan

Susan wrote me several times over the years, always remembering Ashley's birthday. She too had lost a child. Although I never made formal contact with her, her letters were always precious to me.

Through the Red Cross, Nancy of Coronado, California, contacted me. We began corresponding not long after the bombing. Several letters and photographs were exchanged, and finally, a little over a year later, she designed and sent me an Ashley doll. The doll is exquisite and an almost perfect likeness of my daughter. Her little dress, hat, and umbrella match the outfit Ashley wore to Michael's and my wedding.

May 25, 1996
Dear Kathleen:
I hope you like your doll. Her hat and umbrella are enclosed in the box, and the umbrella fits through both hands. I hope you think she looks like Ashley. (A doll can never be as cute as a child.) There are only 2 Ashley Megan dolls in the world, yours and mine (Mine has brown painted eyes).

Please don't worry about me marketing your doll. I would never do that. I will save the molds forever, so just in case a piece breaks, I can replace it. If you look under her hair on the back of her neck, you can see her name engraved and the date and my signature.

If you know another mother, or Grandmother, who has lost a child, please tell them to write me. I never charge anyone who's lost a child and would like a doll.

Thank you for your sweet letter. I admire your strength. I read your article in Ladies' Home Journal. *I hope and pray, you get your surgery to reverse your sterilization procedure. If you'd like me to try to get the hospitals and doctors to do a donation surgery like they did for Edie, I would be happy to try here in San Diego and Los Angeles. Please let me know.*

I'll always try to stay in contact with you, so if you need doll replacement parts, you will be able to find me. We do move quite often. I hope your doll arrived in perfect condition.

Love,

Nancy

Many gifts came through the mail. One was from Sheila, who lost her husband tragically and was having trouble coping. She sent her "Wings of Hope," a beautiful gold charm of angel wings that she designed and marketed herself.

Here is the letter that accompanied her gift:

March 22, 1996

Dear Kathleen & Mike,

I spoke with Mike on the phone today and wanted to also tell you my story.

When I was 29 years old, my husband was abruptly killed, and I had 2 small children to raise—(3½ and 5½ yrs. old) Then, a few years ago, my little 8 month old niece suddenly died from a muscular disease.

They were the saddest times of my life. I wanted to turn it around and have something good come of it.

Suddenly, all I kept drawing were "angel wings" . . . the same side-view of angel wings over and over again. I was driven to create them in some type of 3 dimensional form, so I could tangibly see and feel them.

First, I designed a large mold and made large paper wings from it. I framed them and was very pleased with how they looked. I felt comfort every time I looked at them.

But then I wanted to have them smaller, in the form of jewelry, so I could wear them every day and touch them whenever I wanted to. Therefore, I designed these smaller "Wings of Hope."

I read the article in Journal *magazine, and I felt strongly that you, too, should have the "Wings of Hope." I think they will help you.*

The next step I'm doing is making them into tie tacks, so that men can wear them and derive comfort from them daily.

I hope you get as much out of the "Wings of Hope" as I (and others) have. Please drop me a note letting me know, you did receive them.

Sincerely,
Sheila

This letter was written by the family who used to baby-sit Ashley and Zachary when I lived in northeast Oklahoma.

Kathy,

We are very, very sorry to hear about Ashley's tragic death. She was always a happy active little girl. She always had that outgoing love. I really enjoyed her and Zack at Ramms Day Care. I missed the kids really bad when you moved, but I always thought about them, their love they gave to me, their helpfulness and being my buddies. I loved them, as if they were my own children. We will never forget Ashley or Zack. We will always love them. Our thoughts and prayers are with you and your family.

Love Claudia & Dickie
Prior Creek, OK

I was amazed by the number of letters that poured in. Each time I opened one, I realized how much people wanted to offer hope.

Dear Kathleen:

After reading the article in the paper about your parents and Ashley's, I felt the need to write to you. Not knowing if you will receive this or not, I still have hope.

I'm a grandmother, and my grandchildren, 7 and 16, live near me. They have been my life since they were born. I am so sorry for your terrible loss. I have put myself in your place, and there is no way to describe the way you are feeling now. I can only say, may God grant you peace from your hurt.

They say time heals, and friends help, and by the look on Ashley's face in her picture, I know you have lots of loving friends and family. Everywhere I go, people like my two grand-girls, and tell me how much they enjoy being with them and talking with them. I'm so glad I could share your grief by reading the story in the paper. We have prayed at our Church and home for all.

Sincerely,
Carol
Meyersville, PA

I've stored each letter carefully away for safekeeping. Along with the correspondence came many trinkets, statuettes, handmade items, jewelry, and books. I treasured the books the most. I read each one carefully, line by line, hoping for a glimmer of understanding. There were days when the kindness from strangers became my sanity, the very thing that kept me going. But I was seldom able to extend beyond my own grief to thank them for their compassion.

The letters from those who'd experienced loss were the most helpful. They assured me, line by line, it was okay to feel the way I did. Each time someone reached out, my burden became a little bit lighter. I began to understand the expression, "Misery loves company." Their words offered comfort, empathy, and understanding, born simply from the fact they'd traveled that road before me.

From around the world compassionate people sowed fragile seeds of faith. In turn, I've reaped a bountiful harvest of blessings. Thanks to my earth angels, what was meant for evil miraculously become much more—a beautiful, God-inspired tapestry of love.

Nine

Epiphany Among the Lilies

I love to think of nature as an unlimited broadcasting station through
which God speaks to us every hour, if we will only tune in.

GEORGE WASHINGTON CARVER

I awoke with a start. It had happened again. Why, God, why am I still tormented so? Over the last several months I had tried to escape through sleep but could never get away from depression's powerful grasp. The deep sorrow, loss, and devastation haunted me in the form of recurring dreams. Each night as I lay tossing and turning the images would come, uninvited, into my mind. As in a continuous rerun of a bad movie, I'd helplessly watch myself enter LaRue's home.

Suddenly I'd see Ashley as she ran out the front door. In her sweet way she'd turn, glance in my direction, and giggle. In a fraction of a moment I'd be off, chasing her, desperately calling her name. But Ashley was always just beyond my reach. As I pleaded for her to stop, she'd look over one shoulder, giggle, then continue running. Through woods and valleys we would go, Ashley just ahead, and me falling behind, a mother desperately in pursuit of her child.

Through a heavy mist I could barely see it, a bridge stretching across a deep, dark abyss. As I chased Ashley to the end, she would open her wings and fly a short distance, hovering just over the chasm. As my body teetered precariously on the edge, I'd hear her say, "I love you, Mommy, but you can't go now. I will see you later. Bye-bye." Clouds, illuminated from within, would begin to part, revealing a light too bright for my eyes. Then Ashley would give me one of her tender, nose-wrinkling smiles, wave, and fly away. Each time I'd awake, thrashing about, sweating, and crying out her name. I grew to dread the dream's arrival. I didn't understand why it tortured me so, why it wouldn't let me rest in peace.

I stumbled to the kitchen for a glass of water. Why, God? Why do these images continue to haunt me?

But it was more than just dreams. Even my waking hours were spent searching for Ashley. In public I'd look at every little honey blond girl I saw, fully expecting that child to be mine. Each giggle would turn my head and rip at my heart.

One day at the mall I saw a young girl who resembled my precious angel. She was with her parents, overjoyed at receiving a new bicycle. She rode in circles as she sang, "I've got a new bike! I've got a new bike!" When her parents called her Ashley, tears rolled down my cheeks. As the family drove away I was once again hit by reality. No matter how I tried, I couldn't face my daughter's death. When I last saw Ashley, she'd been whole and full of life. My heart still believed she was coming back.

As I glanced out the window, I saw flowers beginning to bloom. I stepped onto the front porch, sat down on the bench, and looked across my yard. The iris Ashley and I planted seemed to reach out to me. It was beautiful, so full of life. I went over to the little garden and sat down.

I was swept away to a sunny afternoon not so long ago. I remembered pulling a big box out of the garage. Ashley was so excited. She skipped and twirled ahead of me as I walked to the spot I'd prepared for my mother's precious memories. She knew the bulbs belonged to her grandma Pat—a grandmother she'd never met. Ashley understood how special they were. She was wearing a little navy blue gingham dress, pink tennis shoes, and lacy anklets. Her hair was pulled back in a ponytail, which she'd swing back and forth as she skipped along.

I saw wonder in her eyes as she looked into the box. "Mama, can I have one?" she whispered. I nodded, and gently she lifted a bulb out of the container. "Can I plant this one in my own garden?"

"Show me where your garden is, Ashley." She led me to a shady area under some cedar trees that we'd recently cleared for the children to play in on hot summer days. "No, baby, this just won't do. Flowers need the sun to grow, and these trees will keep out the light. Why don't you help me plant them in my garden, and they can be our flowers. We can share."

She smiled brilliantly. "Can I have a special place just for my flowers, just for me?"

"You bet! How about right here?" I pointed to a spot on the end. Ashley quickly went over and planted a half dozen bulbs. I watched her as she carefully removed the dirt. "There, that's just right." We put the bulbs in the ground and covered them with soil. Ashley was so cute, kneeling down in her little dress, a smudge on her cheek and dirt up to her elbows. When she caught me watching, she'd give me one of her brilliant smiles.

Before long she saw the boys splashing in the sprinkler and ran off to join them. The yard was filled with the joyful sounds of children playing and laughing. It was a day I will treasure in my heart forever.

Each afternoon Ashley tended her flowers. Daily she'd ask, "When will they bloom?"

"In the springtime, around April," I told her. "But for now they are sleeping, gathering strength so they can put on their beautiful, delicate wedding dresses just for you."

Ashley never saw that spring day, never saw her flowers bloom in their joyous display of life. She'd been taken to heaven before she could see the culmination of her handiwork. How she would have loved the flowers. She always found tremendous joy in the beauty of God's creation.

How I longed for my daughter to pick the flowers today, to watch the soft petals caress her face. I knelt down in the grass, overcome with the sense of her presence. Seeing her flowers in full bloom was like receiving a hug from heaven.

I was suddenly overwhelmed with my need to hold her just once more. My tears fell on the petals, then slid to the soil. I looked up to the heavens. "*Oh, God,*" I cried, "how could you let them take my precious daughter from me? I just need to understand. What did I do to deserve this pain? Why am I being punished so harshly?" I collapsed onto the ground and lay there sobbing uncontrollably. "Why? Why? Why?" I wailed.

As my heart continued to break, words of comfort came softly. "Don't you remember, Kathleen? I also lost my child. Like yours, he suffered a cruel, needless death. I know your pain. I did not cause it. But I gave all my children the choice to love and obey me. This is the price of their disobedience."

"But, God," I pleaded, "I'd returned in faith. I was setting my life on the right path. I don't understand. Why are you punishing me now?"

"My child, I am not punishing you. Others have caused your heartbreak. It was their choice, and they chose death."

"But you were supposed to protect me from this. Why did you let this happen to me?"

As I lay on the cool grass, my mind flashed back to a time right before the bombing. We'd decided it was good for our family to worship together, to be in the presence of God. And so we did. Each Sunday I felt my heart's desire grow stronger. I wanted to get more involved with our church but wasn't sure where I could most be of service. One day I went before the altar and rededicated my life to God. I wanted to be a strong voice for Him, to bear fruit, to help a hurting world. I realized the one thing I was good at was sharing my heart. As I knelt before Him I prayed for a powerful message, something that would open the doors for me to talk to many about my faith, my Christian walk, about the hope of God. I never dreamed I would have to lose a part of myself, my child, in order to receive that message. I thought I was praying for wisdom, for God to use my past to help others.

Suddenly an overwhelming sense of guilt swept over me. Had my prayer caused my daughter's and in-laws' deaths? I've always been told, "Be careful what you pray for, because you just might get it." Could this have been what happened? Had I brought this horrible tragedy upon my family? The thought overwhelmed me, and once again I started to weep. The mere possibility I'd asked for this was more than I could bear. "Just take me now, God! My life is over. I can't handle this anymore!" How could I face my family, knowing somehow I'd brought this devastation upon us?

I prayed for the earth to open up and swallow me. I was giving up, defeated. I had succumbed to the darkness that flooded my soul. But then an inner voice, the one I've come to know as the still, small voice of God, began to speak. "Your prayers did not cause this evil, Kathleen. Others caused this pain. Because time, for me, is eternal, I've always known this would occur. Even though I did not stop the bombing, I did not ordain it. Your prayer was merely an offering to use your life for good. You are not responsible for what others have done. But I will take this tragedy and build great things from it through you, and others, who are willing."

As waves of relief washed over me, my thoughts were directed to another time. I remembered sitting at my computer and designing Ashley's birth announcement when God cautioned me about my child's future: "Ashley will not grow to be an adult." Could I have prevented the tragedy from happening?

What about the warnings I'd received regarding my tubal ligation? The doctor had tried to discourage me from having the procedure. He told me I was very young, only twenty-six, and a lot of things could change over the next few years. This operation was not easily reversed, and even if it was, the chances for me having more children were slim. He felt I should wait a few years before I made such a drastic decision. Why hadn't I listened?

And what about Ashley's strange question right before the bombing. "Mommy, would you be sad if I died?" Had she been warned too? Was that why she didn't want me to go to work that morning?

Everything was beginning to make sense. God had been trying to protect me from pain, but I wouldn't listen. I had refused to heed His repeated warnings. He had known all along what was going to happen and had tried to prepare me, to protect me from harm.

I sighed heavily. "What am I supposed to do with this wisdom now, God? It's too late for me to go back and change anything."

"Be patient. Everything will unfold before you, and in time you'll understand. But first, you must begin to live."

I gazed at Ashley's flowers. They seemed to be radiating from within, almost pulsating with the spirit of my daughter. My eyes swept the perimeter of my yard. In that moment I had a clear, newfound understanding and a sense of inevitability. I could not change what had happened in the past, but I could still make choices. Two possibilities were before me—I could choose to live, love, and laugh again, or I could choose to be bitter. I knew, for me, the latter meant death.

I thought of Michael. He'd been such a tower of strength, his words filled with comfort and wisdom. Michael had always been there for me. Even though he was devastated as well, he managed to hold me up. Michael wasn't just my husband; he was my best friend. I could talk to him about anything, without fearing judgment or ridicule. Our relationship was so good, so positive, I knew he was a gift, one I couldn't afford to lose. We'd both been given a second chance at true love. It was clear, hurt and anger would push him away from me. If I became bitter I'd risk losing the love of my life.

I thought of my sons. Even though David was not my biological child, I loved him. He was my golden boy, with his white-blond hair and beautiful blue eyes. In a way he was a reflection of Michael. He made me smile. It had been difficult blending our families. For many years David was an only child. Getting him accustomed to sharing his father had been the greatest challenge. We were all still getting used to our roles and working things out as a family when tragedy struck. One thing was certain, David was Michael's son, and I was determined, with love, we could work it out. I knew if I let myself become bitter and angry, he would withdraw further from me, and my example would scar him for life. He'd already been through such hardship by the age of nine, how could I put him through more?

Then there was Zachary. What a surprise he'd been. Never had another person changed my life so much. From the day he was born I loved him with a fierce intensity. His arrival grounded me and caused me to think of someone other than myself. He was such a beautiful little boy, with dark skin, blue eyes, brown hair, and dimples in both cheeks. When he smiled I simply melted. I thought of how much he loved and protected his baby sister. What would happen to this joyful, loving little boy if I became a bitter, angry woman or, worse, if I died? By six years of age he'd been through so much, how could I put him through more?

All my "men" needed me. Each one of them was a gift from God, each was meant to be in my life, and I was meant to be in theirs.

Ashley in the dress she wore as a flower girl in Michael and Kathleen's wedding, April 1994. Michael and Kathleen carried this picture with them while they were searching for Ashley. This is the dress that was buried with Ashley.

top: Luther and LaRue at a family picnic.

bottom: Luther, LaRue, Brad, Abby, and Ashley at Michael and Kathleen's wedding reception, June 1994.

top: Michael and Kathleen's wedding, June 1994.

bottom: LaRue hugs Kathleen at her wedding. This was when she whispered in Kathleen's ear that she was the wife she had always wanted for Michael.

I am a Treasure

Ashley

above: Ashley's handprints done at Vacation Bible School, 1994.

right top: Ashley playing on the merry-go-round, fall 1994.

right bottom: Ashley at Christmas, 1994.

top: Ashley and her older brother Zack, fall 1994.

right: Ashley and Zack, winter 1994.

top: Ashley, winter 1994.

bottom: Ashley and Zack, spring 1995. This was the photograph used at the trials.

Graffiti written by one of the rescue teams on the wall of the *Journal Record* building on the day of the bombing. It was requested that the message be left as is to serve as a permanent reminder of the passion the rescuers felt in their mission.

left: Rex Haymaker
gives the eulogy at
Ashley's funeral.

below: Kathleen and
her family at Ashley's
funeral.

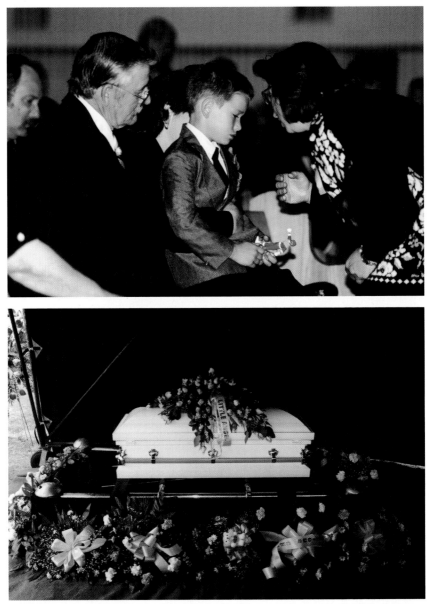

top: Zachary and Nathan at Ashley's funeral. Waynett Martin, Zack's Cub Scout den mother, offers comfort.

bottom: Ashley's casket.

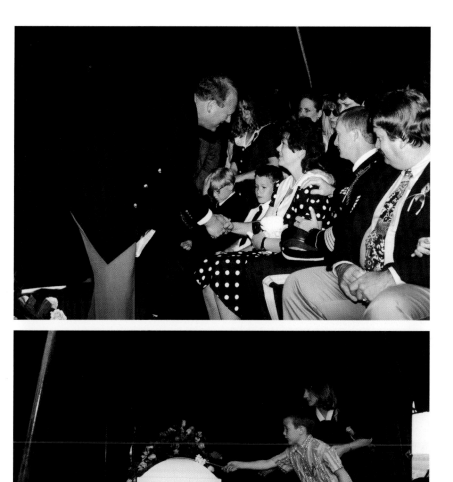

top: Rex Haymaker offers comfort to Kathleen and Mike at the gravesite.

bottom: After Ashley's funeral, Janice and Ben Mobley pause to lay flowers on her casket. Ben was the young boy who got up at Ashley's funeral and said, "Ashley was my good friend and I will miss her."

top: Exhibition of the design submissions for the memorial. More than fifteen thousand people viewed the designs, from which five were selected for final judging.

bottom: Presentation of the Oklahoma City National Memorial design to President Clinton in the Lincoln conference room in the White House, fall 1997.

top: Opening of the Oklahoma City National Memorial, April 19, 2000. The number of people who attended was enormous.

bottom: The Oklahoma City National Memorial 9:01 gate in front of the reflecting pool.

Ashley's chair at the Oklahoma City National Memorial.

top: Twilight at the memorial with a view of the Methodist church overlooking the compound. The reflecting pool is designed so that visitors can see their reflection as "those who were changed forever."

left: Luther and LaRue's chairs and the Baptist church that also overlooks the memorial.

right: Jesus Wept statue. This is not an official part of the memorial but is placed across the street. The larger-than-life statue of Jesus has its back to the 9:03 gate facing the memorial wall.

below: The Survivor Tree. This American elm withstood the full force of the blast and survived, damaged but not destroyed. It has become a living symbol of all who believe in the message the memorial imparts.

To: The Parents Of Broken Hearts

I am very sorry your child have died. I prayed every night for you.

Your frieng
Samantha

Letters and cards from well wishers.

Dear Miss Love Katie
Traynor
I hope
htat you
are feeling
better
I am srry
htat your
baby didy

Letters and cards from well wishers.

Letters and cards from well wishers.

April 27, 1995

Dear Parents,

I am sorry about what happened to your child or children. I wish there was something I could do to help. I just want you to know that I care And I know you're in alot of pain now. My whole family is worried.

My class and I planted a sycamore tree it is a fast growing tree. And every time it blossoms we will think of your child.

Sincerely your's
Brandilyn
Class 43

Letters and cards from well wishers.

April 27, 1995

Dear Parents,

I am sorry about what happened to your child or children. I wish there was something I could do to help. I just want you to know that I care And I know you're in alot of pain now. My whole family is worried.

My class and I planted a sycamore tree it is a fast growing tree. And every time it blossoms we will think of your child.

Sincerely your's
Brandilyn
Class 43

We Care

La petite

PHILIPPE

Dear Oklahoma Victims

Don't worry, be happy.

I wish I could change the Past. I'm very sorry.

Blessed Sacrament Fr. Katie

Letters and cards from well wishers.

April, 26, 95

Dear family of Ashley Treanor

I had heard about the terrible accident that accursed. I hope you will have another little girl just like Ashley. I am really sorry about this. The police is sure not going to let this happen again.

I am sure that alot of people including me cares about what has happen. And You got to stand up for yourself. Don't give up Your Hopes Think about the happy times before your had Ashley. They are alot people out there in the world that needs help. Maybe you could help them as much as you could.

Yongrui
6th Grade

Letters and cards from well wishers.

Dear People of Oklahoma,
My heart is sad because
a terrible thing has happened
to so many people in your
city. We pray for you all
and will continue to lift
you to God everyday.
Love, Melissa,
O.L.P.H.-Glendale, Az.
1st Grade

Letters and cards
from well wishers.

Dear Mrs. and Mr. Treanor,

Your daughter is very pretty! You must have alot of feelings going through your mind. You probably left her room just the way she left it. The Oklahoma bombing was very series. My heart goes out to your family and all the other victims of the Oklahoma bombing.

Lots of luck,
Shannon

Dear Mrs. and Mr. Treanor,

Your daughter is very pretty! You must have alot of feelings going through your mind. You probably left her room just the way she left it. The Oklahoma bombing was very series. My heart goes out to your family and all the other victims of the Oklahoma bombing.

Lots of luck,
Shannon

Letters and cards from well wishers.

Letters and cards from well wishers.

4-26-95

Dear Families,

I feel bad for what happened to your child or children. I know they were little and smart kids. When I hear that people have been killed, I start feeling bad. When people are killed, the rest of the people that is in their family will come to see them. Some families are so sad that they can cry for a long time. A lot of people have been getting killed and some haven't. Some live their life just fine and some don't. People don't deserve to be killed. If people would stop hating and fighting each other the world would be a better place to live and there will be peace. I hope you feel better soon families.

You friend,
Marco

Letters and cards from well wishers.

Letters and cards from well wishers.

Dear Mr. and Mrs. Eckles,

I cannot know how you feel. This is one of the greatest tragedy that I have ever seen. The question on the mind of everyone in the U.S. is why? Why would this happen to anyone. Though I don't know you, there was probably no more of a reason for this to happen to your daughter than to anyone else. I'm sorry.

sincerely,
Danny
, age 13

Letters and cards from well wishers.

May brooks, trees and a singing hitls
Join in the chorus too
And every gentle wind that brong
Send happiness to you!

Love
Matthew

Letters and cards from well wishers.

right: Statue in Ashley's garden. It was sent by a couple who owned a nursery and wanted to help with the garden.

below: Newborn picture of Kassidy with her daddy, Michael.

In Memory of
Ashley Eckles

The playground constructed in Ashley's honor.

Family photo. Clockwise front to back: Kassidy, Kathleen, Michael, David, Zachary, summer 2001.

I needed to put myself back together—for them. My family was relying on me to get through this. I had a responsibility to set a good example, to learn to live again.

On a larger scope there were countless people around the world who'd been touched by Ashley's story. Didn't I need to share my faith with them, to show how God can bring His people through times of trouble? This was the very opportunity I'd asked for. Surely my prayers had been answered. I'd been given a powerful message. I wanted God to use me. All I needed to do now was pull myself together, to lean on faith for strength and begin to live.

I knew it wouldn't be easy. There were still unanswered questions and many steps to take. I had much to learn, and more wounds to heal. As I looked at the monumental task before me, I wondered what the future would hold. Then I quietly shook off my concerns. Trust in God, I thought. Take each day, just one step at a time.

A verse from the Bible came to mind. Although I'd memorized it in my childhood, at that moment the words offered fresh comfort: "To appoint unto them that mourn in Zion, to give unto them beauty for ashes, the oil of joy for mourning, the garment of praise for the spirit of heaviness; that they might be called trees of righteousness, the planting of the Lord, that He might be glorified" (Isaiah 61:3).

Suddenly images from my dream raced through my mind. Only this time, instead of panic, I was offered fresh understanding. A sense of peace and purpose enveloped my being. Perhaps the dream was not a cruel reminder of my loss after all but instead God's comfort, Ashley's comfort, attempting to lift from my presence the dark, unspeakable grief. My daughter had gone to heaven, and no matter how hard I chased her it wasn't time for me to go. Ashley was waiting for me, but for now my place was on earth. I knew then, my dream was a metaphor for the way I'd been living. I'd been chasing her for so very long.

What about Ashley's question only a few days before the bombing? Would I be sad if she died? My natural instinct had been to shudder at the unthinkable, to tell her I'd miss my little girl terribly. Yet in her innocence she'd offered words of comfort. Ashley had reminded me she'd be in heaven with Jesus, that she'd be an angel watching over me.

Suddenly it all made sense. I couldn't change what had happened, but I could continue the mission which Ashley's short life had set me upon. She had a new home now, and for this moment in time I couldn't join her. I knew she was in heaven, and I would see her again one day—she told me so in my dreams.

I got up, wiped the tears from my eyes, brushed the grass from my body, and began to move about the yard. My pink climbing roses were in full bloom, and the air was filled with their sweet fragrance. I caressed their delicate petals and inspected the trellises. They were sorely in need of attention.

I went to the garden shed, took out my tools, and got to work. I removed the weeds and began pulling up bulbs. The daffodils needed tending. I replanted the iris. Throughout the day I worked, moving daylilies from the back of the house to the front, lining the porch. I set a border around the lilac bush and cleaned out the weeds beneath it. I trimmed the dead limbs from the climbing roses and tied the branches to their trellis.

As Michael came down the drive from work, I looked up. I must have been a sight. He approached me with a knowing smile as he brushed the dirt from the bridge of my nose. "Well, it's about time you joined the living. What have you been up to all day?"

"I've been communing with Nature. I really missed you," I said, as I hugged him around the neck. Michael gently pulled away, then looked at me closely, trying to read between the lines. "Are you okay?"

I shrugged. "I hope you're not tired. We have a deck to finish."

Michael smiled broadly. "Give me just a minute." He went into the house just long enough to get a cup of coffee and change into a T-shirt. When he returned I was waiting with hammer and wrecking bar in hand.

We went to work tearing out the old deck. It had rotted in many places and needed to be replaced. We worked side by side, and planned the renovation as we went. When we came to a place where Michael didn't understand what I wanted, we'd stop, sit down, and talk.

I didn't tell him what had happened to me that morning. I was still trying to understand it myself. Instead, I drew strength from his quiet presence and gentle enthusiasm. We worked hard until dark, together once again. It was the first time since the bombing I had not spent the entire day crying. The hard work had other benefits too—I was exhausted. That night I rested soundly, not relying on my prescription drugs to fall asleep. As I slipped into blissful oblivion, I knew change was in store.

On that beautiful spring morning, God reached deep into my soul and performed a miracle. Although He'd been patiently waiting, guiding, and offering comfort all along, I hadn't always felt His presence. I understood this healing was not dependent on my own strength, or even the strength of my family, but on God alone. It was His strength that enabled me to cope. He'd spoken to my heart and given me reasons to go on, to walk out of the darkness and into the light. He understood, had been where no one else could go, saw the depths of my heart's cry, the inner workings of my soul. He quietly offered His extended hand, a way out of my torment. I had only to reach out and accept the help I so desperately needed.

I knew then as I know now—in Him is strength, joy, life, and purpose. The decision was up to me. With a thankful heart I reached out and took His hand. I chose God. I chose my family. I chose to live.

Ten

Planning the
Memorial Garden

Many a humble soul will be amazed to find that the seed it sowed in
weakness, in the dust of daily life, has blossomed into immortal flowers
under the eye of the Lord.

HARRIET BEECHER STOWE

One relatively quiet afternoon my phone rang. It was Cindy Jones. At first I didn't remember her. Then, with a little coaching, I recalled our meeting at the First Christian Church. She'd been the conservatively dressed woman with Dawn from *The Geraldo Rivera Show*. She wanted me to sign her petition to get control of the permanent memorial while it was still in the early planning stages. She explained she'd left repeated messages with the governor's office, as well as the mayor's, but her calls had not been returned. As far as she knew the establishment was going forward with limited input from the victims' families.

After that call we talked almost daily. I shared Ashley's angel story, and we cried together. Before long we became close friends. There were days when our phone calls became semicounseling sessions. Time after time I'd pour out my heart while Cindy patiently listened. Even though I hardly left the house, Cindy managed to offer comfort with her gentle voice.

Eventually she got me moving in the right direction. I started writing letters. I must have sent out nearly one hundred copies to government officials, requesting the victims' families be allowed to choose the memorial that would be placed at the bomb site. I received many responses from concerned individuals who agreed.

Senator Lucas made it a point to call. At first I was a little dumbfounded that a state senator would call my home. But I managed to explain the situation and to enlist his help in contacting the proper authorities.

Within a few days he called again, armed with names and phone numbers. He gave me the mayor's office number as well as a number for Bob Johnson. The mayor, it seemed, had assigned Bob Johnson, a prominent local attorney with the largest law firm in the state, the enormous task of forming a committee to organize construction of the memorial. I immediately jumped on the leads and called, leaving messages with both offices.

Then one afternoon I was watching the news when a story appeared about a new city project. It was a huge reconstruction proposal for downtown Oklahoma. Architects were invited to display potential designs. Then the report briefly mentioned that the same people were designing the bomb site memorial. How could they appropriately honor people they didn't even know? I pulled myself together and called Cindy.

"I need to organize a press conference. Can you reach some of the family members who are interested in this project, and find out when we can meet at the bomb site?" She promised to handle it immediately and, true to her can-do personality, she did just that.

Within a few minutes my phone started ringing. The first caller was John Cole, the godfather of Aaron and Elijah Coverdale. He expressed the same concerns I had, and since neither of us was able to get through to the mayor's office, we agreed a press conference would resolve the situation.

When we hung up I received several more calls. It was clear; I was not alone with my feelings. We were on our way. I called several TV stations, as well as the Associated Press, and arranged a time to meet downtown.

The next day we gathered and stated our concerns. We weren't asking for anything unreasonable. We simply wanted some answers. Yes, we understood plans for a memorial were under way, but why hadn't the families been contacted first? After all, planning the memorial was akin to choosing our loved ones' headstones; we needed to be involved.

When I got home there was a message from Bob Johnson on my answering machine. I called his office again and was able to speak with him immediately. He explained why he'd been appointed by the mayor to chair the 350-member task force to oversee construction of the permanent memorial. I asked how many of the families were represented by this large committee. He told me Phillip Thompson, whose mother was killed in the credit union, and Toby Thompson (not related to Phillip), whose brother was killed in the Social Security office, had agreed to cochair one of the ten subcommittees. These subcommittees would be made up of interested people from the families and survivors. They were planning to announce a meeting soon to explain what groundwork had been laid, and how the families and survivors could be involved. He took my name and address, and told me when, and where, the first meeting would be held, then strongly encouraged me to attend.

I called Cindy and asked her to pass the word. Everyone interested in attending needed to call Bob's office to get on the list for future notifications.

I attended the first meeting, in the middle of July, with nervous anticipation. Much to my dismay it resembled an organized lynching. Although we tried to sort through the tasks at hand, many were dealing with so much rage it sometimes became displaced. It was reiterated over and over: Nothing would be built until the families, and survivors, had the opportunity to offer their input. Then Phillip, Toby, and Bob explained the structure of the task force and how decisions would flow.

That night I met Cheryl Vaught. Cheryl had agreed to cochair the families and survivors subcommittee. She was an attorney and lead counsel for the Oklahoma City Chapter Red Cross. When I looked in her direction, I did a double take. We shook hands and exchanged the usual introductions. "I'm sorry," I said, "You look familiar to me. Have we met before?"

She looked puzzled. "I'm not sure, I don't think so." It would be several months before I'd put it together. Cheryl had been the Red Cross volunteer at the First Christian Church—the one who'd offered me comfort right after the bombing.

Over the next month or so I spent hours talking with Phillip and Bob, trying to understand how this task force worked. Phillip told me when he first heard about the memorial he wasn't entirely sure one should be built. He was afraid it would become a monument to the act, and not to the victims themselves. It was this fear that motivated him to get involved. He was determined to see the memorial built right.

I agreed. I felt Mike's mom and dad wouldn't want a monument erected in their honor. They were simple people who did not ask for or need any recognition. They'd just done what was right, and what was good. I couldn't see them endorsing this endeavor unless it had a lasting effect on the people who came, or they could take something away from this place—a learning, life-changing experience. Their memorialization would have embarrassed them.

For me, the physical structure was never as important as the "ministry" it could offer. I tried to look much further ahead. For this memorial to be enduring, people a hundred years from now needed to see the good that came from tragedy. They needed to understand, these people were not just sacrificial lambs but decent, hardworking, law-abiding citizens, many of them public servants. It was clear to me, the memorial needed to be both proactive and reactive, reaching people who may consider doing this again and possibly helping people who'd lived through tragedies of their own. If we could encompass all that, the project would be worthwhile.

Phillip Thompson had lost his mother, Virginia, who was an employee in the Federal Credit Union. I was surprised to discover our purpose was similar too. Phillip, like myself, didn't believe there should be a memorial, but because public outcry was so loud and adamant he felt it would be pointless to try to stop it. He decided to get involved just to make sure it did not become a tribute to those who did this terrible deed, or that it in any way dishonored our loved ones' memories. I told him about Mike's mom and dad, their lifestyle and beliefs. We agreed. The memorial needed to offer healing to all who came.

Toby Thompson had lost his brother, Mike, in the bombing. Mike worked in the Social Security Administration. We like to think Mike and my family may have been together in their final moments. Toby was particularly creative and passionate in his role with the memorial. Mike was his only brother, and they were extremely close. Toby got involved to honor his brother's memory. I came to know him as an eloquent spokesman.

While we were busy planning in earnest, others seemed to be exploiting the tragedy. A bachelor hero calendar was about to hit the market. The full-color extravaganza, featuring twelve rescue workers, mostly firefighters, was being promoted with fanfare. On the flip side the names of the victims were listed. Several survivors and family members flew into a rage. I was one of them. What in the world were they thinking? What would possess them to mix publicity with tragedy? Angry letters were written, interviews were given, and within a week the names of the victims were removed from the product.

The next months flew by. Between working on the memorial, taking calls from people wishing to express their condolences, and talking to the press, I'd grab any moment I could to toil peacefully in my garden. Michael labored right beside me. He was glad to see me outside once again, moving about.

I went to the garage in search of the water garden kit Ashley and I had purchased together. I was finally able to take it out of the box and incorporate it into my garden. How Ashley had dreamed of this day.

As I prepared the setting I realized I was creating my own private memorial for my daughter. I moved flowers we had planted into its parameter. I purchased three small weeping willow trees and planted them carefully. For me the willows symbolized the multitude of tears I'd shed for Ashley.

Cindy helped too. She was able to obtain a piece of granite from the Murrah Building and gave it to me in my daughter's memory. I took it to our local monument company and had them engrave the words ASHLEY'S GARDEN across the stone. I picked it up, walked to my own little memorial, and carefully placed it amidst the lilies.

Over the next few years the committees became a positive, therapeutic focus in my life. Unlike others, who benefited from counseling, I didn't feel it helped me at all. But each committee meeting allowed me to come to know many of the families and survivors. Each gathering would bring a few more people into my world. I began to realize I wasn't the only one having problems with depression and anxiety. I felt the walls fall away and my world open up a little more. Each time someone shared a story, my heart was touched, and a little more healing entered my soul. There were so many others, just like me, who had cried a river. Everyone's wounds were still open, and all our hearts still ached. Over time we became brothers and sisters. It was clear, we needed each other. Realizing I was not alone was my first step toward recovery. Somehow being in a sinking ship with someone else alleviated my desperation and gave me the strength to persevere. Each meeting for me became a sort of group therapy session. I looked forward to them yet dreaded them.

Many gatherings were charged with distrust and anger. There wasn't consistency to our healing because people came and went as they needed. Many entered at different stages of the grief process. Sometimes they'd pull me back into despondency and anger. But mostly I tried to remain focused on the goal. It took nearly nine months to work through those feelings and come to some type of consensus. It was time well spent.

Before long I volunteered to produce a newsletter for the memorial in an attempt to keep everyone informed. My first edition went out in September. Over the next several months the newsletter became a forum to inform families and survivors of any events that had been established for our benefit, and any assistance that had been offered.

During that time Cheryl became my closest friend. We'd speak almost daily. She seemed to realize just how much I needed positive strokes. The more she encouraged me, the more I'd try to do. I agreed to cochair the Family and Survivors' Subcommittee and the Public Relations Subcommittee, and to work on the Public Input Committee. For the first year of the task force's existence, I was involved in almost every aspect of the memorial. Soon I was volunteering forty to sixty hours per week. The first year after the bombing, I worked myself to a fevered pitch. I volunteered, or was volunteered, to sit on several subcommittees.

Our first priority was to write a mission statement based on a submitted collection of ideas from the victims' families and survivors. For many months we gathered around long tables discussing expectations for the memorial—what it should be, what it should not. Most of the submissions were deeply emotional, consisting less of what the memorial should look like than of the powerful feelings it should contain.

Some individuals were adamant that their loss was greater than anyone else's. There was one woman in particular who presented an enormous challenge to me. From the beginning she seemed to attack everyone involved. Nothing we did was good enough. Most of the time she was in a total rage. I grew to dread seeing her. Yes, I understood her pain, but I felt it was detrimental to others' quest for healing. I would often go home shaken from my encounters with this bitter woman. It was difficult enough trying to deal with my own loss, but trying to calm her down too was nearly impossible. Sometimes I found myself drawn into her rage, but I'd quickly attempt to shake off those feelings. We had several disagreements over the years, but all the while we respected each other, and our losses, and eventually came to an understanding. Everyone grieves in his or her own way. We were all struggling. No matter how different our responses were, we shared a common bond.

I soon realized the memorial was bigger than I'd imagined. I had to look beyond my personal loss and find compromises we could all live with. My actions and words were meant to honor and respect the memory of my loved ones. I carefully measured everything I said and did, trying to consider how Luther and LaRue would feel, what they would have wanted. At times, I must admit, it was a difficult cross to bear, and on occasion I became overwhelmed by it all.

Then I met Priscilla Salyers. Priscilla was a survivor. As we sat at a roundtable discussion I watched her carefully. For some reason I was drawn to her. I think it was the haunted look in her eyes. At first she hardly spoke, only nodding in agreement with others. Then the discussion turned to survivors. We asked if we had any at our table. She shook her head in affirmation and took a deep, trembling breath.

"I was employed by the Secret Service on the fifth floor. I'd just gotten to work and was sitting down at my desk. My best friend and co-worker,

Paul Ice, just stepped in to say good morning when the entire building shook and everything went black. When we heard the noise, our eyes locked. I vaguely remember falling through the air but do not remember landing. When I came to, I was buried under concrete and debris. I couldn't free myself, but I could move my arms, just a little. I felt around and found a hand. It was still warm. I held on to that hand as if it were a lifeline. I felt it grow cold, but I never let go."

As I listened to her soft, sweet voice, I came to understand the level of pain this woman was holding inside. She paused as tears slid down her cheeks, then slowly continued. "I lost many friends in that building, but I am still alive. I don't understand why I was spared. I didn't ask to be a survivor, but I am." I reached across and squeezed her hand. As she continued to share her story, I began to weep with her, for her. I could see the tortured look in her eyes was guilt, born from the understanding she had made it out alive while others had not. She went on, "Sometimes I wish I hadn't survived."

I gasped. "Oh, Priscilla, I've never heard your story before. I'm so glad you survived." I hugged her. "If you hadn't lived, I would never have heard your story. I think this is the reason you survived. Maybe if you look hard, you will discover that too."

She reached out to me. "But you lost so much, your little daughter, your mother- and father-in-law."

"I cannot fault you for living just because they didn't. You didn't set the bomb, nor did you have any idea what would happen. I imagine if you had any clue this tragedy were about to occur, you would have moved heaven and earth to empty that building and help everyone to safety. We must place the blame and guilt where it belongs, not on ourselves."

From that moment on we drew from each other intense comfort and healing. We became close friends. I was with Priscilla when she vaguely remembered that, months before the bombing, Timothy McVeigh had cased the building by coming into her office to ask for a job. The memory tortured her, the images inflicting more guilt as she wondered if somehow she could have prevented the entire tragedy.

I recall the first time I met Kari Ferguson-Watkins, now the executive director of the memorial. Her job was to handle the media and communication issues. She had been a producer at Channel 4, our local MSNBC affiliate, for some time and decided she wanted to get involved in this project. She looked so scared. It was a night when tensions were high. By the time the meeting was over, I thought Kari would run for the door, but she didn't. She asked me to help her form a communications committee.

Over the next few years Kari and I got to know each other quite well, speaking almost as much as Cheryl and I did. Kari "got it" right away; she understood where we were coming from. I never sensed any agendas or underlying motives. She just had the clear desire to do the right thing. She's been instrumental in keeping us on course and neutral on some of the tougher issues. Later, when she became executive director, I cheered her selection, knowing she would do right by all of us.

That winter Bud Welch came to one of our monthly meetings. He'd been to several previous meetings, and I'd come to know and admire his strength. That night he pointed out the Survivor Tree that sat across from the Murrah Building. He told us when the bomb went off, the explosion blew away the tree's leaves and destroyed many of its limbs. "My daughter, Julie"—he paused, and then went on—"would try to get to work early so she could park under that tree. It has special meaning to me. But I would like to point out, this tree should have special meaning for all of us. This tree is a survivor. It survived the tragedy, but it's now suffering and possibly dying. I think we owe it to ourselves to try to save it and incorporate this tree into the memorial as a symbol of who we all are—survivors." After he spoke a quiet murmur blanketed the room. I saw people nodding their heads in assent. This was the perfect symbol of who we'd become.

Before the end of the evening we unanimously agreed the Survivor Tree would be a part of whatever design was selected. Bob Johnson promised to write up a resolution for its incorporation as one of the elements. Bud Welch's tender presentation was the beginning of our group coming together as a family. It was the first thing we'd unanimously agreed on. From that day forward we began to make substantial progress. Each committee meeting brought forward new ideas and feelings.

My contact list continued to grow by leaps and bounds. With each call I made it a point to get to know the person on the other end of the line. This was how I met Doris Jones. We had a lot in common. She too had lost a precious daughter and, unbeknownst to me, she'd also lost her unborn grandson. Not many people knew about the unborn children. They were not discussed, nor were they included in the count of persons killed. Doris told me her daughter, Carrie, was very excited about having a baby and had just gone that morning to have an ultrasound. Others who saw her that day said she was showing off her pregnancy when the bomb went off. We wept together when Doris told me she'd never get to see that ultrasound, because it had been buried in the rubble.

We spent many days trying to help each other understand what we were supposed to do with the rest of our lives. Recently Doris went to work full-time at the Memorial Center. She told me she feels close to Carrie there, and feels that by her work she is able to continue honoring her daughter. I also understand she found the ultrasound photograph among the items recovered from the building. It was another of the rare "angel gifts" that occasionally touched our lives. Doris values that picture as a sacred treasure.

In December of 1995, Mike and I determined it was necessary for me to go back to work. I was feeling guilty taking the checks from various charities who had graciously supported me for almost nine months. Besides, I felt I needed to get back, as much as possible, to the way things were before. But I was afraid of going too far from home. My self-confidence and security had been shattered. I needed to be close to the boys. The fear of losing either of them gripped my heart.

Soon I heard of a position at a law firm in Guthrie. So I pulled myself together and applied. I was hired immediately, and on January 2, 1996, I went back to work. At first I felt a bit lost and confused, but I plugged ahead.

I continued to volunteer with the memorial. In the evenings after work, I'd try to put the newsletter together, as well as field calls and requests for media interviews. I was stretched to the limit. I found myself struggling to find balance between my family, a full-time career, and volunteering for the memorial.

The committee for the mission statement was moving forward. I was extremely honored to participate and knew this would be the driving force behind the process. I didn't miss a single gathering. There were twelve of us, somewhat like disciples—those who lost someone, survivors of the blast, and the rescue and recovery community.

Beth Short facilitated the meetings, and Yvonne Malone was appointed "reporter." Both of them were volunteers, but they gave as much to the process as anyone. Beth asked the hard questions. She used creative and insightful ways to get us to look at things from another perspective, to explore every aspect of a word or phrase. As we grew closer and closer to the defining statement, every word was packed with meaning and substance. We decided the memorial would be a "gift of remembrance" to the world and to anyone who came to the site. We wanted to remind people why they were there—"We come here to remember . . ." We were very careful not to exclude anyone who had been affected—"Those who were killed, those who survived, and those changed forever." Even the order of those phrases was important.

We recognized that those changed forever could be almost anyone in the world. We hoped that, through an interactive learning center, the public could share the impact the bombing had on our lives and become a part of the memorial by sharing their stories with the world. The next line we envisioned as a prayer—"May all who come here know the impact of violence." We didn't try to define the knowledge, or what we expected people to learn, but hoped they would see firsthand how this evil had destroyed so many. Then the last line—"May this memorial offer comfort, peace, hope, and serenity." We all agreed, the best way to honor our loved ones and their memories was to continue their legacy. We hoped this memorial would develop outreach to other communities who had suffered acts of violence. It was to be a quiet place where anyone could come to remember, mourn if necessary, or even pray.

When I first read the completed work, I broke down in tears of joy and of sorrow. I was glad to be a part of this group—of people who could inspire such community genius, but I felt sad, it was finished. It was by far my most difficult accomplishment, yet my most rewarding. When we presented the work to the Family and Survivor's Subcommittee, it was met with a short pause, then with cheers, tears, and applause. I went home feeling satisfied, and totally drained.

My time and energy were spread pretty thin, but I still felt I needed to be involved. Sydney Dobson was chosen as the executive director, and it was announced an administrative assistant would be hired in the near future. Even though I now had a job, I desperately wanted this position. It would give me the outlet I needed to work on the memorial every day and still help support my family. It was the best of both worlds. I applied for the job, confident I'd be selected. I'd basically been doing the work for the last two years anyway. Why wouldn't I be chosen?

Cheryl Vaught watched intently as I burned the candle at both ends. She saw my exhaustion building. She felt I needed a vacation and made all the arrangements for Mike and me to get away from the turmoil. She and Kay Gable, one of the many counselors who assisted us in the planning phase, took it upon themselves with their own financial resources to book airline, hotel, and rental car reservations. Thanks to these lovely women, Mike and I were headed to Key West. We prepared joyfully for what we termed as a second honeymoon, since our first had been local to save money.

When it was time to head out, I picked up the mail. On the plane I opened what I thought was the notification for my new position with the memorial. Instead, I read a rejection letter. I had been fired, by form letter no less, from the only thing that had held me together for the past two years. I cried all the way to Key West, and unfortunately allowed it to put a dark cloud over our vacation.

When I got back to Oklahoma City, I called Cheryl immediately, primarily to thank her for the lovely gift but also to tell her about the job. I tried to be strong but instead broke down. I explained my utter disappointment. It seemed I'd been good enough to perform my services for free but not good enough to be paid for them. For me it was rejection in the worst possible way. Cheryl comforted me, but the decision had been made by others. From that point on I pulled away emotionally from much of the memorial process. Besides, I reasoned, my family needed my attention more.

Once I realized I was neglecting the needs of my children, I knew the rejection was nothing short of a godsend. The desire to be a part of the memorial had been my way of keeping my daughter's memory alive, but in the process I was sacrificing the well-being of my two boys. Although I continued to volunteer, I began to cut back my hours and got my sons some much needed counseling.

David was having trouble in school. We'd confirmed he had attention deficit disorder and put him on Ritalin to help him concentrate in class. It seemed to help for a short time, but eventually his health deteriorated. He became thin and drawn. He looked like an addict and hardly spoke to anyone. When we tried to talk to him about his feelings, he flat-out refused to discuss them.

Zachary was a bit easier. We'd watch home movies of Ashley together, or look at pictures. Just allowing Zack to talk about his sister seemed to help. I realized right away, venting is good therapy.

We were still struggling to come together as a family. Since Ashley had been small, she'd helped to blend everyone. With her gone we were split right down the middle—my son, your son.

David and I struggled to come to terms. He resented me for being there, and I resented his resentment. He told his counselor he wanted his real mom to move back with his dad and wanted me to go away. He held me responsible for the death of his grandparents, and for the horrible reality he had to face every day. It was a huge mountain to overcome.

David and I went to war. He was determined I leave, and I was determined to stay. I guess you could say I won, because I am still here, but I've changed a lot to accommodate his feelings. And David, bless his heart, has changed too. The minute I stopped nagging him about his homework, his medications, or the cleanliness of his room and just turned him over to God was the minute we started to come together.

All the while, Ashley's garden continued to grow. Plants spontaneously arrived, as did a lovely fountain depicting a little girl with a watering can. They were donations from beautiful people who wanted to be a small part of our healing.

Michael and I took cuttings of LaRue's flowers and included them in our memorial. I even planted a few vegetables in honor of Luther—the farmer of the family. We added pools and a waterfall. Before long Ashley's garden took on an eclectic style from the hodgepodge of plants and decorations that arrived.

Each day I toiled in Ashley's garden, I nurtured the wounds of that fateful April morning. I soon realized, my daughter's spirit had never really left me. I could still see, and feel, her in the colors of the flowers and in the loving generosity from complete strangers.

One quiet afternoon I was contacted by Kelly Rice, a young woman from Indiana. Kelly wanted desperately to do something for us. At the time we didn't understand what our future needs would be, but I knew Ashley would have loved a church playground. Luther and LaRue had prayed about one for years.

My cousin was working with her congregation to raise money for the project. I told Kelly the plans that were in motion, and she promised to see what she could do to help. I didn't hear from her for a while, but when I did she had good news. Tim, a playground designer from Indiana, was moved to donate and build some equipment. Kelly and Tim organized a statewide campaign to raise money for bringing the playground to Oklahoma.

In just a few weeks Tim and his wife, Shelly, were on their way. They drove straight through, not stopping for a moment because of the unusually wet spring. When they arrived Tim got straight to work, toiling all morning in the miserable damp weather. By mid-afternoon he finished. The minute he did the sun came out, and we were blessed with a rainbow. It was a smile from God—another promise. The next day Tim and Shelly stayed for Sunday services. They were given a standing ovation by our little congregation and made honorary church members.

Although the gift was incredible, there was still a backlash. When Tim first arrived he seemed a little agitated. He didn't discuss many details but briefly explained he'd no longer be with his company when he returned. Tim felt they were trying to capitalize on the project, and he didn't approve of their tactics. He was repaid for his kindness by losing his job and nearly losing his home. He and his family, because of their generosity, had become victims of the bombing too.

I watched helplessly as the repercussions of the explosion went on and on. After all they had done, I couldn't do anything to help. I haven't heard from Tim and Shelly in over a year and can only pray things have gotten better for them.

After the equipment was assembled, a local manufacturer donated a chain-link fence. The men at church pitched in to construct it, a park bench was donated, and pea gravel was laid. The playground was finished.

As I made the final selection for Ashley's headstone, I mentioned the playground to the owner of the monument company, who immediately donated a small marker for the gateway. It said, TOYS DONATED IN LOVING MEMORY OF ASHLEY MEGAN ECKLES. Today when I gaze at the beautiful playground, I'm keenly aware of the good inside all of us, and the kindness of strangers, evidenced by the multitudes who reached out to say, "We care."

In October 1998 it was time to break ground for the bomb-site memorial. The international competition had been held, and the design selected. Bids were taken for the construction, and we were ready to begin.

Vice President Gore arrived. He laid a lovely wreath on the site. Families and survivors who attended were given shovels and asked to gather around the grassy area for the groundbreaking. In unison we dug in and turned over the rich, black soil. As we did Zachary began to cry. It was the first time he'd sobbed since the funerals. I held him as his tears fell on sacred ground. There was nothing I could say; I knew his sobs were cathartic. I reached down and grabbed a handful of moist dirt. I tenderly placed it in his hand. "Zachary," I said, "Ashley's, Luther's, and LaRue's blood is all a part of this soil now. Take this and treasure it as a small piece of them." He quietly nodded and clutched it into a small ball; it still remains in his room.

The next day several hundred people arrived to move the fence. We sang hymns, held hands, and quietly prayed. As I grasped the chain-link fence, still cluttered with the many gifts people had left in memory of the victims, I realized we were taking a huge step in releasing these sacred grounds to the world, to strangers. Before long the memorial would be built, and we would have to share—our Wailing Wall, our leaning post, and the memories of those we'd lost.

Eleven

Pulling Weeds

*Trials teach us what we are; they dig up the soil, and let us see what we
are made of; they turn up some of the ill weeds on to the surface.*

CHARLES H. SPURGEON

We learned fairly quickly that Luther had severely leveraged himself financially. He had several outstanding loans and had borrowed against his life
insurance to the tune of over $110,000. That was more debt than I could
imagine. The biggest chunk went toward the eighty acres he'd been purchasing over the last fifteen years. Luther had made a deal with the owner.
He'd pay the interest on the $60,000 until he could get ahead and start
working on the principal. Unfortunately, "getting ahead" never happened.

A few days after we buried Luther and LaRue, the phone rang. It was
a representative from the bank where my father-in-law had taken out his
loans. He wanted to know when he could expect payment in full. He indicated he had no obligation to hold these loans over for us, and he'd start
foreclosure proceedings if an arrangement could not be made immediately. He went on to say he was not familiar with our family, and therefore was uncomfortable doing business with us. I grew angry at his

implications and told him he was legally obligated to wait until the estate could be worked out.

We'd already made arrangements to meet with an attorney to help settle matters. Through the Unmet Needs Committee, we'd been provided with free legal assistance. Unfortunately, Luther had not left a will, so this would be more complicated. It had only been a few months since my daddy had passed away, and we were still settling his estate. I understood the mechanics of the process and tried to use my limited knowledge to help Michael. Unfortunately, all this did was add to my stress.

After I hung up the phone I immediately called our attorney. "In the midst of everything else," I told him, "I don't want to lose my home too." He assured me I didn't have to worry, because legally the bank couldn't do anything until the estate was settled. He promised to send a letter asserting that he was our attorney.

Soon it came time to talk to the attorney and designate the administrator of the estate. I wasn't allowed in the discussions, and I wasn't really interested anyway. I figured it was cut-and-dried. Michael, being the oldest, would be the administrator. However, all four siblings became administrators, and decisions had to be made by a majority. We would be at this forever.

Not long after that our attorney called to say he'd contacted the Unmet Needs Committee and found a businessman who was willing to donate his time to help us with the estate. His name was Frank Bolen, and he wanted to meet with us as soon as possible. We had our first meeting in our attorney's offices, and Frank outlined what needed to be done. He would put us in contact with a good farm implement appraiser to check the equipment. He'd also help us resolve any issues that couldn't be agreed upon, and determine what was important and what was not. Over the course of time Frank essentially became the estate's administrator.

Frank is a savvy negotiator and had an easygoing way about him. He was able to diffuse most of the problems, but the estate meetings were usually tense nonetheless. Decisions had to be made, a survey of the land had to be conducted, appraisals of the house and its contents needed to be developed, and cattle needed to be sold. There was so much to do and no money to do it with. Since the estate was in debt, with no prospect for income, any items the four siblings wanted to keep had to be purchased for their appraised value. Michael and I bought as much of the equipment as we could afford, with the intention of farming the land in the future.

In the beginning Michael, Debbie, and Mark wanted to continue the farming operation together and try to pull the estate out of bankruptcy. Our purchasing some of the items put a little into the account to help feed Dad's cattle. There were over 160 head grazing the pasture when Dad was killed. Plus, he had about 60 at a feedlot near the little town of Meridian. He was planning on feeding them out for sale later that spring.

For Dad buying and selling cattle was like playing the stock market. For us, not knowing the game, it was a disaster. We watched in horror as the cattle market plummeted. We experienced spring flooding and an incredible drought in the same year. By the time we were able to get a buyer for the cattle in the feedlot, we barely broke even. The cattle at home were no better off. We decided to winter them out in the hope the market would recover.

We all pitched in. Mike and I mended fences. Mark, Debbie's husband, Buddy, and Mike took turns feeding the livestock. And everyone planted the winter wheat we hoped would feed them.

Late that fall Buddy was drilling the wheat in the old long tractor. I could hear the chugging of the motor across the creek. Before long he drove up in his car, visibly agitated. The treads had completely come off the big tires. Dry rot had set in. Pulling the huge grain drill loaded down with wheat seed was more than they could handle. It would be a painful expense to replace the tires, but we had no choice. We'd already bought the wheat seed, and it needed to be planted right away.

We called Frank and told him about our predicament. He promised to see what he could do. A day or so later he called back. The Unmet Needs Committee would help with the cost of replacing the tires on the big tractor as well as the little one. He also suggested we look into other farm maintenance issues, because there were more ways the charities could help.

It was welcome relief. The cost to replace the tires on the big tractor alone was over $1,600. Now to some that may not seem like much, but when there is no income it is a huge expense. Although with the help we were able to finish planting the seed, we lost it later to a winter drought. One disaster seemed to follow another.

Every other night Mike patrolled the fields in his truck. He'd feed the cattle, throw them hay, and look for strays or sick cows that needed veterinary care. On the last day of February, he found a baby calf nearly dead in a tuft of hay. February is dreadfully cold in Oklahoma, and this day was no exception. Typically a newborn is not left until it is at least able to stand on its own. Michael stood back and looked around for the mother. He even waited a bit, but she never arrived. He finally concluded that the mother had abandoned her baby. Either the mama was immature or she was too sick to do what came naturally.

Michael gently picked up the calf and placed her on the floorboard of his truck. Then he drove straight into town to the vet. After an examination it was determined the little heifer had pneumonia. The vet gave her the proper medications and handed Michael the additional treatments to keep her alive.

On the way home Mike stopped by the feed store and picked up the formula she would need until she was old enough for solid food. Imagine my surprise as he carried the little dark red bundle into our kitchen. She was still shivering cold, and her eyes were glazed over. Her nose was wet and burning hot. It was obvious; she was near death. Together we wrapped her in a thick blanket and put her over one of the floor vents.

Before long she managed to get up on her feet and began crying for something to eat. Feeding a baby calf its first bottle is a real experience. First, she didn't know what to do. So I put a little formula on my fingers and gently placed them in her mouth. Once she got a taste of the sweet milk, she went to town. In a few seconds she had emptied the bottle and decided to lie back down for a nap.

We let her ride out the night in our laundry room, so she could warm up and have a little time to recover. The next day we could move her to our small dog pen just outside the back door. It was just the right size for a baby calf. She'd only need a little hay to sleep on and, of course, constant feedings.

In the wee hours of the morning, we heard little hooves tippa-tapping on the laundry room floor. I got up and went to check on her. She was hungry and followed me around the kitchen while I prepared her bottle. Her eyes now had a healthy, delicate appearance. As I watched her eat heartily, I somehow knew she would make it.

Later that morning the boys helped feed our little one in her new home. Soon she began to thrive. We named her Sadie because she'd been found on Sadie Hawkins Day. Michael grinned and told me, "There's no gettin' rid of this one. Once you've gone and named an animal, you can never get rid of it. Now she's a pet." That didn't really matter to me. I was just glad she was alive and thriving. The thought of another baby dying was too much to bear. We had saved her; of course she would always be ours.

In some small way Sadie helped me care vicariously for my little girl. She was an outlet for my desire to nurture, which I'd lost when Ashley was taken so abruptly. I felt that by bringing Sadie back from certain death we'd won a small victory over darkness.

Michael found a couple more calves in need of care. We named them and bottle-fed them all, but Sadie was the one who'd remain. In fact, she's still happily living on our farm today.

With a sick calf on the mend, we were back to financial reality. No matter how much we tried to fight it, we were unable to afford the note of $60,000, or $750 per acre, that we'd need to purchase the land. The appraiser said it was overpriced for unimproved farmland. Michael and I offered the owner $550 per acre instead, but he refused and put it on the open market. One of our neighbor's sons bought it. We were sorry to see it go but couldn't do a thing.

At one point the banker came out to the farm while we were vaccinating the cattle. He said he was just checking on his investment. We were furious. Mike told the banker if he showed up unannounced once more, we would file a protective order and have him arrested for trespassing.

We kept the cattle for one more year, hoping beyond hope we could pull it out. Each month we struggled to come up with more money for feed. The natural prairie grass that covered the acreage grew ragged and thin from overgrazing. We knew there were far too many cattle for the small plot of land. Fortunately, some of the charities helped us pay the huge cost of feeding them through that last winter.

The next spring we gave up. Michael, a few of his close friends, and I rounded up all of Dad's herd into our trailers and took them lock, stock, and barrel to the auction to be sold. The cattle had grown painfully thin and many were sickly. We knew we wouldn't get premium dollar for them. But we didn't know how bad it would be until we saw the checks. We were expecting the livestock to bail us out of the financial burden Dad had left us with. However, by the time all the equipment and herds were sold or dispersed, we were still in the red nearly $50,000.

Time had taken its toll on the siblings. While they were trying to settle the estate, tensions rose. Each child had a different idea of how Dad would have wanted things handled. I think all of them were right, in their own perspectives, but sometimes compromises have to be made, and at that point none was willing to make any concessions. It was just too hard to talk about, too hard to deal with. We knew at some point, though, that we'd all have to bite the bullet and take out loans of our own. It was just a matter of when and how much.

Soon the question of our house and Michael's loan from Dad came up. All Michael's brothers and sisters knew Dad had purchased the house, and Michael was paying him back over time. Fortunately, Mark had talked with Mom, and she had verbally confirmed this arrangement not long after we'd given her our last payment. I went through ten years of canceled checks to find the proof we needed—our last payment was made on April 1 of that year.

When push came to shove, Mike and Mark stood their ground. "Everyone knows Dad never charged any of us interest when he loaned us money. If anyone wants to get tough about this, then we all need to come clean about what we owed Dad. Every one of us needs to pay back the money with interest." It was never mentioned again.

We discussed keeping the land as a whole and continue sharing the farming operation. However, the previous years had shown us how expensive it was to comanage the farm. We needed to be free from the financial burden. It wasn't that we didn't trust each other. It just didn't seem right, and it was going to be an accounting nightmare. The separation of the land was inevitable.

Our attorney informed us that the entire property had to be sold as one lot. For legal reasons, it couldn't be divided until it belonged to someone else. One of us would have to purchase all the land and then sell portions to the other. Michael and I were the only ones with enough liquidity to do so.

We asked our loan officer to front us $80,000 to purchase the entire acreage. Then it was another three months before the rest of the sale could be finalized. When the dust finally settled we were in debt for about $20,000. But at that point it didn't matter. I was just glad I no longer risked losing my home. The thought of moving away from the last place Ashley had lived was more than I could bear. Now it was clear: this was my land, my home. No one could ever take it away from me. It was a day of thanksgiving.

I reflected back to a day long ago. I'd gone to the Oklahoma City Interfaith Ministries to pick up a check for the headstones and met a young woman. "Well, at least you're rich now," she said. I didn't understand what she meant. I suppose she was implying all the money pouring into Oklahoma to assist the bombing victims had gone straight to us. I laughed at her comment. Even though I knew millions upon millions of dollars had been sent to Oklahoma City to help with the rescue and recovery, none was spent to help us pay this debt. The charities were very careful, just as they should have been, about the way they dispersed the funds. Some helped to buy food for Dad's cattle. Some helped us recover lost income. But what we needed most was for the debt to go away. In the end we had to rely on our own resources to make that happen. Unfortunately, it was at great cost financially, emotionally, and spiritually. The settling of the estate caused a chasm between Mike and his siblings. It has taken a great deal of time to heal the wounds that a proper last will and testament might have prevented.

After going through all the complications my father's estate had involved, we'd asked Luther if he had a will. When he said no we begged him to have one made. We even offered to pay for it, but it was no use. He was firm: "All I'm going to leave you is debt. There won't be anything for you to fight over." If only he had known.

I don't believe we've finalized the estate yet. There are still a few farm implements that need to be sold, but the major things are finished. The bank is satisfied, and all the siblings have settled into their own ways of life. I've learned, intimately, how quickly loving families can turn to anger in the process of resolving an estate. I've also learned that time, and distance, usually heals those wounds.

I'm glad Debbie and Mark own the land around us—it's always good to know your neighbors. Today Debbie's kids often play with mine. Mark recently got married to a wonderful young woman and is now living in Texas. He and his wife are joyously expecting a baby. Mark still owns the land with the hundred-year-old farmhouse. They plan on moving back to Oklahoma City as soon as he is vested with his company and can request a transfer. Eventually, he and his wife will undertake the complete refurbishment of the farmhouse from the ground up. I'm sure LaRue would be happy about that. Brad and his wife have two more children and still live nearby in town. We see them occasionally. If they were still alive, Luther and LaRue would have fourteen grandchildren. How they would have loved that. They were always so proud of their growing family.

I know it would have broken their hearts to see the breach in the family their sudden, untimely deaths caused. But I also think they'd have been proud of the final outcome. Even with all the tension, in the end, we're family and have managed to get through the hurts this tragedy caused. I know now, the anger was simply the early stages of grief. I also know I've been guilty too. It is my prayer that over time the wounds will heal, and we will be a close family once again.

Twelve

Fields of Confusion

Every flower is a soul blossoming in Nature.

GÉRARD DE NERVAL

The day after Ashley's funeral my phone rang. I shuffled toward the receiver, with barely the strength, or desire, to answer it. When I mumbled a weak "hello," the man on the other end identified himself as an Oklahoma City police officer. He hesitated, then inquired about Ashley's funeral. When I explained we'd already buried our little girl, he seemed disappointed.

He cleared his throat, then told me he was the one who had found Ashley. Eventually the story came forth. When he heard the bomb go off, he was in his patrol car at the corner of Broadway and Fifth. The impact from the explosion threw debris across his vehicle. After sitting stunned for a moment, he pulled himself together, then quickly drove toward the scene of destruction. However, because of the remnants in the street, he couldn't get much closer. He decided to walk the remaining block to the building.

His voice began to tremble as he told me he discovered a woman in a blue dress trying desperately to get to the day-care center. He cautioned her to wait. Then he went around to the south side of the building and crawled down to the "pit" to search for survivors. He spent the remainder of the morning digging through the rubble looking for babies. He continued to hand the little ones up to other officers and firemen on the edge of the structure, because no one would come down to help him. He was finally forced by the threat of a second bomb to move away.

He wasn't allowed back into the interior of the building. The FBI had arrived, and a protective structure had been put in place. He was relegated to crowd control.

He seemed traumatized by his experience. His emotions fluctuated between sorrow and anger. We talked for several minutes, but because I was still incoherent, I took his phone number so we could talk more later.

Over the next few months we stayed in touch. During one phone conversation toward the end of that year, he told me he was having medical problems because of his time in the building but wasn't getting assistance from the police insurance. I contacted caseworkers at the American Red Cross and Feed the Children to see if they could help this deserving man.

Soon afterward I saw him doing a television interview in which he said, "I took all the children out of the day care." Then, I knew something was wrong. Ashley wasn't in the day care. Had it all been a mistake? Maybe he was confused about which child Ashley was—there had been so many. Maybe when he talked about the "pit" he was referring to the entire building. However, unable to handle the perplexing emotional roller coaster, I never contacted him again.

Even though it seems he was not who I thought he was, I had no doubt his struggle was sincere. No one can fake that kind of hurt. I heard it in his voice, and I saw it on his face.

After the first anniversary of the bombing, Linda Cavanaugh from Channel 4 did a beautiful, hour-long photojournalistic essay about some of the families affected by the tragedy. She chose our family because we had "lost so much." As soon as it aired my phone rang. This time it was Chet Clark, a fireman with the Oklahoma City Fire Department. He wanted me to know he'd been the one who found Ashley. I was confused. I told Chet about the other officer. He became agitated. "I don't know what he told you, but he couldn't have found your daughter." Then he described everything Ashley was wearing that day, even the color of her hair, and many details about her no one else knew. It became apparent to me then, Chet was probably Ashley's true rescuer.

I continued to listen with morbid curiosity. I needed to know what had happened to my daughter. We spoke for almost an hour. He told me how he and his lieutenant had crawled into the pit and found a pocket of people who'd been thrown against the wall. His unit had already removed one body when he saw a little foot sticking out of the rubble. He decided she would be next. At first Chet thought she was a little boy because Ashley was wearing blue jeans and a T-shirt. He started digging and didn't stop until the wee hours of the morning. Many times the officers tried to pull him and his team out, but he wouldn't leave until he'd recovered her body. He told me he knew there were some parents out there worried beyond belief, not knowing if their child were alive or dead. At least if she were recovered they would know the truth. Chet had lost his infant son less than a year earlier, so he knew intimately the pain parents feel when their child dies. "All the time I was digging," he said, "your child was my child."

I didn't know what to say. All I could do was mutter, "Thank you." I wrote down his name and phone number, because I knew when I'd sorted things out I would want to talk with him again. Unfortunately, his contact information was somehow misplaced.

In the fall of 1997, at a meeting for the memorial, I learned through the fire chaplain, Ted Wilson, that many of the rescuers were having extreme problems coping with the tragedy. It became apparent that we had to focus on bringing the rescuers together with the victims' families or survivors whose lives they had touched. And I felt it needed to be more intimate than a public meeting.

After the meeting I approached Ted and told him everything I knew about the fireman who'd contacted me. At the time I couldn't recall his name, but I gave Ted as many details as I could. I was in luck; Ted thought he knew who it was.

Within a month Ted called. He believed he'd located Ashley's rescuer. I was elated. I had neglected the most important part of my healing—I needed to know the man who'd found my daughter. He had experienced a part of Ashley that no one else ever could.

Since it was so close to Christmas, we agreed it would be too difficult to plan a meeting right away. Ted said he'd contact me after the first of the year. Around February he set the wheels in motion. Chet called me at home. I sensed he was uncomfortable but also felt we needed to meet. I let him decide whether to bring his family or come alone. We agreed to meet at a restaurant near Tinker Air Force Base, where I worked. I hung up and immediately called my sister. As I suspected, she wanted to come too.

As Mike, Darlene, and I pulled into the parking lot, I spotted him. He was dark-haired and husky. The minute I got out of the car, I hurried over, grabbed him, and hugged his neck. I didn't want to let go. I felt a powerful, instantaneous connection with this man. I had brought a picture of Ashley in a pretty little frame. I handed it to Chet. "This is for you. I want you to remember Ashley this way, not the way you found her," I said.

Chet gently took the photograph from my hand. "You don't know how much I appreciate this. I have a small picture of her on my desk that I cut out of a magazine. This will be much better."

I hugged him again, then brushed away my tears. He had brought his wife, but his three children had opted not to come along. We went into the restaurant, sat down, and ordered lunch. As we waited we talked about their work, their family, and their life. Chet was a soft-spoken, compassionate man. I could see the hurt in his eyes as he struggled with what he needed to say. Finally, he took a deep breath and said, "I want you to know, I never left your daughter for a single second. I cared for her like she was one of my own." I smiled at him. "Thank you, Chet. I can't tell you how much that means to me." I tried to speak more but choked on my emotions.

He nodded and proceeded to tell us the whole story. Several bodies had been thrown against the parking garage in the back of the Social Security office. A team had gone in and removed one body, and then it was his turn. He moved some rubble, saw her little foot sticking out, and knew instantly, this was a child. He started removing the surrounding rubble to get to her. He didn't remember exactly how long he was there, but he did remember his supervisor asking him to come out. But he wouldn't. He explained, "This became very personal to me. I knew how it felt to lose a child, and I knew how important it would be for the parents to have that child back with them. I couldn't rest until I was done."

Normally the bodies would be handed out to firemen waiting on the outside, but Chet wouldn't give Ashley to anyone. He carried her all the way to the morgue. He told us Mom was with Ashley. He knew it was LaRue because of her long, silver hair. No one had hair like she did. He helped recover her body as well.

Then Mike chimed in. "Let me ask you something that's been buggin' me all this time. A friend of mine was on the site and had taken several pictures. He described a picture of what he'd been told was my mother. He said the picture was a solid slab of concrete with only two legs sticking out. From that picture, we assumed Mom was crushed, but from what you are telling me, this doesn't seem possible."

Chet looked a little puzzled. "I am certain your mother was in the pit near Ashley. It's possible the photograph he described was later identified as someone else. There was a lot of confusion during that time. It could be a mistake, or it could be she was trapped that way and he saw the other side."

"One other question. We were told Mom and Dad weren't found together. Is that true?" Chet seemed to remember Dad being there too, but he wasn't sure. There were several people found in the pit together, and he thought he remembered a redheaded man there, but he just couldn't be certain. He promised to check with the guys in his unit and let us know.

There was a long silence, and then I broke it. "I just want you to know, even though you don't think of yourself as one, and that you were just 'doin' your job,' you are a hero in my book. You can say what you like, but I think you and your guys went above and beyond the call of duty. No one should ever have to do what you and so many others did willingly. I am proud to know you, and thankful you were there for Ashley, Mom, and Dad. You have become a part of our family. Like it or not"—I chuckled—"we will be inviting you to all our family functions, so just be prepared."

He laughed softly, then shyly murmured, "Thanks."

During that couple of hours we discovered we shared many interests. My sister breeds draft horses, and Chet used to be in the Draft Horse Club. His daughters were in 4H and barrel raced, and he dabbled with farming.

"Chet, Mike's sister, Debbie, and his aunt and uncle, LaRue's brother, asked me to locate the fireman who recovered Mom and Dad. Since you were in on that, would you mind meeting with them too?"

"That shouldn't be a problem," he said.

We asked him to come to my sister's farm in the spring because that was when her mares were due to foal. His kids would love it. Darlene added, "I'll have Nathan hook up his wagon team, and we'll do a hay ride and a barbecue. Just plan on makin' a day of it."

Chet nodded and grinned. "That sounds like great fun. We'll plan on being there."

Unfortunately, with all the chaos surrounding the aftermath of the disaster, barbecues, horse-drawn carriages, and picnics reuniting families never materialized.

Just as we were leaving Chet took Mike and me aside. "I have some pictures of the site, my own personal photos. I've never shared them with anyone. But if you should ever feel the need to see them, I'd be happy to make copies for you." We thanked him. Then I hugged him and his wife and said our good-byes.

As we drove away from the restaurant, a sense of peace washed over me. I felt I'd almost completed my journey. I'd finally met the man who last held Ashley in his arms. He was a kind, loving, gentle family man who seemed completely sincere. I couldn't have asked for anyone nicer to hold my daughter in those last, sacred moments. I said a prayer for Chet and his family. I sensed he was still struggling with the horrific sights he'd viewed that terrible April morning, and that it had forever changed the dynamics of his family. I knew one day our paths would cross again. And I prayed he would find peace.

Thirteen

Cultivating Justice

Vain are the thousand creeds
That move men's hearts; utterly vain;
Worthless as withered weeds,
Or idlest froth amid the boundless main.

EMILY BRONTË

The pretrial was about to begin. I arrived early at the Oklahoma County Courthouse and took my place in line. Together we stood, survivors of the blast, family members of the lost, sharing the bonds of a grieving community none of us had asked to join.

We waited for several hours, and I watched in disbelief as the Nichols and McVeigh families waltzed by the long line to be seated at the front of the courtroom. I didn't mind waiting, I just resented them getting preferential treatment.

Rick Fugate, president of the Oklahoma Crime Victims Center, was with me. He offered words of wisdom: "Kathleen, this is just the beginning. You're about to experience many 'injustices' in the 'justice' system." How I wish I'd understood the depth of his warning.

Finally it was time to enter the courtroom. One by one we filed inside, seeking understanding, seeking truth, and seeking justice. I found an empty spot behind a wall of attorneys. But I could barely see the defendants. I felt my anger grow.

I began to tremble as I watched Tim McVeigh saunter into the room, closely followed by Terry Nichols. McVeigh was laughing and joking with his attorneys, clearly unmoved by the whole process. Nichols was subdued and quiet.

I focused my anger on McVeigh. Did he have no compassion? No understanding of what he was being charged with? Did he care? I stared angrily at him as he sat at the defense table. I kept thinking, If I can only get my hands around his neck, I can choke him into submission. I wanted him to hurt the way I hurt. I wanted him to grasp what it felt like to bury your child in pieces.

Eventually a recess was called. I rose but was unable to move. My hands gripped the back of the bench in front of me, and my knuckles turned white. Rage welled up inside me. There was a dark battle for my sanity. If I'd let go of the bench that day, there's no doubt I would have been arrested. I continued to glare at McVeigh as he rose with his attorneys. Apparently he felt the intensity, because suddenly we locked eyes. I stared bullets at him and mouthed the words "baby killer." I watched with some satisfaction as the smile dropped from his face and he hung his head. It was a small victory, but a victory nonetheless.

I listened to the rest of the proceedings with only half an ear. I was having a hard time understanding why they just didn't take the boy out and hang him like they did in old western movies. I left during the afternoon break and drove home, utterly exhausted yet still on fire with rage. I swore that day, if I were given the opportunity to take the stand against this man, I would do so readily.

I followed the judiciary proceedings carefully. With disbelief I watched as the trial was moved to Denver, Colorado. I felt helpless knowing it would be impossible for me to attend the daily court proceedings. I couldn't afford the trip but, more important, couldn't afford to be away from my children, my home, and my job.

Soon, because of public outcry, arrangements were made for closed-circuit television transmission to the Federal Aviation Administration building in Oklahoma City. It wouldn't be the same as being there, but everything hadn't been taken away from us.

Then came another shock: Judge Richard Matsch determined that anyone who viewed the courtroom proceedings wouldn't be allowed to testify. He was convinced that watching the proceedings would corrupt our testimony. Each of us was forced to decide whether it was more important to testify or to view the trial.

Almost immediately legislation was brought before the Senate to make it possible to do both. The decision caused Judge Matsch to rescind his ruling. But he reserved the right to interview witnesses to determine if any portion of the trial had influenced their testimony. A few brave souls tested the waters and did both. I didn't have the strength or the courage. Too much of my sanity was riding on being able to look McVeigh and Nichols in the eye once more.

Each day without fail Darlene attended the trial. During jury selection she took detailed notes, then called to fill me in. At times I wanted to join the others, but, determined to testify, I stayed at home waiting for Darlene's feedback and the nightly news.

As the trial grew closer I became more apprehensive. I'd never been in a courtroom before. I knew I was expected to perform within strict limitations. I wondered if I would be able to do it, but I was determined that McVeigh, and the jury, needed to hear our story.

In mid-June the Justice Department asked me to get ready. Within a week they'd fly Michael and me to Denver. I called my husband's work to arrange his absence. The scramble was on. We made plans for the boys to stay with our friend Janice Mobley in the evenings. Michael's aunt and cousin would watch them during the day.

As we packed I realized the time had come for me to tell this man what he'd done to my family. Then my mind wandered to the jury. I'd learned from Darlene that they were taking the evidence pretty hard, and the courtroom had been extremely emotional.

Helena Garrett, whose son, Tevin, was in the day care, was one of the first to testify. She stated that she'd arrived at the building on foot shortly after the explosion searching for her son. She found the children laid out on the playground in a makeshift morgue. She testified how upset she was to find them in that condition. "We don't want our babies laid on glass," she said, and wept.

Judge Matsch was keeping tight reigns on the courtroom, limiting how many atrocities the jury members were subjected to. He shut many of the witnesses down in midtestimony. That upset me. I began to fear the judge would stop me, before I'd shared everything I needed to say. Michael offered reassurance: "Everything will be fine, Kathleen, you'll be able to accomplish everything you need to." However, the week before I gave my testimony, I spent my nights tossing and turning, asking God for wisdom, for comfort, for justice.

Finally the day arrived. We headed for the airport, held hands, and boarded the plane. It was a packed flight. Almost immediately Michael and I were separated. He was seated at the rear of the plane, and I was at the front. As we waited on the tarmac for what seemed like eternity, I bit my lip. Eventually the captain announced there was a minor problem with the plane's air brake switch, so we'd be experiencing a slight delay. That "slight" delay took over an hour. By the time we took off, I was almost in tears.

When we landed in Dallas I called the attorneys' office and asked them to take a note to my sister, who was in the courtroom. They promised to do their best. However, when we arrived in Denver, Darlene was in a panic. "Where have you been?" she asked. "When you were late, I got so worried." I told her what happened, and how I'd called to let her know, but she'd never received the message. Things continued to progress downhill.

Exhausted, we went to our hotel room and settled in. Unfortunately, we weren't told what to do next. We were afraid to go anywhere, believing we should stay close to the phone. Michael and I spent our time unpacking, reading the local papers, and watching a bit of television. Finally, after waiting for hours, we left for dinner.

When we returned to our room the message light was flashing. We were to call the witness center to make arrangements to meet with Vicki Behenna the following afternoon.

In the morning Michael and I quickly showered, dressed, and drove to the Safe Haven, an area set up in the basement of a Catholic church that was a short walk from the courthouse. The church provided a big-screen TV, games, and lunches for those who'd been displaced because of the trial. Reporters were not allowed in, nor was anyone else who might harass or upset us. We were greeted by people I'd come to know through the memorial process. It felt good to be among friends.

So many were scattered when the trial was moved to Denver. Darlene had flown out a few weeks before us, and kind friends had taken her in. She was determined to watch as much of the proceedings as possible. Many of the victims' families doubled up in hotel rooms and shared transportation to conserve resources. Each morning Darlene got up at 3:00 and stood in line so she could be assured of a spot in the courtroom. And each day she watched as the McVeigh and Nichols families walked in a few minutes before the session began. It didn't seem to matter that she had severe back problems, or that she'd stood for hours in the snow waiting for a seat.

Soon the victims' families began to work around the system. Once Darlene and a friend paid a couple of homeless men to hold their places in line so they could rest. The men felt bad about taking the money, but the women insisted.

Finally, after what seemed like years, both sides rested. The jury was asked to make their decision: guilty or not guilty. So much depended on those twelve individuals. They held in their hands our families, our hearts, our very sense of peace. We waited for a verdict, and we waited for justice.

That evening we met with Vicki. She informed us we were to testify during the sentencing phase of the hearing. Once the jury pronounced McVeigh guilty, the victims and their families would be allowed to speak. She was not completely sure of the witness order but felt my statement would be toward the middle.

Together we reviewed my story one last time. I told her I was terrified. She hugged me and said, "You'll do just fine. Just tell your story to me, and I will question you to elaborate on points that need to be heard. Just focus on me and nothing else." I nodded in agreement. As she moved toward the door we quietly said good night.

Later that evening Michael held me as I wept. I wasn't sure I could do it. But in spite of my fears I needed to express everything I'd come to Denver to proclaim.

Each morning we'd go to the Safe Haven and watch for the verdict. Hours turned into days. We feared the jury wouldn't be able to find McVeigh guilty. Periodically the foreman approached the judge for clarification on points of law.

Finally the verdict came. Everyone who could rushed to the courtroom. The rest of us gathered around the big screen on the edges of our chairs. We held our breath and our hands.

The jury was seated. The judge addressed the foreman. The reporter quoted after the judge:

> In the United States District Court for the District of Colorado, Criminal Action No. 96-CR-68, United States of America vs. Timothy James McVeigh. We, the jury, upon our oaths unanimously find as follows:
>
> Count 1, conspiracy to use a weapon of mass destruction, guilty.
>
> Count 2, use of a weapon of mass destruction, guilty.
>
> Count 3, destruction by explosive, guilty. Do you find that the Government proved beyond a reasonable doubt that the crime or crimes committed by the defendant, Timothy James McVeigh, as found above, resulted in the death of one or more of the persons named in the indictment? Yes. Was the death of such person or persons a foreseeable result of the defendant's criminal conduct? Yes.
>
> Count 4, first-degree murder of Mickey Bryant Maroney, guilty.
>
> Count 5, first-degree murder of Donald R. Leonard, guilty.
>
> Count 6, first-degree murder of Alan Gerald Whicher, guilty.
>
> Count 7, first-degree murder of Cynthia Lynn Campbell Brown, guilty.
>
> Count 8, first-degree murder of Kenneth Glenn McCullough, guilty.
>
> Count 9, first-degree murder of Paul Douglas Ice, guilty.
>
> Count 10, first-degree murder of Claude Author Medearis, guilty.
>
> Count 11, first-degree murder of Paul G. Broxterman, guilty.

Pandemonium broke loose in Safe Haven as we hugged one another and cried. Relief washed over me. It was over. He was guilty. Court was adjourned, and everyone came back to join us.

While Safe Haven celebrated I needed to find a quiet place to pray. I ran up the stairs to the sanctuary and sat down on a wooden pew. Waves of grief washed over me, and I wept. Finally I regained my composure and began to pray. I thanked God for the justice we'd sought. Then I asked Him for guidance, wisdom, and strength for the many days to come.

When I returned to Safe Haven, Michael and I went outside to greet Darlene. There was a huge procession of attorneys, reporters, and others from the courtroom, as well as law enforcement trying to keep a rein on the crowd. I saw my sister and ran across the street toward her. We stood on the corner, hugging and crying. "We've got him, Kathleen. He can't hurt us, or anyone else, ever again. We've got him."

We spotted the prosecution team. It was like seeing a group of avenging angels. These were the people who had sacrificed two years of their lives for this trial. They had put everything on hold to see justice through. They had fought the fight for us. We owed them much more than gratitude—we owed them our lives. I ran over and hugged Joseph Hartzler and then turned to hug Vicki. Cameras were everywhere. Reporters fired a barrage of questions. We ignored them.

We moved inside the Safe Haven. When the prosecution team entered they were given a standing ovation. They looked surprised and a bit embarrassed. Joseph Hartzler addressed the crowd. "Today was a victory for all of us. We have lived this journey with you, and suffered alongside of you. We share your joy." Then he reintroduced the team. "The next few days will be much harder for many of you. We have the conviction, now we must go for the sentence. For that, we will rely on the testimonies all of you have so eloquently shared over the course of our investigation." He went on to outline how the next few days would progress; then the "meeting" broke up, and we all mingled.

I was still a little disappointed that Luther, LaRue, and Ashley were not among the victims named. The count was so small. The charges should have been for 168 counts of murder, not just 8. But we would have to be satisfied with the way things were, at least for now.

On Thursday, June 5, it was my turn to face McVeigh. Before our testimony we were called to a location near the courtroom to wait. Michael and I sat with a handful of other witnesses and tried to ignore what was happening across the street. The room was filled with nervous chatter and long silences. I could feel my muscles tensing and my throat constricting. I wasn't afraid of McVeigh, I was afraid of the judge. My hands were sweaty, and my face grew cold.

Soon it was my turn. We were moved to another room to wait for the bailiff. Michael was brought to the auxiliary courtroom to listen. Without him, I felt terrified. As I sat, waiting to be called, my fear grew.

Within moments I was escorted into the courtroom; I was certain everyone noticed my uncontrollable shaking. First, I looked at the judge. His eyes and nose were red and swollen. It looked as if he either had a terrible cold or had been crying. He nodded to me as I entered. Then I glanced toward the jury. All their eyes were red and swollen too. Many already had sympathetic looks on their faces. I was sworn in.

I looked toward Vicki and was reassured to see a familiar face. Behind her I could see Darlene. After taking a deep, trembling breath, I looked toward McVeigh. He was bent over his table with his attorney by his side. McVeigh looked at me, and his expression was almost apologetic, you might even say pleading. Yet I saw no sign of remorse. His eyes were not red and swollen. It was clear he wasn't grieving for the lost. I clenched my teeth and waited to begin.

DIRECT EXAMINATION BY MS. BEHENNA:

Q. Where do you live, Ms. Treanor?

A. I'm sorry?

I was startled by Vicki's first, simple question. I was still trying to calm my nerves and stop shaking, and had been looking around the courtroom trying to find familiar and friendly faces. I saw many people I'd come to know over the last few years. I prayed silently I wouldn't disappoint them.

Q. Where do you live?

A. I live in Guthrie, Oklahoma. It's about thirty miles north of Oklahoma City.

Q. Are you married?

A. Yes, I am. My husband's name is Michael Treanor.

Q. How long have you been married?

A. It will be three years in a couple of weeks.

Q. Is this a second marriage?

A. Yes, it is.

My answers were terse. I was afraid to elaborate for fear the judge would stop me at any moment. I tried desperately to stay focused on Vicki.

Q. Do you have any children, Ms. Treanor?

A. I had three children. I have two boys remaining, David, who is eleven, and Zachary, my son, who is almost nine.

Q. And you had a little girl?

A. Ashley. Ashley Eckles.

Q. How old was Ashley?

A. Ashley was four and a half.

Q. Would you consider yourselves to be a blended family?

A. Oh, yes. David is Michael's little boy from a previous marriage, and Zachary and Ashley were mine. The funny thing about Ashley, though, is she was so very young when we—our families came together, she was the bridge. She called Michael "Daddy," and she loved him as a daddy. I can remember one morning—or one night, actually, whenever she called him into the bedroom and she said, "I'm the luckiest little girl in the world, because I have two daddies that love me very much." And he came out of the room that night and he said, "Thank you for giving me a daughter."

I choked on the last few words, remembering that night and how sweet Ashley was. I began to tremble beyond control. My heart was racing, and I was sure everyone in the courtroom could hear it. Again I glanced over at McVeigh, hoping for any signs of remorse. He didn't look up from the pad of paper in front of him. Steven Jones, his attorney, was slightly turned away from him, alternately watching Vicki and me as I testified.

Q. You and Mike don't have children together.

A. No, ma'am. I can't have any children anymore.

Q. I'm going to show you Government's Exhibit 1489. Okay? And it will appear on that computer screen in front of you. Can you identify that?

It was a picture taken in the spring right before the bombing—of Zachary and Ashley at a Japanese garden. They were seated side by side, and Ashley had one of her brilliant smiles on her face.

A. Yes.

Q. You've seen that before?

A. Lots of times.

Ms. BEHENNA: Your Honor, I'd move for the admission of Government's Exhibit 1489.

MR. JONES: No objection.

THE COURT: Received. It may be published.

Ms. BEHENNA: Thank you, Your Honor.

BY Ms. BEHENNA:

Q. Describe for the jury who that is and what they're seeing on this photograph.

A. That's my son Zachary and my daughter, Ashley.

Q. When was that picture taken?

A. Not very long before the bombing. Probably a couple of months.

Q. Sometime in 1995?

A. Yes.

Q. Spring of '95?

A. Yes.

Q. You stated that you lived in Guthrie. Do you live on some land in Guthrie?

A. Yes. As a matter of fact, we live on about a quarter of [a] 160-acre section that belonged to my mother-in-law and father-in-law, Luther and LaRue Treanor. There are approximately four houses on that quarter acre of land—quarter section of land.

Q. Who lives out there?

A. Michael and I have a house; and his sister, Debbie, and Buddy Price live behind us; and also his younger brother, Mark, has a house there as well. Before the bombing, Luther and LaRue lived there as well.

Q. And that's Mike's mother and father?

A. Yes.

Q. Let me show you Government's Exhibit 1208C. I'd ask you if you can identify that.

A. Yes. That's LaRue. LaRue Treanor.

Ms. BEHENNA: Your Honor, I would move for the admission—actually, I believe it's already admitted on a chart, Government's Exhibit 1208.

I looked at the picture of LaRue on my view screen. It was the best and most recent picture we were able to find of her. She had been cut away from this particular shot. I listened as the discussion went back and forth between Vicki and the judge.

THE COURT: All right. So this is off of that chart.

Ms. BEHENNA: It's off the chart, Your Honor.

THE COURT: All right. It's received.

BY Ms. BEHENNA:

Q. Can you identify that picture for the jury, Ms. Treanor?

A. Yes. That's LaRue Treanor, my mother-in-law.

Q. Let me show you Government's Exhibit 1208D. And who is that?

A. That is Luther Treanor, my father-in-law.

Q. And they lived out there with you on the eighty acres of land as well as the other people that you've identified?

A. Just a hop, skip, and a jump away.

Q. Did Luther Treanor work?

A. From the time he was eleven years old, he worked. He was a milkman for Townley's Dairy.

Q. Did he also farm?

A. Yes. He loved his farm. He so loved his cattle. He had just about every one of them named. He could tell you what one of them was doing at any particular time. He knew what was going on every second of the day with his farm.

Q. What about LaRue Treanor? Did she work?

A. She did at one point. She had a slip-and-fall accident and was confined to the house. Her work was taking care of the children for us.

Q. And the children that you're speaking of are your children and Mike's children? Right?

A. All of her grandchildren, and she had eight great-children at the time—at the time.

Q. Ranging in ages from what to what?

A. Let's see. David would have been the oldest at that time—he was nine—clear down to a tiny baby.

Q. And how long had she taken care of her grandchildren?

A. Since David was a tiny baby.

Q. For a long time?

A. For a very long time, yes.

Q. Your in-laws were not federal employees, were they?

A. No, ma'am.

Q. I'm going to direct your attention to the morning of April 19, 1995. You worked outside the home.

A. Yes.

Q. And LaRue Treanor, your mother-in-law, took care of Ashley for you?

A. That's right.

Q. She wasn't in school at that time, was she?

A. No, ma'am. She was getting ready to start school in the fall, and she was very excited about that. She was looking forward to it.

When I said those words, I thought of the many conversations I'd had with Ashley about starting school that next year. She loved being with Nana—LaRue—but she was a very social little girl and longed for more companionship.

Q. And your mother-in-law also helped get the two older boys off to school?

A. Yes. As a matter of fact, that morning I had gathered the three children up in my car, and we made the short drive over there. By habit, I would spend fifteen to thirty minutes in the morning just to visit with Mom and to make sure that the kids were situated before I left for work, just kind of was a routine, kind of helped me get my day started; and I did that morning as well.

Q. And then you left the house, leaving David and Zachary and Ashley with their grandmother?

A. Gave all of them a hug and kiss; and as I was leaving, Ashley ran up to the door and threw her arms against the doors and gave me one of her little, mischievous grins and she said, "You cannot leave." And I said, "But, Ashley, I have to go to work today." And she said, "You cannot leave until you give me another hug and kiss." So I leaned down, and she threw her arms around my neck; and she gave me a real hard kiss on the lips and hugged me again, and we rubbed noses.

By then I was softly sobbing. Every muscle in my body was drawn tight, and my chest began to hurt. I clutched the stand and bit the inside of my cheek to maintain control.

Q. And then you went to—

A. And then I went to work.

Q. When did you learn that your mother-in-law and your father-in-law and your daughter were downtown in Oklahoma City?

A. It was about 10:30 in the morning.

Q. Up until that moment in time, you had no idea that they had gone downtown to the federal building?

A. I knew that they had an appointment downtown, but I did not connect that it was at the federal building. My sister—

Q. I was just going to ask how did you learn that your in-laws as well as your daughter were downtown in the Murrah Building?

A. My sister called me. I had just started a new job, and she wasn't certain exactly where I worked downtown; and she was worried about me. She thought I might have been hurt. And she called and begged me to come home. And I told her no, I needed to stay close, just in case I could do something. And I asked her, because the phone lines were so jammed—I said, "Please call Mom and let her know that I'm okay, so she doesn't worry." And she said she would. And we hung up; and of course, I watched the video on the TV for a while. And then about fifteen to thirty minutes later, she called back. She managed to get through and she said, "Kathleen, where is Ashley?" And I said, "Well, Ashley is with Mom." And there was a big pause, and she said, "Did you not remember that Luther and LaRue had an appointment at Social Security today?" And I said, "Well, yeah, I remember, but that's over at the capital complex; that's nowhere near where this building is." And she said: "No. I worked downtown. I know that

Social Security is in that building." And I argued with her for probably five minutes, before I realized she was right, and she knew what she was talking about.

Q. And you made a call, then, to your in-laws' house, didn't you?

A. I hung up with her, and I called the house, because I couldn't believe it.

Q. Who did you talk to when you called the house?

A. Brad, Mike's little brother, answered the phone, and he was there.

Q. And he tells you what?

A. I asked him, "Where are Mom and Dad?" He said, "I don't know. I think they had an appointment downtown. I'm going right now to see if I can find them." He gave me his pager number, and we hung up. When I hung up from him, I called the Red Cross and I described Ashley, everything that she was wearing right down to her little panties, because I dressed her that morning.

Q. You not only called the Red Cross, but you called other hospitals in downtown Oklahoma City?

A. All of them. I made the whole circuit.

Q. And at one point in time, you decide to head downtown to St. Anthony's to see if you can find your in-laws and Ashley; right?

A. I had called Michael and asked him to please come. I needed him to be there with me, because I didn't know what else to do. And my boss at the time—he said: "Come on. They're putting a list up at St. Anthony's. We need to get you down there and see if she's somewhere in the city, if she had been found." So we went there, and I ran right over to the wall; and I scoured the list, looking for any sign of any one of them, and none of them were there. So I just sat down and waited, and finally Michael came; and we waited and we waited all day long, we waited.

Q. And you leave St. Anthony's Hospital later that afternoon and you go—

I was building momentum. My fear had subsided, and I was able to talk without Vicki dragging every word from my mouth.

A. About 5:00 that evening, they told us that any information would be given to the First Christian Church and that we should move there and we would be made comfortable. So we did.

Q. And you go to the First Christian Church, and you provide the people there with information about your daughter, Ashley; right?

A. That's right.

Q. As well as—

A. And we sat down with the medical examiner, and he asked for any kind of medical records or dental records or any kind of identifying scars or marks that might be able to identify them.

Q. You also provide information about your in-laws.

A. Yes.

Q. And you go home?

A. No. We waited there for probably four or five hours.

Q. And eventually go on home?

A. And finally we did go home, and we had to tell our boys what had happened. At that point, we hadn't given up hope. We still thought they might be found.

Q. At some point in time, you were called by the law enforcement officers wanting to come over to your house and dust Ashley's things for fingerprints.

A. And I told him that wouldn't be necessary. My husband was a reserve police officer; and he had taken all three of the children down with the Cub Scouts to take their fingerprints, kind of a child-protection-service thing.

Q. And you provide those fingerprints to the law enforcement officers?

A. Yes.

Q. Do you remember the day that you do that?

A. Yeah.

Q. Was it April 21, 1995?

A. Yes.

Q. Did you receive a call later April 21, 1995?

A. Yeah, between four and five that evening, we got a call, I believe, from the medical examiner's office, asked us to please come down to the First Christian Church; that they had some information for us.

Q. And you get to the First Christian Church. You're notified that they have recovered and they've identified your daughter, Ashley?

A. Yes.

Q. Do you also tell the medical examiner's staff at that time not to call you again until both LaRue Treanor and Luther Treanor have been found and identified?

A. Yes. Actually, Michael asked them to do that because we were all down there and we were all in utter shock, you know, from losing three people from our family at one time. It would have been more than we could have taken to be dragged there two more times, so we asked them just to limit it to one.

Q. And you later receive a phone call about Luther and LaRue Treanor having been found?

A. When we came back from Ashley's funeral, we called from the church. And we had four messages from the medical examiner's office asking us to please come down to the church again; that they had more information for us. So once again, we gathered all the family together, and we went down to the First Christian Church.

Q. Now, that didn't end your contact with the medical examiner's office, did it, Ms. Treanor?

A. No, ma'am.

Q. As a matter of fact, you receive a call from the medical examiner's office in November of 1995, don't you?

My throat constricted as I realized where she was leading me.

A. Yes.

Q. And the voice at the other end of that telephone conversation tells you that he has some more information for you. Do you remember that call?

A. Yes. It was Ray Blakeney.

Q. What does Mr. Blakeney tell you?

A. He says, "I'm very sorry, but I have to tell you this, so I know what I need to do." He said, "We have recovered a portion of

Ashley's hand; and we wanted to know if you wanted that buried in the mass grave, or if you would like to have it to do with what you need to do." And I said, "Of course, I want it. It's a part of her, and I need to have it where I know it is." So we called our funeral director, and he made arrangements for us.

Vicki appeared nervous and began shuffling her papers. She kept glancing back and forth from me to the judge. As soon as I was finished with that last statement, she moved to complete the examination.

MS. BEHENNA: All right. I know this is difficult, and I'm sorry to have to ask you that. Your Honor, that's all I have.

THE COURT: All right. Any questions?

MR. JONES: No questions for this witness.

THE COURT: All right. Mrs. Treanor, you may step down. You're excused.

MR. JONES: Your Honor, may I approach the bench?

THE COURT: Yes.

I was confused; there was so much more. Why had Vicki stopped me? I got up and left the room as the attorneys approached the bench. I walked down the hallway, sat down, and sobbed. Soon Michael joined me, and I fell into his arms and wept. "I blew it. I blew it," I said over and over. "I choked and couldn't talk. I was so scared."

He hugged me. "You did fine, honey. I think the jury understood."

Later I was informed that because of my testimony there were to be no more last kisses, and no more second funerals mentioned on the witness stand. It was too difficult, and the jury had heard enough. Vicki felt the judge was about to end my testimony, so she cut it short. Although the explanation brought some relief, I was still disappointed. Did the jury, did McVeigh, even begin to understand my loss?

We went back to the hotel and packed our bags. I was ready to go home. I desperately missed my children. But there was something more I missed in Oklahoma. I'd built a safe and comfortable prison there, and I was determined to go back where I could hide from the world once more.

Fourteen

Snake in the Grass

As I have seen, those who plow iniquity
and sow trouble reap the same.
By the breath of God they perish,
and by the blast of his anger, they are consumed.

JOB 4:8–9 RSV

It was late 1997, and the long-awaited trial of Terry Nichols was about to begin. Fortunately, much of the groundwork had been laid by the McVeigh proceedings. I followed the daily news reports and on-line transcripts from home. But even this information couldn't give me the intimate knowledge of what was going on in the courtroom. I was looking for details—the demeanor of the jurors as well as the judge, and how the prosecutors were holding up against the defense team. My lifeline, once again, became my sister, who faithfully attended the proceedings every day.

After jury selection she called with concern in her voice. "I'm worried," she said. "I don't believe this jury is as good as the one in the McVeigh trial. There are two, in particular, who seemed uncertain about the death penalty. I'm concerned, very concerned about this."

"Don't worry so much, Darlene. I'm sure our attorneys will give us what we need. Besides, the evidence is overwhelming." But even though I tried to reassure her, fear gripped my heart. I was losing faith in the system.

Because of limitations in seating, only a handful of families were brought to Denver, for a week at a time, at the expense of the United States. If more came it was on their own dime. However, that didn't stop the determined. Several people moved to Denver for the duration of the trial. Jannie Coverdale was one of them. She even took a job in the community, holding on for the long ride.

I cringed when I heard that, just as with the McVeigh trial, the defendant's family members were being escorted inside ahead of everyone else.

Every day Darlene scrutinized the jurors. She was horrified when a few times she thought she saw a couple of them napping. How could they make a decision regarding someone's life if they were sleeping on the job?

As the trial progressed my anger and frustration grew to exponential proportions. My family had been put through so much. The proceeding had been moved several states away, and with the revictimization from the judicial system, it was simply more than I could bear. I was angry because I lost my daughter, and because no one seemed to care. I was angry because I couldn't attend the trial. I was angry because I wasn't pregnant. I was just flat-out mad.

It was the holidays, and David was struggling with school. He was bringing home failing grades, and nothing I did seemed to help. Each evening I'd sit with him for hours, helping with work he refused to do in school. Even though we'd put it in his backpack, he simply wouldn't turn it in. The friction in our home ran high while the children dealt with the loss, Mike struggled to hold the family together, and I struggled to control my anger.

Since I'd had the surgery to reverse my tubal ligation, I was still waiting for a sign a baby was on the way. By this time I was convinced it wasn't ever going to happen. I was despondent, and I couldn't do anything about it.

On December 23, 1997, the news arrived. Terry Nichols was found guilty of the bombing conspiracy but acquitted of the two felony counts blaming him for the attack. The jurors found him guilty of eight counts of involuntary manslaughter for the deaths of eight law enforcement agents.

I was horrified at the mixed message the jury seemed to be sending. What were they trying to say? He was guilty of planning it but not guilty of carrying it out. Huh? Wasn't this man just like a crime boss who plots to kill someone but sends somebody else to do the "dirty work"? Terry Nichols had gone to great lengths to help McVeigh. According to testimony he'd purchased the fertilizer, stolen the blasting caps, and helped construct the bomb. He made several conscious decisions to aid and abet McVeigh in killing 168 innocent people. Terry Nichols could have stopped the tragedy at any time, but he chose not to. Why was this obvious concept so hard for the jury to get?

Like it or not, the verdict had been decided, and it was time for the penalty phase to begin. Just as expected I received a call. They asked me to come to Denver to testify. It was a few days after Christmas, and my emotions were at a peak.

Another holiday had passed without my daughter. Zachary and I often sat together, watching family videotape of our previous Christmases together and talking about how much we missed our little angel. We laughed and cried as we watched Ashley play with the Spin and Twirl Barbie she'd received the year before she was killed.

Since the bombing Christmas had become a somber occasion. I used to decorate weeks ahead of time, spreading the spirit to all corners of the house. Ashley would help by handing me the delicate ornaments to hang on the tree, and by choosing the special spot for each one. Before the bombing lights would cover the exterior of our home while bows, ribbons, and evergreen branches were splashed inside and out. But not anymore. It was everything I could do simply to erect the tree and place a few ornaments on it.

Christmas shopping was incredibly painful. Everywhere I went, there were children with their parents, gleefully entering stores and coming out with armloads of gifts. I'd just bite my lip and buy a few simple things for Mike and the boys. There were only a couple of packages under the tree. It still didn't seem right to celebrate, even after so much time had passed.

Our traditions had changed. No longer did we make the short trek over to LaRue's house on Christmas Day to open presents and share a festive dinner. My mother-in-law always made beautiful decorations and cooked up a delicious meal, punctuated by the clear knowledge that this was Jesus' birthday. For the last Christmas we'd celebrated together, Michael and I had made LaRue a new top for her dining room table. We cut it from a four-by-eight-foot sheet of wood, finished the edges, then carefully stained and varnished it. Every time we sat down at that table she'd mention how proud she was of it, and how wonderful it was to seat her whole family in one special place.

As I made the flight to Denver, images of a family destroyed by violence ran through my mind in a never-ending loop. Michael decided to stay at home with the children this time and asked Darlene to be my moral support. She was waiting for me when I arrived. All the rage and frustration I'd felt over the past two and a half years were bubbling right below the surface. As hard as I tried, it was getting next to impossible to control my hostility.

After I'd settled in I spoke with Geoffrey Mearns, an attorney I'd never before met. Mr. Mearns certainly seemed nice enough, but this unexpected change rattled me. We talked for about an hour, went over my testimony, and then he sent me to the courthouse to wait my turn.

It was New Year's Eve. There were several people in the staging room. A few nervously chatted back and forth. For a couple minutes I attempted to make polite, idle conversation, but then I backed away, trying instead to concentrate on the enormous task before me. By the time my name was called, I was shaking with a mixture of rage and fear. I entered the courtroom, took several hard breaths, was sworn in, then sat down in the witness box.

THE COURTROOM DEPUTY: Would you raise your right hand, please.

I spelled my name for the court clerk. My eyes swept the crowd looking for my sister. I found her at the back of the room, behind the Nichols family. I watched as Geoffrey Mearns took the podium to question me.

THE COURT: Mr. Mearns.

MR. MEARNS: Thank you, Your Honor.

I looked at the faces of the jury but saw nothing—no sympathy, no apparent comprehension. This was not what I'd expected. Then I looked over at Terry Nichols. I wanted to see remorse, but what I got instead was a cold, flat stare. I began to shake uncontrollably. I was sure the sound of my knees knocking together was loud enough for everyone in the courtroom to hear.

By Mr. Mearns:

Q. Good afternoon, Ms. Treanor.

A. Hello.

Q. Where do you live?

A. I live in a little town just outside of Oklahoma City, about thirty minutes away. It's called Guthrie.

Q. How long have you lived in the area of Oklahoma City?

A. Since I was born. I went to school there. Met my husband that I'm married to now there. Went to school with his brothers and sisters there.

Q. What's your husband's name?

A. Michael Treanor.

Q. When did you and Michael Treanor get married?

A. We got married June 16, 1994. We were high school sweethearts originally; but life had separated us, and we married other people and had children by other people. And I had a little girl, and little boy, and he had a little boy by a previous marriage.

Q. What was your son's name?

A. Zachary Eckles.

Q. What are your two children's names?

A. Zachary Eckles and Ashley Eckles. David Treanor was his son.

Q. And was your daughter, Ashley, and Michael's two parents killed in the explosion in Oklahoma City?

A. Yes, sir, they were. They went down to Social Security that morning to file for Luther to retire. He was getting ready to retire.

Q. And Luther Treanor is your husband's father?

A. That's correct.

Q. And what is—what was Luther's wife's name?

A. LaRue. LaRue Treanor.

Q. And how was it that your daughter, Ashley, was with Luther and LaRue Treanor on the morning of April 19?

A. LaRue watched all of our children for us. All of the—all of her children's children. She had eight grandchildren, and they all stayed at her house. And as it turned out, Ashley was the only one that she had with her that day. And she just went along with Luther. I mean, it was just going to be a quick little trip. They were just going to be there for a short time, sign some papers. And then they were going to make a day of it. Maybe do some shopping and have lunch, that kind of thing.

Q. And those three members of your family were killed in the Social Security office that morning?

A. That's correct.

Q. How old was Ashley at the time of her death?

A. She was four and a half.

Q. How long had you known Luther and LaRue Treanor?

A. Almost as long as I'd lived in Guthrie. Mike's little brother, Mark, and I started school together, first grade. We grew up together. I mean, it's a small town. Everybody knows everybody. And—and it's just like one big, happy family. We went to a little community church together. Mike and I started dating in high school, as a sophomore in high school, and we were baptized in this little church. Luther and LaRue were kind of our mentors and guides, and such, as we were teenagers. I—I'd known them almost my whole life.

Q. Tell us, if you would, what Luther Treanor did for work.

A. He was a milk delivery man for Townley's Dairy. He had started the job as a temporary job twenty-seven years ago and just never left. He also farmed. He had 240 acres outside of Guthrie where he had cattle and wheat. And he had done that all of his life, since he was a little boy. He had grown up on a farm in Oklahoma. He loved it. Wouldn't be anywhere else. He—he just loved the earth, was really close to the earth and he loved his farm. Loved his kids. And he loved his wife.

As I spoke, I hoped the Nichols family were truly listening. This man their son had helped murder was a farmer, just like them. A simple man, just like them. I hoped they understood.

Q: I'd like you to take a look at Government Exhibit 1208D.

I looked at the screen. It was the picture of Luther and LaRue taken at a picnic a year or two before they were killed. Only Luther was shown.

MR. MEARNS: At this time, we'd offer that photograph, Your Honor.

MR. TIGAR: No objection, Your Honor.

THE COURT: Received. May be shown.

BY MR. MEARNS:

Q. Who is that picture of, Ms. Treanor?

A. That is my father-in-law, Luther Treanor.

Q. Tell us what kind of a man Luther Treanor was.

A. Oh, he was a good Christian man. He was a pillar of his community. He was a charter member of his church. We tell a story about Dad. He goes to work. He would go to work 2:00, 3:00 in the morning. And one day, he was going to work, and he looked over and he saw a house on fire. And he pulled off the road, and he tried to wake the people up by beating on the door. And finally, he just broke the door down and helped the people get out and saw that everything was okay and under control and calmly got back in his truck and went back to work.

For weeks and weeks afterwards, the TV and radio was looking for the man who had saved this family's life. And he told us he didn't need any recognition, he didn't need any glory; he just did it because it was the right thing to do. And he wouldn't have had it any other way. But that was just the kind of man he was.

He loved his kids. Every one of us. Even if we were married kids, to him, there was no difference. He loved us all the same. There wasn't anything he wouldn't do for us. If we needed money, he was our banker. If we needed moral support, he was there for us. If we needed encouragement, he was there for us. There wasn't anything he wouldn't do for us at all.

Q. How many children did Luther and LaRue Treanor have?

A. They had four children. Three boys and a girl.

Q. And how many grandchildren did they have?

A. At the time, they had eight grandchildren.

Q. I'd like you to take a look now at Government Exhibit 1208C.

The photograph flashed on my viewing screen. It was the other portion of the picnic photograph, showing LaRue. I smiled when I saw her; she was so beautiful.

THE COURT: Received. May be shown.

BY MR. MEARNS:

Q. Who is that, Ms. Treanor?

A. That's LaRue Treanor.

Q. Tell us, if you would, what kind of a woman LaRue Treanor was.

A. For me, LaRue filled a very special hole. She was my mother. My mother had passed away, committed suicide, a few weeks before my son was born. And LaRue seemed to recognize that I needed her. She was my friend. She was my confidant for quite some time. She seemed to know that I needed a mother figure in my life.

I smiled as I remembered LaRue's sweet spirit toward my family.

She was a beautiful woman. Very creative. Very joyful. Loved to sing. Loved her grandkids. She had a shirt that she'd made. It was so sweet. It was a little teddy bear Santa, and Santa was holding a scroll with the list of names and he was checking it twice. And it was all of her grandkids. And as she would have a grandchild, she would add a name to that shirt. And it didn't matter that my children were step-grandchildren. They were still her grandchildren, and she loved them just the same.

Q. I'd like you to take a look now at Government Exhibit 1489.

It was the picture of Zachary and Ashley in the Japanese garden.

MR. TIGAR: No objection, Your Honor.

THE COURT: Received. May be shown.

BY MR. MEARNS:

Q. Tell us, Ms. Treanor: Who do we see in that photograph, please.

A. It's my son, Zachary, and my daughter, Ashley.

Q. What kind of a girl was Ashley?

A. She was a beautiful child. She was the sunshine of my life. She still is.

Q. What kind of a relationship did she have with her two brothers?

A. She ruled our home. Anything that Ashley said, those boys, they marched right to her tune. And nobody could pick on Ashley, but those two boys. They just would not allow it. They loved their little sister. She was—she could do no wrong as far as they were concerned.

She had such a joyful spirit. I mean, she'd sing all the time. She'd sing to her dolls. She'd sing this, she'd sing that. It didn't matter if she knew the words. She'd make them up as she'd go. She was just so full of life.

We had had some kittens not long before the bombing, and she picked these little kittens up. And she'd come running in the house; and she said, "Mommy, Mommy, the cat had kittens." And she was holding this little kitten right up next to her, and she was being so careful and so gentle with it.

And I said, "Honey, you've got to take the kitten back, or you're going to upset the Mommy cat."

And she said, "But I just want to love it." And she was so careful with these kittens, and she just went and took and laid it right back in the box with the Mama cat. And she just stayed there the whole time and just—you know, that's just who she was. She just loved life. She was so full of joy. She was so special to all of us.

Q. What kind of a relationship did Ashley have with your husband, Michael, her stepfather?

A. You know, we have a blended family; and that's—that's difficult at best. And every night, when we'd tuck Ashley into bed, and she'd run in and she'd say, "A kiss and a hug for Mommy." And I'd go in and I'd tuck her in, and I'd give her a kiss and give her a hug. And we'd talk a little bit and say our prayers.

And when she was done with me, she'd say, "A kiss and a hug for Daddy." And Michael would come in, and he'd do the same.

And one night after he had done that, she told him, "You know, I'm the luckiest little girl in the world because I have two daddies that love me very much."

Michael came out of the room that night, big tears rolling down his cheeks; and he said, "Thank you so much for giving me a daughter."

Q. What has been the impact on your family with the loss of Luther and LaRue Treanor?

A. I don't even know where to begin. After the bombing—well, before the bombing, we all would gather at Mom and Dad's house for holidays. That was the place we came. And it didn't matter what differences the brothers and sisters might have had; they all stopped at the door. And we came in, and we were one big, happy family, and we would always fellowship together. We would love, and we would have a really good time, and all the cousins would get together and they would play. It didn't matter.

Since the bombing, we haven't—we haven't even been able to stay in the same room with each other. It has torn our family apart. We—we can't see eye to eye on where Dad wanted us to go with what he was doing. Dad had bought several acres of land, and thousands and thousands of dollars' worth of cattle, and he mortgaged himself to the point where you could see that this man was not prepared to die financially. He had leveraged himself financially to the point where he knew, he was going to be around, and it was going to take him some time to get out of that.

After the bombing, not knowing, he left us no instruction, no will. We didn't know what we needed to do with all these cattle and all this land. We lost the cattle. We lost most of the land. And finally, after all was said and done, all of us had to take out mortgages and—to keep from losing our homes. We all lived on this one acreage—all of us, except for Brad, who lived just in town. And that was something we had holding over us through this whole two and a half years. We—we didn't know if the—the banks were going to come and take us out of our homes. We'd already lost our family, and then we had to worry about this.

Q. What has been the impact, the effect, on you and your family of the loss of your daughter, Ashley?

A. There was a great deal of—of pain, as you can imagine. It took me a long time to just find the will to live, to go on. Ashley was the sunshine of my life. She was such a beautiful child. The last day I saw her—normally, Ashley would get up in the mornings when we would get up, and she would greet us at the—at the door when we would be coming out of the bedroom.

But not this morning. This morning, she didn't want to get up. She cried and screamed and I had to—to sit on the bed and dress her. Normally, I didn't have to do that. And she begged me: "Mommy, please don't go to work today. Please stay home with me and play with me today. I need you to stay home today, Mommy." And I couldn't. I had just started a new job.

At this point I began losing control. I started thinking about the what ifs. I started to cry as I related our last moments together.

A.   And so I took her to Mom's house that morning and—and left her, and she was okay then. I mean, everything was okay. And she threw her arms around me and she kissed me one last time. And the next time I saw her was in a box. I buried a little, white box. I never saw her again. And I had to live with the guilt, the guilt of being a mother that had to work.

I cried even harder. I was furious at the obvious lack of concern on Nichols's face. All the anger that had been building up in me over the past three years started to overflow as I testified about how this man had changed my life, about who had been taken from us.

And I wanted to die because my daughter was gone. She was taken from me. She was taken from my family. I have no daughter now. I have no future with my daughter.

The first day of school, I sat there in the parking lot, remembering that we had been counting the days. We had 137 days until she started school. And I sat there in that parking lot for most of the day, and I cried because we weren't going to get that. It was gone. It was stolen from me.

With surprise and fear, I felt my fist hit the stand as I punctuated my last words. I realized my voice was rising but didn't grasp how much. I was just so hurt and angry, no one seemed to get it. The lack of compassion from the jury, and from the defendant, was more than I could bear. I was thankful I was done, but I had a gut feeling I had failed. I was escorted from the courtroom sobbing. Later I would learn what was said:

MR. TIGAR: If the Court please—

MR. MEARNS: Thank you. I have no further questions.

THE COURT: We're going to take the recess; and we will clearly complete, I think, the testimony yet this afternoon and perhaps earlier than five. But of course, you know what I'm going to say about the witness you've just heard, and the outburst of anger that you just heard. Understandably, the woman lost control. And as I said to you in some detail this morning, when these people come in and get asked about these things, that, you know, are so sensitive for them and touch the basic emotions here—you know, this woman lost. And the volume with which she expressed her anger is something that may have been intended to suggest more to you than she was asked. And you'll have to disregard it. Obviously, that was inappropriate. But we're not here to deal with anger, we're not here even for the people on the jury to deal with grief and sorrow and revenge and vengeance.

Darlene met me in the debriefing room. She was sobbing as well. There was a counselor present, but it was no use. "I blew it," I wept to my sister. "I lost it, and I didn't mean to. I was just so angry, and he just sat there and didn't care."

"It's okay, Kathleen, you did fine. Those people needed to see how much you hurt—right or wrong. I hope he burns in hell for what he's put us through." We sat there for a bit while I tried to regain my composure. Finally I stood up and asked to go home. I needed to be with my family, my children, and my husband. I had failed them and needed to ask their forgiveness.

We were set to leave on the next plane out of Denver. There was about a two-hour wait, so we decided to have a quick meal. Darlene went to get our food while I looked for a seat in the overcrowded airport dining room. I spotted a couple of chairs adjoining the table where a small family was having their dinner. I leaned over and asked if my sister and I could sit next to them. They agreed and moved their packages aside to make room.

Their little girl, Emily, appeared to be the age Ashley would have been if she were still alive. While I waited for Darlene to return, I watched this sweet, young child interact with her parents. She was playing with a very lifelike wooden snake that her parents had bought in Phoenix. It tore at my heart to see her, but at the same time her joy made me smile for the first time in ages.

When my sister joined us, she struck up a casual conversation. Suddenly Emily reached up and hugged Darlene. Pointing to me, my sister whispered, "She could really use a hug right now." Without any hesitation Emily approached me and gave me a tight squeeze. Her innocent tenderness sent a fresh wave of tears across my cheeks. As I held her tight all the disappointment and bitter frustration washed over me. "I really needed that hug," I told her.

Darlene leaned over to the parents and briefly explained where we'd been. I watched their faces carefully as expressions of parental caution turned into compassion, an outpouring of love. The mother's eyes filled with tears. She sat back, sharing her daughter with a complete stranger.

"Would you like me to read to you?" Emily asked.

"I'd like that very much," I answered.

She dug a book out of her travel bag, climbed into my lap, and started reading. As I attempted to eat my lunch, Emily stayed right by my side. It was as if Ashley had sent her to comfort me. Soon enough we said our good-byes and boarded the plane. All my anger, frustration, and hurt seemed to have melted away under a little girl's gentle touch.

It wasn't long before an envelope arrived in the mail.

Dear Kathleen:

Since our meeting at the Denver airport, you and your family have been on our minds, and in our prayers. . . . Karen, Emily and I are very sorry for you. Emily has talked about you a lot. You made quite an impression on her.

While that Wednesday was a bad day for you, you should realize, you had quite an effect on Emily, Karen and I. I think we have a whole new perspective on how lucky we are, and how lucky we are to have Emily.

I've enclosed a picture, and please feel free to write to us, or to Emily, anytime. I wanted you to know how special you and Darlene

are to Emily, Karen and I. You will continue to be in our thoughts
and prayers, and we wish you and your family the best.
> *Your friends in South Dakota,*
> *Keith*
> *Rapid City, SD*

I believe there are angels who walk among us. You only have to look a short distance in order to find them. And sometimes they find you. This family, like so many others, became some of the many angels who rose up in the aftermath of pain and destruction to help put my life back together. Their small acts of kindness soothed my aching spirit.

The next day I learned the defense attorney Michael Tigar had moved to strike my testimony. The trial was to come to an end.

But what the judge said—"And the volume with which she expressed her anger is something that may have been intended to suggest more to you than she was asked. And you'll have to disregard it"—hurt the most.

From the minute I arrived home, reporters were calling nonstop. I declined any on-camera interviews but spoke briefly with a couple of newspaper journalists I knew. I was just too emotionally drained to offer more.

Several days later the jury came back with a nonverdict. They couldn't unanimously agree on a sentence, so the fate of this man was left to Judge Matsch. Although he couldn't impose the death penalty without the jury, Judge Matsch did say he felt Nichols deserved to die because he had murdered the Constitution. As his best alternative, he gave him life in prison without the possibility of parole.

That just wasn't enough for me. My attention shifted to the coming state prosecution of Terry Nichols. This man needed to take responsibility for his crime, and he needed to pay with his life. I'd always felt capital punishment should be applied to cases like these, but being involved made me even more of a believer.

To this day, I continue to draw great criticism because of my need to see this man pay for his crimes with his life. People have told me to "move on," "get over it" and, my all-time favorite, "try a little forgiveness." Most of these people have never had to bury three members of their family in less than a week, or face the repetitive trauma the trials and the criminals continue to cause us.

In the face of adversity, I turned to Scripture. I'd heard opponents quote from the Bible about overturning the death penalty, but I hadn't heard much from those who were in favor of it. I wasn't sure if my spiritual beliefs conflicted with my need for justice.

Sure, I knew about the Scriptures requiring "an eye for an eye," but were there more? Eventually I found a collection of verses on the topic. One in particular jumped out at me: "Think not that I am come to destroy the law, or the prophets: I am not come to destroy, but to fulfill" (Matthew 5:17). This verse helped me understand that as a Christian I had to take the Bible as a whole, not just the feel-good parts. God gave us the law to protect the righteous from evil and to assign penalties for certain crimes. The Old Testament law still holds true today. "Thou shall not kill" is correctly translated from Hebrew as "Thou shall not murder."

I realize the Bible can be used to make a pretty good argument on either side of the issue. But for me, in the face of such heinous evil, capital punishment just made sense. I began to look at the death penalty as simply sending *them* to a higher court. Death for McVeigh, and Nichols, meant an end to my family's suffering, clemency so to speak. Some called it vengeance, but I called it justice.

Fifteen

Harvest of Faith

They shall come and sing aloud on the height of Zion,
and they shall be radiant over the goodness of the Lord,
over the grain, the wine, and the oil,
and over the young of the flock and the herd;
their life shall be like a watered garden, and they shall languish no more.

JEREMIAH 31:12 RSV

Before Mike and I married, we'd discussed having kids of our own. I'd even checked with my OB-GYN to find out more about the surgery that could reverse my tubal ligation. However, the price tag was far too high. Besides, the procedure offered only a 50 percent chance of success. Since we already had three children combined, we didn't feel we could afford the luxury of such an option. On occasion we discussed what our kids might have looked like if we'd had them together. It was our little fantasy.

The night of the bombing I turned to Mike and told him we had to go through with the surgery.

"You can't replace Ashley," he reminded me.

"I'd never try to replace her," I cried. "How dare you imply I would?"

Although I understood Mike's heart, over the next few months the thought of surgery began to fester in my mind. Edye Smith, one of the moms who had lost both her young sons in the America's Kids day care, announced on television that she wanted to have the operation. I watched in amazement as a doctor in Texas agreed to perform it for free. I carefully considered this option. However, after much soul-searching, I felt for me I should resort to prayer.

At that time I'd been in close contact with Katherine Casey, a reporter for *Ladies' Home Journal.* She'd kept a running log of my life from the moments after the bombing until the first anniversary. I inadvertently told her my "secret." I didn't intend for her to print it, but she included it in her story.

After the article ran a woman who worked at a fertility clinic in New Jersey contacted me. After reading the story she had convinced the head surgeon at her facility to perform my operation without charge.

After several long discussions, and consulting with the doctor, I decided I just couldn't be away from my family while I underwent surgery of this magnitude. Besides, Mike was dead set against my leaving Oklahoma. He argued that if it were meant to be, my doctor, whom I knew and trusted, would be able to do the procedure herself. I agreed and declined their generous offer.

From that day forward I prayed God would send me a sign—not just any sign but one that would be abundantly obvious. I call those the beat-me-over-the-head signs. That way, I reasoned, I'd be sure it was God's will. Within a few weeks Mike's company changed their health insurance policy to include a three-thousand-dollar lifetime benefit to assist with the expenses of sterilization reversal surgery. With that help, along with the cash donations that had come to us through the mail, we were able to afford the operation. I made the arrangements with my doctor.

The surgery was performed on my birthday, August 14, 1996. Although the procedure went smoothly, the recovery was excruciating. I spent two days resting in the hospital, and it was several days before I could walk upright again.

Now I met each passing month with anticipation. Could I be pregnant with Michael's child? Yet each time I was devastated. As the months turned into a year, I became depressed. It seemed God had said no to my dream. But how could that be? He'd provided a way financially, hadn't He?

One day my sister gently reminded me that the stress of the trials was probably preventing conception. I simply shrugged my shoulders. No matter what anybody said, I was fairly convinced—it just wasn't going to happen.

Even my doctor tried to reassure me. Although the national average success rate was between 50 and 60 percent, all the women on whom she'd performed the surgery had become pregnant. She had a 100 percent success rate. Her statistics gave me the faintest shred of hope.

At times I berated myself for having had the operation. What difference had it made? Finally I quit wondering why, quit blaming, and simply gave up.

In April 1998 we began a large addition to our home. It was a substantial financial undertaking, but it was a project we'd planned long before the bombing. I was both apprehensive and excited. What if one of us lost our jobs and we weren't able to pay back the note? What if one of us got hurt? But the thought of spreading out a bit and having room for all the stuff we'd accumulated drove me onward. Remodeling drives wedges between some couples but not us. Michael and I thrive on it.

At the end of May, Michael left for two weeks at summer army training. I spent the downtime in his absence searching through books for additional decorating tips and contacting subcontractors for work we couldn't do ourselves. With the framework up and the roof on, our project was beginning to take shape. I could hardly wait to move all the bedroom furniture into our new master suite. I'd finally have a home office and a bright sunroom for all the plants I'd been given at Ashley's funeral. There was even a spot to display the multitude of angel figures I'd received from around the world.

Michael was still away on June 3, when I went to my doctor for my regular checkup. I gathered my nerve and asked about my failure to conceive. My doctor suggested doing an exploratory procedure to see if there was any blockage; after that she recommended I consider taking fertility drugs.

I cringed at the thought. I associated fertility drugs with multiple births. I was sure I couldn't handle having more than one baby at a time, and there was no way I'd opt for selective elimination. I told her drugs were out of the question, but we could have a quick look to make sure the initial surgery went okay. She suggested I schedule the appointment as soon as my next cycle was over.

While walking back to my car, I felt crushed by the weight of my future. In my innermost fantasy I'd been sure she'd say I was pregnant. Tears of utter defeat fell down my cheeks.

It was nearly mid-June when I first suspected something. I'd been waiting for my period so I could schedule the exploratory, but it just never came. I rarely missed, but my hopes had been dashed so many times, I didn't want to believe it was possible. But eventually I shared my suspicion with Michael.

"So, what makes you think you could be?" he asked.

"I'm having all the signs I had with Zachary and Ashley," I said. "I think this is the real thing this time." He looked at me suspiciously.

Finally, on Father's Day, I couldn't stand it anymore. After church I bought a home pregnancy test. During the drive home I could hardly contain myself. The car had barely rolled to a stop when I jumped out and ran into the house. I quickly read the instructions and performed the test. The color changed almost immediately. It was positive—we were going to have a baby! I was on cloud nine.

I ran outside to show the test to Michael, who was faithfully unloading the groceries. He looked at the test, not quite comprehending. "Does this mean . . ."

"Yes! You're going to be a daddy again!" I threw myself into his arms for a loving embrace. At that very moment, out of a relatively cloudless sky, came a tremendous clap of thunder. The lightning that accompanied it must have struck very near, because the ground shook so much it felt like a small earthquake. We grabbed hands and ran for the open garage. Once inside we hugged each other and looked out to the Oklahoma horizon. Michael smiled broadly and said, "Well, God, you sure know how to put an emphasis on your work!" We laughed and hugged, relishing the utter joy of a miracle.

We knew what we had to do next. We walked into the house and called the boys.

"Guess what?" We paused as they looked at us with great anticipation. "You're going to have a baby brother or sister soon."

"*Yessssssss,*" Zachary yelled as he started to dance around the room.

"All right," David chimed in. "When?"

We told them that although we weren't sure it would probably be sometime in February.

"It's got to be a sister," Zack declared. "I don't want another stupid brother."

I laughed. "We won't know for some time yet whether it's a brother or a sister. Only God knows for sure. We'll just have to be patient."

I was bursting at the seams with the news. I wanted to shout it to the world, but Michael was cautious. "I'm not sure how accurate these tests are. I think you should go to your doctor, just to be certain."

I was devastated. "Can I at least call my sister?" Darlene had been a labor and delivery nurse, and she'd be able to tell me if I was crazy or not. I picked up the phone, dialed, but got the answering machine. Disappointed, I left her a message. "Darlene, it's Kathleen. I have something important to tell you. Give me a call as soon as you get in." A few moments later my phone rang.

The second I answered Darlene asked breathlessly, "What is it? What kind of a message was that—'I have something important to tell you'? Tell me, tell me, before I go nuts."

"Well"—I giggled—"I went to the store and got a pregnancy test—and it's positive!"

Darlene screamed. "A baby, we're going to have a baby!"

"Shhhhh," I said. "It's just a home pregnancy test. Michael wants me to go to my doctor before I start announcing it to the world. He doesn't trust its accuracy."

"Well . . . those tests sometimes give false readings. However, they never give a false positive, you can bank on it. You're pregnant!"

I was ecstatic. But to humor my husband I called my doctor's office the next morning. The receptionist immediately transferred me to the nurse, Starr. "Honey, you're going to get basically the same test here. You can believe it. You're pregnant. But let's have you in for a check anyway."

The next morning I went in, and Starr confirmed everything. The office seemed to glow with a holiday atmosphere. I hugged my doctor. "It was your hands that made this possible. I can never thank you enough."

Each passing month found me dancing on air. The years of grief and sorrow seemed to lift from my soul. The promise of the baby reaffirmed God's love. This was truly an answered prayer. My doctor told me, "You've been through so much, you deserve this baby."

"I don't really deserve anything," I explained. "I'm just glad God answers prayers." It was obvious that she looked forward to the birth as much as we did. Each visit she'd ask me, "How is our miracle baby today?"

It was at my next visit, in July, that I first heard my little one's heartbeat. As the strong, steady pulse resounded through the room, I cried tears of joy.

When September rolled around, it was time for an ultrasound. Mike took off work, and Darlene met us at the hospital. I wouldn't allow myself to dream this baby would be a girl. I even chose some boys' names, just in case. I was shaking as I disrobed for the test. I could hardly sit still while the technician began scanning my abdomen. She did the necessary measurements and told us our due date was February 14. How appropriate—our baby would be arriving on the day celebrated for great love. Then she asked the question we were all waiting to hear—did we want to know the sex of the baby? In unison we shouted, "Yes!" Not knowing what we'd been through, she looked at us like we were crazy. My sister briefly explained what had happened to Ashley. The technician nodded in understanding.

A few moments later she whispered, "Nothing there."

"What?" I asked. "What does that mean?" I looked at my sister.

"It's a girl," Darlene said, with a mischievous glint in her eye.

"Are you sure?" I was still reluctant to believe.

The tech moved the scanner again. "See? Nothing there."

"I don't understand. What are you showing me?"

"Let's get a closer look," the technician said as she pointed to the monitor screen. "See? Three lines—a girl."

I stared at the monitor. A lump welled up in my throat. I was completely in awe of God's grace. I got dressed, hugged Michael and Darlene, and together we left the hospital. A girl, a girl . . . *a girl*!

For months we'd been scanning the baby name books, looking for a name that would fit perfectly. As we drove home I looked at Michael. "How does the name Kassidy Caitlin grab ya? Her initials will be KC, so if she's a bit of a tomboy (and with two big brothers, there is little doubt about that) she can use her initials instead. It's a good Irish name to go with Treanor. Kassidy means 'clever and curly headed' and her middle name, a derivative of mine, means 'pure.'"

"I love it," Michael proclaimed.

So it was decided—Kassidy Caitlin—absolutely perfect.

The next months were spent in joyful preparation. My sister and some of my friends from the memorial orchestrated a shower with almost a hundred people in attendance. There were mountains of presents and more than enough hugs to go around. I had no idea that so many people cared so deeply. Later that week I sent out this letter.

Dear Friends and Family:

Michael and I were pleased, and overwhelmed, so many of you were able to celebrate the impending birth of our daughter. So pleased, in fact, for the first time I can remember, I was speechless, while I wept tears of joy.

Over the last 4 years, you have each, in your own special way, shared our tears and sorrow from the tragedy that's forever changed our family. Because of that, it was equally important for you to be able to share our joy, as we wait to celebrate the birth of our daughter.

Many of you know Michael and I wanted to have children together long before this. However, circumstances and finances would not allow it. So many things had to happen first, and so many people had to come together to make this little miracle a reality. I can honestly say, without your continued prayers, and outpouring of love and generosity, we might not have made it through as joyous and triumphant as we have, and quite possibly might not be celebrating the miracle of this baby at all. To Michael and me, this baby is confirmation, God loves those who love Him, and He really answers prayer.

It has brought us a measure of peace thinking Ashley, Luther, and LaRue went to heaven and personally selected this little spirit for us to love and cherish for a time here on earth. Because of that, in some small way, we feel a piece of them has been returned through her. If the truth be known, if they were still here, we would not be having this baby.

As we welcome our daughter into this world, we pray all the love you have shown us will filter through to her, and she'll grow to be a joy and inspiration to individuals everywhere. We pray each of you, in your own special way, will continue to show her all the beauty and joy that is in the world, and help us to shelter her from anger and destruction. Help us by praying for her, and praying for God to give us the wisdom and courage to be good parents.

With Gratitude, Love & Joy,
Michael & Kathleen Treanor

On the thirteenth of February I experienced labor pains. I was glad, but when the same thing happened the next day, and the next, I became frustrated beyond belief. Michael and I went to my doctor's appointment on Tuesday the sixteenth and voiced our concern. The doctor just chuckled and said, "Babies have their own schedule." But when she checked the chart with my latest tests, she added, "Well, your proteins are elevated, so let's just get this show on the road." I knew what elevated proteins meant because of my experience with Zachary. I'd begun swelling and feeling breathless, like when I was preeclamptic, but it was mild this time, so I hadn't paid my symptoms much attention.

The doctor left the room and came back shortly with a tiny white tablet. She held it up and explained, "This is my magic pill. I will put this in your cervix, and within twenty-four hours we'll have a baby."

Finally! I was so excited, I would have let her do a cesarean right then and there. Even though my baby had been a part of me for nine months, it wasn't the same as looking into her face and falling in love with the little person she'd turn out to be. "I'll see you tomorrow," the doctor said, as I practically danced out of her office.

I called my sister from the cell phone in the car and shared the news. She was elated and made me promise to call her the minute I was on my way to the hospital. Then we called the boys and gave them the news too.

Michael and I decided to stop by the mall and have a leisurely dinner with just the two of us. It would probably be quite a while before we'd be able to do that again. As we were walking in the contractions started coming. Not hard, but they were definitely the real thing. We walked the length of the mall, talking about Kassidy, wondering whom she would look like and what might happen the next day.

When we got home Zack met us at the door. He wanted to skip school the next morning and go with us to the hospital. I put my foot down, explaining he'd drive me crazy and time would pass much faster if he and David kept their normal schedules. Besides, that way I wouldn't have to worry about them. Someone would pick them up and bring them to the hospital after the baby was born.

"But I want to see Kassidy being born," Zack exclaimed.

"But I don't, and I always win," I retorted, winking at him to ease his disappointment. Then I called Aunt Lanita and told her Kassidy was coming. She opted to come over and spend the night so she could help if she were needed. Bless her heart. Aunt Lanita wanted so much to fill the role LaRue would have taken if she were still alive.

That evening I finished packing while humming to myself, stopping frequently to handle the contractions, or just to smile and pat my tummy. Michael was right beside me. He scurried around making sure the car was gassed up and the baby seat properly installed in the back. Finally, exhausted, we went to bed to try to get a little rest. Michael lay down beside me and held my hand while he cradled my tummy. With every contraction he'd tenderly rub my stomach, then squeeze my hand when it was over. At my insistence he finally succumbed to sleep while I catnapped between pangs.

Early in the morning labor began in earnest. I had to get up, walk around, and brace myself through the contractions. Finally it was time to go. We made the drive to Mercy Hospital and checked into Room 717. It was the seventeenth, and it was Ash Wednesday, three sevens, three very biblical numbers, another reminder for me that God was working.

Before long my doctor came to check on me. I hadn't progressed far.

"Break my water; strip my membranes," I begged.

"Okay, but I will have to put you on a Pitocin drip, and you probably won't like that."

"I don't care. Just get this going." I was calling on my previous experiences to try to hurry this along. I was so ready for my baby.

After the Pitocin hit my veins, contractions started coming hard and fast—as a matter of fact, way too fast. I wasn't able to recover and catch my breath between them, and before long I started to hyperventilate and lose control. I asked the nurse for some Demerol or Stadol to take the edge off. She went down the hall to retrieve the medications.

I didn't see her again for several more strong contractions. I was starting to panic as the pains came harder and faster than they ever had before. The nurse came back, and I asked for my medication. "Oh, I forgot," she said. "Let me go get that right now."

"Forgot? What do you mean, you forgot?" I nearly went nuts. If I could have reached her, I would have strangled her.

When she came back again empty-handed, I said, "To heck with natural childbirth, get me an epidural now!" I was livid. My sister went straight to the head nurse and complained. And I was more than annoyed. All my plans for natural childbirth had flown out the window.

Fortunately the anesthesiologist showed up quickly. I was grateful beyond belief. By that time I was about to lose consciousness. The contractions were coming every two minutes, and I was still only 50 percent dilated. The doctor had me sit up and lean forward into Michael's chest. The nurse and her student hovered in the background. Michael took one step back from me and promptly fainted. The student nurse caught him and helped him gently to the floor. Although a bit pale, he quickly recovered.

"I locked my knees," he said. "I knew when I took that step I was in trouble. The next thing I knew," he said, "I was picking myself up off the floor." Everyone had a good chuckle at Michael's expense, and he graciously took it in stride.

When the epidural hit my system I began to itch and burn. Huge red welts rose on my arms and chest. I was having an allergic reaction to the medication. Quickly the nurse brought some Benadryl and added it to my IV. As soon as the Benadryl flowed through my veins, the itching stopped, and I promptly fell asleep. I spent the rest of my labor peacefully snoring—with the evidence forever preserved on tape.

Around noon I was finally fully effaced and dilated. I waited in my drug-induced stupor as the nurse said, "Let's just give it twenty more minutes."

Sure, I thought. What's another twenty minutes? But I was still puzzled. Where was the doctor? Soon the nurse returned with her student in tow. She put me up into the stirrups and got the room ready for delivery.

"We're just going to give you a quick test push," she said.

Yeah, whatever, I thought, still heavily medicated, and assuming the doctor was on the way.

"One, two, three, push," she recited.

I pushed, you betcha, and Kassidy crowned immediately. A look of sheer panic crossed the young nurse's face. "Oh my, I didn't expect that. I'm not supposed to be delivering babies."

"What?" I almost screamed. I could see Kassidy's little head in the mirror. I watched as it turned from healthy pink to deathly blue. Then everything seemed to progress in slow motion. The nurse hadn't called the doctor; in fact, she didn't even have her number. From the corner of my eye, I saw the student nurse dart out of the room while the one in charge frantically got my doctor on the phone.

Soon several other nurses rushed in and took control. Kassidy had the cord wrapped around her neck. The head nurse gently cut the cord while she was still in the birth canal. Blood went everywhere, and Kassidy came forth with a rush. I held out my hands for her, but something was wrong. She was still blue. She wasn't breathing.

I watched in terror while she was immediately taken to an incubator, where a pediatric nurse and several others worked fast to get her breathing.

My sister hovered in the background. It was obvious she wanted to jump right in and help. "I wasn't scrubbed, or sanitary, or anything, but I wasn't about to let our baby die while I stood there doing nothing," she told me later.

As Kassidy slowly regained her pink tone, Darlene assured me she was all right. Then my doctor arrived and quickly assessed the situation. "No one told me this was an emergency," she said, as she looked pointedly at each of the nurses. "If I'd known, I would have run right over. I took time to put on my gear thinking everything was under control." It was clear she was angry.

Just like us she'd awaited the birth of our little miracle with great anticipation. Even though she'd brought so many children into the world, this one was different. It was her part of the healing in the aftermath of the bombing, and this error had robbed her of that joy. Later she gave the nurses a real dressing-down. "Not that it did any good," she told me, "but it made me feel better anyway."

When the emergency was over and the doctors had checked her out, Kassidy was wrapped in a warm blanket, and Michael held his baby daughter for the first time. Tears coursed down his cheeks as he said, "Hello, my beautiful Kassidy. We have been waiting for you." It was such a tender moment. I watched, my own eyes welling up with tears, as my husband gently held his daughter and stroked her little cheeks. Her tiny hand reached up from the blanket and grabbed his finger. The bond was set—from that day forward the two were inseparable.

When the linens on my bed had been changed, Michael brought my beautiful baby over to me and placed her in my arms. Kassidy, the smallest of the three children I've given birth to, was beautiful. She weighted in at only seven pounds, five ounces. I'd forgotten how tiny newborn babies are, and almost completely forgotten their dear, sweet smell. She was awake, very alert and attentive as she stared lovingly into our faces.

Michael looked from Kassidy's eyes to mine. "Thank you, again, for giving me a daughter. She is beautiful, just like her mother."

I studied her little hands and face intently, trying to see who she looked like, trying to see any signs of Ashley. I saw hints of everyone: LaRue's hands, Ashley's nose, Daddy's eyes, my dimple; she was a beautiful combination of the best of both families.

Soon our loved ones came to join us. My niece Candy was almost hysterical. Out in the waiting room they'd heard there was an emergency in my room, but when they asked the receptionist what was happening, they were sharply told to wait until family members let them know. Candy said, "All I could do was think we were going to lose another baby, or that you were in danger."

Later that evening NewsChannel 4 came to the hospital and made the birth announcement over the air. Kassidy was only a few hours old, and she was already on TV. I laughed at the irony and wondered if I'd ever return to an anonymous life. Probably not, I thought. This was just one of the ways my world had changed, and I needed to get used to it. It was still hard, after nearly four years, to comprehend the magnitude of the message I'd been given to share with hurting people everywhere.

When our precious newborn was welcomed into the world, Ashley would have been eight years old. Kassidy would have been the thirteenth grandchild of Luther and LaRue. It was bittersweet reveling in her birth yet knowing there were three people missing, three people who should have been there to experience this moment with us.

I will forever hold Ashley in a sacred place, hidden deep within my heart. Nothing, and no one, can take my memories away. Ashley's life, and her death, have brought a new purpose to my existence like nothing else ever could. I'd prayed for a powerful message, and I'd received one—certainly not what I'd expected, but I received one nonetheless.

Kassidy has become an incredible symbol of God's love and restoration. She's brought a joyous end to the terrible ache in my arms. Her birth has allowed me to release Ashley to heaven until we can be reunited once more. Through our difficult journey, our family's become stronger and closer than ever before. With the gift of little Kassidy, we've finally moved forward, dancing in the light of love.

Sixteen

On Holy Ground

And the Lord will guide you continually,

and satisfy your desire with good things,

and make your bones strong;

and you shall be like a watered garden,

like a spring of water,

whose waters fail not.

And your ancient ruins shall be rebuilt;

you shall raise up the foundations

of many generations;

you shall be called the repairer of the breach,

the restorer of streets to dwell in.

ISAIAH 58:11–12 RSV

The fourth Anniversary Remembrance Ceremony was about to take place. We waited on the plaza overlooking the site. The construction workers stood at attention while a huge American flag flew from a giant crane. We listened to the hymn "We Are Standing on Holy Ground."

I was positively glowing. I held my two-month-old baby, Kassidy, tightly in my arms. Mike held my hand, then gently put his arm around my shoulders. Although Zack stood beside us, David had chosen not to come. We understood. He had to grieve in his own way.

I beheld the ceremony in utter amazement. What so many had promised turned out to be true—God does restore. I had living proof before me, in the memorial now under construction and in my little girl, my miracle, Kassidy.

We were each handed a delicate red rose. Then together we dropped the roses over the wall, watching as they gently fell onto sacred ground. As we walked away we knew the next time we returned we'd be gathered within the walls of the finished memorial. So much blood, sweat, and tears was beginning to bloom into fruition.

After the ceremony I deliberately stayed away for a year. I didn't want to ruin my first impression of the memorial, or have it tarnished by the sight of more construction. I wanted to experience it like a beautiful present awaiting the day of its opening.

Although I'd cut back my involvement, I still wanted to be part of the observance. My sister heard that a 168-member community choir was forming. The number was significant. Each choir member would represent one victim. Darlene and I joined and, with excitement, prepared for the event. I was honored. This was my way of giving back to the people of Oklahoma, and the entire nation, who'd supported us over the years.

The evening before the dedication we met for a final rehearsal with the Oklahoma City Philharmonic Orchestra. As we were preparing to sing, a member of the choir came forward with a small brown bag. "I have pictures of each of the victims. Please take one to remind you why you're here. Let's each dedicate our performance to our special individual." We applauded him as tears welled up in my eyes. A lovely lady singing next to me received Carrie Lenz's photo. After the rehearsal I introduced her to Doris Jones, Carrie's mother. When I explained this woman was singing for Carrie, Doris wept as she embraced her.

The media attention surrounding the grand opening of the Symbolic Memorial and the five-year anniversary was at its peak, and I was pressed into service as a spokesperson. There were to be two services that year—a private one revolving around 9:02, for the families, survivors, and rescue workers, and a public dedication in the evening.

The morning ceremony was a beautiful, spiritual service. The roads were blocked off in front of the 9:02 gate, and chairs lined the street. When we arrived thousands were already there. It was good to see so many people I'd come to know and love over the last few difficult years. I tried to stay away from the media. I felt we needed to remember and reflect alone, as a family.

We sat quietly, listened to the speakers, and were moved to tears when a trio again sang "We Are Standing on Holy Ground," the song that had become our anthem.

The mission statement was read. Then we observed the traditional 168 seconds of silence. I was struck with intensity as the moments ticked by. It seemed like an eternity—168 seconds, 168 lives lost. I appreciated the enormity of their deaths. Several church bells began pealing, while four Air National Guard jets did a flyby in the missing man formation. Then each victim's name was read as the family came forward to be escorted into the pristine interior of the memorial by honor guards from all branches of law enforcement, fire, and military.

When Luther and LaRue's names were called, we walked up. While we stood in line Ashley's name was called. When the honor guard met us, he asked whom we'd come forward for. We explained we needed to find three chairs, for all our family members who'd died.

For a moment he lost his military composure and looked at the ground as he tried to comprehend what I'd told him. Then he squeezed my hand and tucked it under his arm as he escorted us to Ashley's little chair. It was the thirteenth one in the front row. Then he pointed out on a map where Luther's and LaRue's chairs were, just a few yards away. He moved away to join the other rescue personnel standing at attention along the reflecting pool.

The sorrow of seeing nineteen small chairs, each representing a lost child, washed over me. Still, I couldn't help but wonder about the three unborn children who were not represented. I thought of Doris, her daughter Carrie, and her unborn grandson. I prayed that she too would find comfort in what was erected in their memory.

Now that I was seeing the completed memorial, five full years of hard emotional work were in full regalia. I gulped down the huge lump at the back of my throat. I had vowed not to cry. This was a day for joy, for remembrance—a day of triumph, not tears. For a moment I was caught up in the gentle sound of water flowing in the reflecting pool. It was a beautiful place that truly captured all the feelings we'd hoped for.

Soon the haunting sound of bagpipes filled the natural amphitheater. As the strains of "Amazing Grace" echoed from the Gates of Time, they brought back memories of Luther and LaRue's funeral. I felt the lump grow tighter in my throat as I watched Zachary and David walk over, dip their hands in the reflecting pool, and then carefully place their handprints on the 9:03 gate. Although I believe they were the first to do so, many have followed.

After we placed armloads of flowers in Ashley's honor, we gathered around Luther and LaRue's chairs. They were in the front row, by one of the loblolly pines, near the 9:03 gate. I stood with our little family on the grass and looked out over the memorial site. So many people we knew were there, all remembering and mourning in their own quiet ways.

I ran into Jenny Moser, whose husband, Calvin, had been trapped in the explosion. She'd become a rescue worker as she rushed to the building to find her husband. She'd cared for the children in their makeshift morgue. The visions of that day still haunt her.

Suddenly someone tapped me on the shoulder. I turned around and looked into the face of a man in full dress uniform. At first I didn't recognize him. Then it came to me. This was Chet, the man who'd found my Ashley! I threw my arms around him and hugged him tightly. "I'm so glad you came today," I cried.

"I needed to come. I haven't been back since that awful day. So much has changed since then. I needed to see that." I caught the hidden meaning in his words. He introduced me to his kids, and I smiled with recognition. They looked just like their dad.

I took him to meet Mike's sister. I gently touched her shoulder and said, "Debbie, this is Chet Clark. Chet is the fireman who recovered Ashley's body and also helped in the recovery of your mom." Debbie's face crumbled into a mass of sobbing tears. "Oh, Debbie, I'm so sorry," I said, "I didn't mean to blindside you that way."

She waved her hands and shook her head, overcome with emotion. "No" was all she managed to say as she threw her arms around Chet and hugged him fiercely. "I'm sorry, I'm sorry," she said over and over again, apologizing for her tears. When she'd regained some composure, she went on, "Thank you, thank you so much." Then she turned away, joined her husband, Buddy, and left.

Chet looked a little embarrassed and shaken. "I hope I didn't make things worse for her," he said.

I shook my head. "No, everything will be all right. Anyway, it was my fault, not yours. I should have realized this would be a shock for her and broken it to her a little more gently. She'd asked to meet you earlier, and I just thought now would be a good time. I'm sure she's fine. Try not to read anything more into it."

I asked Chet if he'd be coming to the evening dedication. He wasn't sure. I told him I'd be there and thought it might be helpful for him to come along too. As we parted he promised to consider it.

When we were gathering our things we ran into Mark Bays from the Oklahoma Forestry Department. It was Mark who'd cared for the Survivor Tree and saved it from an inevitable death. Under his care broken and damaged limbs were removed. The tree was treated for Dutch elm disease, and each year he and his staff gathered seeds and took grafts, to ensure the elm lives forever.

He stood tall, proudly handing out seedlings to the families, survivors, and rescue personnel. I asked him for one for my sister. As he handed over the seedling, I smiled and said, "Mark, I just wanted to thank you for all you've done over the last few years. If it weren't for you, I'm sure the Survivor Tree would have died, and we'd have lost an incredibly important symbol. Your work has been an amazing gift of love."

He seemed a bit embarrassed. "Thank you," he said. "I'm just honored to be involved."

I thought about all the volunteers. Most were like Mark—simply glad to be included in part of our city's healing. It was people like him who restored my faith in humanity.

We went home, rested for a while, and tried to take it all in. We had seen so much, been through so much, yet we'd somehow made it. Later that evening we headed back to the memorial.

As the evening ceremony was about to begin, I stood on the risers with the choir singing "To Remember," an anthem written with the words from our mission statement. When we came to the line "Those changed forever," I caught a glimpse of Chet's face in the audience. Yes, we'd all been changed forever, but by the grace of God we would all find peace.

I looked out over the crowd and saw many rescue workers with torment in their eyes. So many were still experiencing the horror they'd witnessed. More than 60 percent of those who'd been involved had gone through a divorce. Others were still having difficulty coping. Many had left their agencies, and there were some documented suicides. The numbers were frightening. It was good to see so many of these people. I prayed the ceremony would be a healing experience, mending each of their weary and wounded hearts.

It seemed we'd accomplished everything we'd set out to. Through the memorial we'd reached out, and others graciously reached back. For me the memorial successfully encompassed all we'd lost, all we'd been taught, and all we hoped the world would one day understand.

In February 2001 the Memorial Center opened. Families, survivors, and rescue workers were invited to view the museum a few days before the official, public opening. We went on Friday. I was filled with anticipation. This was the part that meant the most to me. It would be the teaching element, the portion I was sure Luther and LaRue would have been proud of.

As we moved through the chapters of the story, we found specific memories of our loved ones. A pair of Ashley's dress-up shoes was placed in her memory box. We hadn't decided what to put in Luther and LaRue's shadow boxes, but later we brought a Townley's milk bottle for Luther's and Mom's Bible for hers.

We entered the room that held items found in the rubble, and Ashley's tennis shoe was on display. I was prepared, but Michael was not. It rattled him to see such a personal item on exhibit.

The following Monday our new president, George W. Bush, honored us as keynote speaker and cut the ribbon. For the second time Darlene and I sang in the community choir. The 145th Infantry Band supplied the music. The director added a joyful atmosphere to the event with his unfaltering cheerfulness.

As each speaker took the stand, the weight of the tragedy became a little easier to bear. It had been nearly six years since the bombing took its toll on our city. In that time, we'd managed to transcend evil. An act of violence designed to destroy, and divide, had done exactly the opposite.

As a fitting end to the ceremony, the musicians played "Oklahoma." The choir spontaneously joined in, singing from their hearts. We wanted the world to know, despite the dark intentions of evil men, the people of Oklahoma had survived. Yes, we were still here—stronger, more aware, and without a doubt triumphant.

Seventeen

Angel in the Garden

Last night, there came a frost, which has done great damage
to my garden. . . . It is sad that nature will play such tricks with
us poor mortals, inviting us with sunny smiles to confide in her,
and then, when we are entirely within her power,
tricking us to the heart.

NATHANIEL HAWTHORNE

The sudden ringing of the telephone jarred me from my sleep. Michael reached over and picked it up.

"Hello," he said wearily.

Who could be calling at this hour, I wondered. After five years it seemed our lives had finally slipped back into the mundane details of everyday existence. Kassidy's birth, the year before, had been the catalyst that put us back on track. I no longer feared such late-night calls. No need to panic, I thought. It's probably just a wrong number.

"Yeah, she's right here, just a second," Michael said, as he handed the phone to me. "It's your brother Jimmy."

I sighed. Jimmy probably just wanted to talk. I didn't mind offering an ear, but it was so late. "Hello," I said, my voiced layered with yawns.

"Kathleen? This is Jimmy." The phone crackled and sputtered. It was hard to hear through the malfunctioning receiver. I jiggled the phone, trying to make it work.

"Hi, Jimmy. Listen, it's late, can I call you back tomorrow?" My day had started at 5:00 A.M., and it hadn't ended until late that evening. All I could think of was sleep.

"Yeah," he said, "but I need to tell you something first. Anthony is dead."

It must have been the connection; I must have misunderstood! "I can't hear you, Jimmy; what did you say?"

"Anthony is dead. He drowned this evening in a swimming pool."

I sat straight up in bed. Anthony was my great-nephew, just a few months older than Kassidy. His parents, Keith and Seana, had brought him, with his older sister, Heather, to my baby shower, and he had been a joyful addition to family gatherings ever since. "What? Oh my God, oh my God, oh my God!" The magnitude of his words were beyond my comprehension. It couldn't be true! "Anthony is *dead*? How can this be?"

"I just thought you should know," Jimmy stammered. Then he offered a quick good-bye and hung up.

I lay back in bed, trying to digest what I'd heard. Not another baby. How could this be happening again? Why was it happening again?

As I handed the phone to Mike I blurted out, "My God, Anthony is dead."

Mike sat up and looked through the dim light of the room. "Anthony?" In his sleep-filled mind, Anthony's name didn't register.

"You know Keith, my nephew? His son."

"What happened?" Mike gasped.

I related the story as well as I understood it. Michael reached for my hand. For a moment, we lay side-by-side digesting the most recent horror in our family history.

We stayed still for a while, afraid to speak or to move. Then, suddenly, reality hit me. Keith and Seana would need help. My sister, I had to call my sister!

I jumped out of bed, put on a robe, stumbled to the living room, and picked up the phone. Darlene was out of town for the weekend, so I dialed her cell number. It rang, but no one answered. I had to find her, had to pull myself together long enough to think clearly.

Like a flash, the answer came to me. My niece Candy! She'd know where to find her mom. I called her cell phone. It seemed to ring forever, but just as I was about to give up, she answered. I heard loud music in the background. "Candy? Where on earth are you?" I asked.

"I'm at a concert. What's going on?" she said.

"I need to reach your mom, and she isn't answering her phone. Candy, this is a real emergency. Jimmy just called me. Anthony is dead. He drowned tonight in a swimming pool."

"What? Oh my God, *no!*"

"I'm not sure of the details. When Jimmy called I was sleeping. At first I didn't understand what he was telling me, but then it all soaked in." The background noise had subsided, and I realized Candy had stepped outside. I started to cry. "Today was Ashley's birthday." For a moment there was a hush as we both wept. "Would you try to reach your mom and let her know?" I choked out the words. "I'm going to find Keith and Seana."

"Okay, I'll tell her. I love you."

I hung up the phone and called Jimmy back. His wife was out of town, and he was home alone. I asked if he needed me there but, true to his nature, he desired solitude. Jimmy gave me a number for Keith and we said good-bye.

I took a nervous breath, then dialed Keith's cell number. Within a ring he was on the line.

"Keith? It's Kathleen. Are you okay?"

Immediately he broke down sobbing. "I tried to save him, I really did, I just couldn't bring him back."

"Oh my God, Keith. How did this happen?"

Keith tried to regain his composure. "We went to Rick's for a visit. Heather was swimming in the pool. I asked her to come in and dry off so we could go home. Anthony was right there with us, playing at my feet while I was talking to Rick. Then, suddenly, we noticed he wasn't there. We started looking for him . . ." His voice trailed off. "Then Seana found him in the pool. We got Anthony right out, and I gave him CPR until the paramedics arrived. But he just wouldn't wake up." Keith sobbed again. "I begged him to wake up, but he just wouldn't. The emergency crew Med-Flighted him to Children's Hospital. They did manage to get a heartbeat just before we landed. But, Kathleen, the doctors are telling us Anthony is brain-dead."

I trembled as I asked, "Are you at Children's Hospital right now?"

"Yes," he whispered.

"You just hang on, I'll be there soon."

I threw on some comfortable clothes knowing this was going to be a long night. Again the telephone shattered the silence. This time it was my sister. I told her what had happened to Anthony. I reminded her it was Ashley's birthday, and we too wept.

"Why is it," she said, "some families go through their whole lives and never have anything like this happen, but our family, we have to bury not one, but two babies? It's just not fair." For a moment time seemed to stand still. Then my sister broke the silence. She'd be home the next day and offered to help in any way she could. We both said, "I love you," and hung up.

I walked through the darkened bedroom, leaned over, and gave Michael a kiss. Then I explained where I was going. Knowing I probably wouldn't be back for a while, I asked him to drop Kassidy off at day care in the morning. I promised to call him later.

"Honey, please be careful," he said, as I made my way for the door. The tone of his voice, the unspoken words between us, made it clear. We had to hold on.

As I pulled out of the garage, I got a call from Candy. She was back home and wanted to meet me at the hospital. I gave her directions, then drove the rest of the way with tears plummeting down my cheeks. My mind swirled with questions and fears. How had this happened? Keith once told me there was a latched fence around the yard. How had Anthony gotten so close to the pool? My mind flashed to Kassidy, who only a few days before had been found kneeling over our pool, playing in the water. Somehow she'd managed to open a locked door and get outside. I was fortunate it wasn't me at that hospital looking over Kassidy's dying body. Was it a warning? Although I'd taken Kassidy to Water Babies classes and felt fairly secure, the thought of losing her brought new terror to my heart.

For a time I'd convinced myself God would protect us from harm because of what we'd previously suffered. I had to remember each day when I dropped Kassidy at day care she'd still be there when I got home. Every day I prayed for protection. Now this. Even though Anthony wasn't my child, he was still my family. My prayers, it seemed, hadn't reached far enough.

My mind raced back to what my sister had said. Our family did have more than its share of suffering. Why? I reflected back over the generations. Many years ago my cousin had been kidnapped, raped, and murdered. My mother had been molested and beaten. There was my mother's suicide, Ashley's murder, and now this.

I felt we were persecuted. We were a good family, raised in law-abiding Christian homes. Why was God allowing us to suffer so? I began to feel like Job. It seemed the moment we worked through one tragedy, another would follow, trouble heaped upon trouble, sorrow upon sorrow. My faith had never been so tested.

Before I knew it I'd arrived at the hospital. I made my way through the emergency doors and headed straight for the ICU. I scanned the waiting room for Keith and Seana. Finally I saw them in the back corner, huddled together. I rushed over to Keith and threw my arms around him. I held him tight as we wept. Only a parent who's lost a child can understand the tears we shared, the bond we felt. "Oh, honey, I'm so sorry. If I could take this from you, I would. I'm so sorry."

"I tried to save him, but I just couldn't," Keith cried.

"It's not your fault. It's just a terrible accident. It's not your fault. It's nobody's fault."

I knew how much he needed to hear those words. Survivor's guilt is one of the dreadful destroyers that often attack after a tragedy. Parents feel responsible for a child's death, even if it was not their fault. I felt guilt that I was not a stay-at-home mom, that I didn't remain with Ashley on that fateful day. There was no doubt Keith and Seana would feel responsible, because they'd momentarily taken their eyes off their young child.

Keith nodded and continued to hold me tight. Over his shoulder I could see Seana. She was in shock. It was like looking at an image of the person I was only a few short years ago. Her eyes were filled with disbelief and confusion. Keith and I grabbed her and held her close. "I'm so glad you came," she said.

"I couldn't let you go through this alone. I know what you're feeling and I thought I might be able to help."

After a few minutes Keith introduced me to the rest of the waiting family. Most were Seana's relatives, and a few were Keith's stepfamily. As it turned out I was his only immediate kin. I was glad I came.

Soon we heard the news. Anthony was on a respirator and, although he was stabilized, the doctor had determined there was no brain activity. Essentially Anthony was dead, although he continued to breathe with the help of machines. Seana mechanically walked back to his bedside while Keith stayed in the waiting room.

He began to explain what had happened. They'd lost track of Anthony for less than five minutes. They blinked, and that was all it took. Keith quietly told me he was considering organ donation but was afraid to bring it up with Seana. He wanted to wait until morning, to avoid filling her mind with images of Anthony being cut up that way. I agreed with Keith, there was still time to make such decisions. Unfortunately, in the end the doctors deemed the procedure impossible.

Eventually I made my way back to the ICU. Anthony lay quietly in the bed. There were tubes everywhere, and monitors all around him, beeping and hissing. If he'd been conscious, Anthony would have been terrified. I went to his side and took his hand. It looked just like Kassidy's, with chubby, little fingers and fresh baby skin. I looked at his golden hair and dark eyelashes as they swept across his cheeks. I thought of Ashley. She'd looked so much like him when she was his age. I caressed his cheek and bent down to kiss him on the forehead. A flood of my tears fell on his pillow.

I walked away and leaned toward Seana. All I could say, over and over, was "I'm so sorry. He's such a pretty baby. I'm just so sorry."

I stepped into the hallway for a moment. I had to hold it together for Keith and Seana. I was struggling with every fiber of my being. This was too personal for me. When I looked at little Anthony, it was Ashley. When

I held his hand, it was Ashley's. When I kissed his forehead, it was Ashley's. All the things I'd been robbed of, those last precious moments, the chance to say good-bye, were happening at this moment. But this wasn't about me. I had to put my own grief aside.

I collected myself the best I could, then walked back to the waiting room. I knew there was nothing I could say that would ease the pain these young parents were experiencing, but I could warn them of what to expect. I began to share with Keith what I'd learned. He was on a journey, and there was simply no turning back. I explained this could destroy his marriage, and he needed to remember grief can make you say, and do, things against your nature. I warned him not to make drastic changes in his life, at least not for a while. Instead I encouraged him to give himself time for everything to soak in, for the shock to subside.

Keith's uncle quietly added, "God won't give you more than you can handle."

I looked steadily at him. "That isn't true," I said. "First of all, God didn't do this. I refuse to believe in a God who kills children. Second, no person can handle something like this alone. Only God has the strength to carry us through such heartbreak. We must rely on Him, not ourselves, to go on. Without His strength, this will be unbearable. Never forget that." They nodded in understanding.

Seana, still glassy-eyed, sat down beside me. I put my arm around her shoulder and pulled her close to me. "Seana, I know the last thing you want to think about is yourself. But have you had anything to eat or drink?"

"I wouldn't be able to keep anything down," she said flatly.

"Would you at least try to drink some water for me? I know you don't want to, Seana, but if you get dehydrated, you might have to be hospitalized yourself. You need to keep up your strength. The next few days are going to be hell. I'm sorry I can't take this pain away from you, but I can try to prepare you for the things to come."

Seana nodded absently and sipped a little water.

About that time Candy arrived, and the tears and hugging started all over again. I took her back to see Anthony. It was obvious by her expression what she was thinking. It was as if Anthony were her baby. Connor, her only son, was the same age as Ashley. When my child was taken, Candy took it hard, and she wasn't faring much better now. Tears coursed down her cheeks as she caressed his hand. "Did you realize, Anthony's and Ashley's names both start with A?" she asked in a strange tone.

I nodded. "Yes, and both children were blond, and this horrible accident took place on Ashley's birthday. Do you remember, our surname, Aniol, means 'angel'? It's almost as if these two angels are linked." Although Candy and I knew it was probably just a coincidence, we couldn't help drawing comparisons, trying to make sense of something senseless, to find order in the chaos. We dropped our heads, and in an unspoken moment understood we'd never really have an answer. Arm in arm we walked back to the lobby.

Keith and Seana looked like they were about to drop. People were getting ready to go home, but they'd be staying the night. I wasn't going to leave. I couldn't.

"Why don't you try to lie down for a while? I know you don't feel like sleeping, but you'll have some tough decisions to make tomorrow, and it will be easier if you've had a little rest. I'll stay with Anthony."

Heather sat down by Seana. "Mama, when will Anthony be coming home?"

My eyes raced back to Keith and Seana. Heather's question hung in the air like an ominous cloud. For now it went unanswered. At eleven years old Heather was this baby's second mother. She'd been the first to hold him when he was born and had given him his first bath. After Anthony was found, she'd taken his ball from the pool and thrown it as far, and as hard, as she could. For her Anthony's death was inconceivable. The answer was obvious. Let her hold on to hope for one more night.

As her grandparents took her home, Seana quietly whispered, "She doesn't know."

"When are you going to tell her?" I asked.

Seana didn't answer but simply stared into space.

"Go ahead and lie down, Seana. You and Keith get some rest. I'll stay with Anthony." She stiffly nodded. I covered her with a blanket.

"I promise, I'll come get you if anything changes," I said. Reluctantly, they both bedded down for the night and struggled to find sleep.

I suggested that Candy go home with the others. I'd call her if anything changed. I walked her to the exit and asked the security guard to escort her outside. Then, after checking on Keith and Seana, I made my way back to the quiet ICU room. I sat down in a rocking chair and began a long conversation with God. I begged Him for Anthony's life. "This family's suffered enough. Why don't you cut us some slack?" I reminded Him, He was the creator of miracles. I knew that to be true. I had Kassidy. He could do a great work tonight. For several hours I cried, prayed, and held Anthony's hand.

Every opportunity I could, I'd question his nurse on the probability of a miracle. She didn't give me much hope. I asked about the donor process so I'd know how to help Seana through her ultimate decision.

Finally, exhausted, I went back to the waiting room and rested. Sleep was fitful, filled with dreams, nightmares, and visions of Ashley and Anthony.

Weary of tossing and turning, I got up and wandered the halls. I decided to check on Anthony again. He looked so helpless, his small body lying there with all the tubes and monitors. I leaned over his bed and whispered, "Good-bye, little angel."

I soon found out that my sister's best friend, Marie, an ICU nurse, would be coming into work at 7:00 A.M. I was glad. Darlene and Marie had raised their daughters together, and for many years they were neighbors. The minute she came in, I explained what was going on.

Soon Keith and Seana woke up. I asked my nephew if he'd contacted his work, but he hadn't. I got the phone number and made the calls myself. I wasn't able to reach the personnel manager but spoke with the receptionist instead. She jumped right on it, hunted down Barbara, and got her on the phone. Both women asked what they could do to help. They even offered to send some of Keith's co-workers to be with him.

Shortly afterward Marie opened a private waiting room. By this time there were fifteen or more family members gathering and, although it was really too small, it was a nice, quiet place for Keith and Seana to rest between visits with Anthony. Sleep hadn't taken the dull expression from Seana's face. I knew that look all too well. I went over and knelt in front of her. "Seana, would you like to hold Anthony?"

Seana nearly jumped out of her seat as her face brightened. "Yes, I would! I haven't been able to hold him since we got here." I nodded and squeezed her hand. "Okay, let me ask if it's all right for you to do that. I'll be right back."

Back in the ICU I found several doctors and nurses working on Anthony. It was more than apparent: he was in trouble. I sat down in a nearby chair, waited, watched, and prayed. I caught Marie and told her how much Seana needed to hold Anthony. She explained he was "crashing" and until they were able to stabilize him that would be impossible. Marie did promise that if everything calmed down she'd make a way for Seana to do that, even if it meant moving the baby over in the bed and letting his mother climb in with him. I nodded, stood back, and let the doctors do their work.

As I watched, and prayed, I lost track of time. I understood how much Seana needed to hold her baby. It was something I still longed for. She needed to say good-bye and, I intimately understood, that included touching her dying child.

Suddenly I looked up, and Seana and her aunt were in front of me. "You didn't come back, and we were worried," Seana said.

"I'm so sorry, I lost track of time. Anthony is having trouble breathing, and the doctors are trying to stabilize him. I was hoping it wouldn't take long, and I'd be able to come back for you." I looked around and realized that with so many of us in the hallway we were hindering the medical staff. "Look, we're all in the way. Why don't we wait in the lobby? I'm sure they'll come and get us soon."

Seana was clearly distressed and didn't want to leave, but she complied. Soon the medical staff came for Keith, Seana, and Heather. The rest of us prayerfully waited.

In a short while—but what seemed like an eternity—Keith came back and told us, Anthony's lungs had collapsed and the doctors just couldn't bring him back. After the tears subsided we made our way to his bedside to say good-bye.

My eyes caught Seana as she sat quietly in a rocking chair, cradling Anthony's little body and gently stroking his hair. She touched him over and over, and kissed his face repeatedly. Heather watched lovingly but stood back, almost afraid. I made my way over to her. "Do you want to hold him too?" I whispered in her ear.

She nodded emphatically.

"Okay," I said. "Let me ask your mom if that would be all right." I gently approached Seana.

"Seana, you hold that baby as long as you want. But when you're done, would it be all right for Heather to hold him too?"

Seana looked at her daughter, then reached out her hand and pulled her close to her side. They talked quietly, and soon Seana got up and put Anthony into Heather's arms. His big sister rocked Anthony gently back and forth, mimicking the movements of her mother.

Cody, Anthony's little uncle, watched from across the room with longing in his eyes. I asked him if he wanted to hold the baby too. He looked up in tears and nodded—he did. Together we approached Seana and asked her permission. She looked at Cody's gentle eyes, hugged him, and quietly agreed.

One by one everyone said good-bye to our little angel. As I watched, I found myself vicariously experiencing some of what I'd missed with Ashley. It was important they do what I hadn't been able to. I knew how meaningful a last good-bye could be.

I thought of Seana's future. I knew the days and weeks ahead would be especially difficult for her. Unlike me, Seana is quiet and reserved. While we were waiting I told her relatives what to watch for in Heather, but I didn't have any clues about Seana. All I could offer was that they should encourage her to talk about Anthony as much as possible, and when she did find the words to speak, they should simply listen, be there for her in every way they could. No matter how many times she repeated herself, they were never to stop her from sharing. I feared Seana wouldn't have the opportunity to open up to others.

I've found many parents who've lost children grieve alone, unable to talk about their loved one or share their sorrow. Often friends and family seem afraid that if they listen they'll somehow invite tragedy onto their own doorstep.

Soon it was time to prepare Anthony for the medical examiner. Heather wanted to stay and help. Keith was against the idea, but after I talked with him he reluctantly agreed. With Marie, Heather helped make his little hand and footprints, and she cut several strands from Anthony's beautiful golden locks. Then, fittingly, the one who'd given him his first bath gave him his last. She gently leaned over, softly kissed his forehead, and whispered good-bye. Although it was gut-wrenching to watch, I knew she needed these final moments with her baby brother.

When they finished Anthony was moved to another room while the hospital priest came and prayed over his body. The rest of the family gathered around, held hands, and bowed their heads in prayer. With the finality of the last amen, I hugged Keith and Seana and made my way home.

The drive was horrible. Finally able to let go, I began to sob. My heart ached for Anthony's family. But my heart also ached for me. I let myself slip back to five years earlier, the long days of not knowing, and then the horrible realization, Ashley was never coming home again.

When I got home I ran inside, hugged my children, and gently broke the news to the boys. I shared with Zachary how much Heather reminded me of him as she tenderly cared for her baby brother. Zachary dropped his head. "I'm glad she got to do that. I wish I could have done that for Ashley." I nodded and hugged him tight. I asked them to watch Kassidy while I tried to get a few hours of sleep. But sleep wouldn't come. Frustrated, I got up and attempted to stay busy until Michael came home. At about 2:00 I couldn't wait any longer. I called my husband and told him I needed him. In what seemed like only moments Michael arrived. I fell into his arms and sobbed uncontrollably.

Soon Keith called to tell us about Anthony's funeral services. I was a wreck. My faith was shaken to the core. I was angry with God for allowing this attack on our family to continue. I was heartbroken and couldn't face the reality of burying another child. God-given forgetfulness had healed me from the horrible memories of Ashley's funeral. Every time I thought of burying Anthony, I was flung back into the dark abyss I'd managed to climb out of. I just couldn't face going back there again. I tried to explain to Keith that I didn't think I could attend Anthony's services, but I detected hurt feelings. I told him I hadn't been to any funerals since the bombing. I knew if I attended, I'd only make matters worse, not only for myself but also for Keith and Seana. I offered, instead, to call family members with the funeral date and time.

One by one I went down the list, still not believing in the finality of it all. Crystal my niece was my last call. She lived in Texas, near her mother, and had the farthest to travel. I told her this tragedy had shaken my faith, and I was angry at God. My words clearly upset her. I'd always been steadfast in my belief. The knowledge that I was wavering was too much for her to bear. "Kathleen," she said, "Mom and I went to the chapel yesterday and prayed for the curse of the Aniol family to be lifted. Since we've suffered so much, we begged God to make the nightmare stop. Maybe we should all pray those words over and over again."

It did seem like a curse. Each tragedy that struck pounded away at our faith. I called Rex, my pastor and my friend, and asked him to plea for a hedge of protection around us. And, just as I expected, Rex did his best to offer comfort and faith.

I knew in my heart that in time I'd be all right, that my spirit would heal and my faith would be restored. But these fresh cuts were deep, and now old wounds had reopened. For days I struggled, slipping back into anger, frustration, and deep depression. I shook my fist at God. I waited impatiently for His reply. But God was silent.

I went to Ashley's garden and sat down in the midst of the wilting flowers. As the hot summer sun beat down on my face, I listened to the splashing of the waterfall in the hope it would bring me a moment of peace. As my eyes scanned the garden, I realized how much I'd neglected it since Kassidy was born. It looked unkempt, almost abandoned. This was a symbol of love for my daughter. It was a gift of remembrance we'd built in her honor. It was my opportunity to care for her, even as we remained apart, and now I was ignoring it. Angrily I knelt and began to remove the hateful weeds.

I reflected back to the day on the grass, so long ago, when God had quietly spoken to my heart. I was reminded of my desire to be a messenger of hope. I'd learned to live again, and God had miraculously restored our relationship, the legacy of my daughter.

In the still of the moment, the words of Dr. Edwin Lutzer began to speak to my soul. He'd so eloquently written of our walk through this world, explaining that when the shepherd sought to move his flock higher, to greener pastures, he'd gather up a few young lambs and carry them over the rocky terrain. The mother sheep would follow her young, through difficult paths, ultimately taking herself and the rest of the flock toward the shepherd.

Had I lost the desire for higher pastures? Had God's precious gift of restoration, my daughter Kassidy, caused me to lose focus? Was the Lord reminding me through Anthony's loss? Had I become complacent? It was time to get busy again and reach out to others.

"Okay, God, you lead, and I will follow."

"Kathleen, if you step out, they will follow."

It was an earth-shattering revelation. I knew I'd never understand why Anthony was taken so young, at least not until the day I met God face-to-face.

After I'd lost Ashley, someone sent me a parable. Its words began to replay in my mind. The parable spoke of a young child watching her mother embroidering. The little one had trouble understanding the image. From the back of the cloth, she saw only dark threads, a collage of confusion, and wondered where its beauty lay. But then her mother turned the cloth over, and the exquisite image began to emerge. Just like God's woven tapestry of our lives, someday His incredible plan will come into remarkable, beautiful focus, but not until we see it from His glorious side.

As I reflected on our family sorrow, it helped to remember Dr. Lutzer's little lambs. They'd keep me walking, step by step, straight ahead, focused on my purpose. I bowed my head and offered a heartfelt prayer. In Him was comfort, this I understood. God would help me make it through this rocky terrain, and help me faithfully bring others safely to the other side.

Eighteen

Seasons of Change

But rebels and sinners shall be destroyed together,
and those who forsake the Lord shall be consumed.
For you shall be ashamed of the oaks
in which you delighted;
and you shall blush for the gardens you have chosen.
For you shall be like an oak
whose leaf withers,
and like a garden without water.
And the strong shall become tow,
and his work a spark,
and both of them shall burn together,
with none to quench them.

ISAIAH 1:28–31 RSV

I was caught off guard by the announcement: Timothy McVeigh had relinquished the remainder of his appeals. Could it really be over? I was suspicious. I'd been on one too many roller-coaster rides, with this man manipulating the controls, to feel truly at ease. But Judge Matsch barely skipped a beat when he set the date for the execution—May 16, 2001. I prayed it would be so. Once it was over I'd no longer be subjected to the continual insults hurled from both McVeigh and his defense team.

I watched as the court proceedings unfolded and the authorities prepared for the impending execution. Soon I discovered there were only eight seats in the chamber; to accommodate all the people who wanted to be present in Terre Haute, Indiana, a lottery would be held. Although I knew many wanted to attend, I felt confident that, just as with the trials, a way would be made for everyone to see this man brought to justice.

Shortly afterward, I received a letter from the U.S. District Attorney's Office in Oklahoma City. It was a survey to determine how many people wished to attend the execution. I sent our response in immediately.

A few weeks before the execution, news came that a biography, written by two reporters from Buffalo, New York, and authorized by McVeigh, was about to hit the shelves. The very concept of this book, based on over seventy hours of interviews with McVeigh, appalled me. One of the reasons for the execution was to prevent this monster from encouraging others to imitate him. Now his words and actions were immortalized. The more I thought about it the angrier I became.

Just as I expected, with the announcement of the McVeigh book, my phone began to ring incessantly. *The Early Show* invited me to New York to express my views. Although I hadn't read the book, and had no intention of doing so, I knew this material shouldn't be out on the street. Its impact on young, formative minds could be devastating.

I was furious with the authors. In my eyes they'd made one critical error—they hadn't spoken with the victims' families first. They hadn't asked how we'd feel about the book's release. Sure, I realized that was a bit unreasonable, but I wondered if they understood the pain they were inflicting on us all over again.

So, with determination burning in my soul, I flew to New York. As the camera light went on, I explained to Bryant Gumbel, "These men prostituted themselves in the name of the almighty dollar and to this mass murderer. Their association with him, and their publication of his words, makes them accomplices."

Bud Welch, who lost an adult daughter in the bombing, and was a friend from my work on the memorial, was also being interviewed. He disagreed. He believed the reporters had good intentions. However, I was, and still am, furious about this publication. I see it as an insult to the many lives this man took. And I believe the book could have been produced much differently; it could have been a psychological analysis. However, their use of McVeigh's words seems to give him credibility.

From excerpts in the paper I knew he called the children in the day care "collateral damage." He had no sympathy for the people of Oklahoma City, and he seemed proud of the mass destruction one man could wage against innocent people. His words made me physically ill. How could we, as a society, have bred such hatred and disrespect for life? I hoped most intelligent, caring Americans would turn away from this book. That morning with Bryant Gumbel, I asked the public for a boycott. I realize I wasn't successful, but I had to try.

On April 11, Attorney General John Ashcroft came to Oklahoma City to meet with survivors and victims' families. He wanted to gain a better understanding of the situation at hand, as well as to gauge our desire to view the execution. I took my lunch hour and waited near the Survivor Tree. I listened intently to the press conference, following Mr. Ashcroft's tour of the Memorial Center. It was obvious he was moved by his experience; compassion was written all over his face. He talked about the many individuals who'd spoken passionately of their need to see McVeigh executed. "Before I came to Oklahoma City," he said, "I had an intellectual knowledge about what happened here. But now after visiting these people, and seeing the Memorial Center, I have an intimate knowledge of the amount of personal tragedy that was experienced here."

I knew then that, as much as anyone from the outside possibly could, he "got it." I felt reassured this man would do right by us. He'd give us this time of healing we so desperately needed. On Good Friday the announcement was made. The attorney general had decided to allow the Oklahoma City bombing survivors and victims' families to watch the execution of Timothy McVeigh on a closed-circuit telecast. "I'm going to do what I can to accommodate the needs of these families," Ashcroft said.

It would be the first execution carried out by the U.S. government since 1963. I realized many of the families, and survivors, were divided on this issue. Some flat-out opposed the death penalty; others didn't need to see it happen. But I did.

I realized from the early days after Ashley's death, I'm a visual person. I had a hard time believing she was in that box because I never saw her again after I kissed her good-bye on that fateful spring morning. It took the news that they'd recovered my little girl's hand to help me understand what my eyes couldn't.

Now I needed to see McVeigh die for what he'd done, and continued to do. Some people may call that vindictive, but I think it's simply the need to see the scales of good and evil firmly in balance once again. As long as this man had life in his body, he continued to be an insult to the goodness of the people he murdered.

I know there is a strong, well-organized, well-funded faction who believe it's wrong to execute a murderer. Although I respect their heartfelt beliefs, I strongly disagree. I believe God has ordained penalties for murder, and the wages of such sin is death. I've always tried to teach my children that there are consequences to each and every action, and they should be prepared to squarely face them. Ultimately, they'll have to take personal responsibility for what they do. Yet that simple reality escapes some adults.

As far as I'm concerned, life in an American prison is not harsh enough for many hardened criminals. There are three square meals a day, a warm bed, and conjugal visits. In all reality it's a state-funded boarding school. I have no problem with attempting to rehabilitate, when and where possible, but there are some crimes so reprehensible that rehabilitation shouldn't be considered. McVeigh was totally unapologetic for his violence against my family and others. He clearly deserved to die. He needed to be silenced before he could influence anyone else to join him in his crusade against the people of the United States.

Many argue against the death penalty by claiming the individual didn't get a fair trial or the opportunity for a strong defense. Yet with the millions of dollars and the multitude of brilliant defense attorneys at McVeigh's beck and call, this was simply not the case. Timothy McVeigh, for all intents and purposes, was a poster child for the death penalty.

When the survey was complete, nearly three hundred people asked to witness the execution. Each had made a very personal decision. Although we all felt strongly, I found no one among us who criticized anyone else's decision. We each understood healing is unique, and each individual needed to do what he or she felt was right and appropriate. The only criticism we received was from some members of the media who accused us of creating the circus in Terre Haute and in Oklahoma City.

On April 13, 2001, my sister showed me an editorial that sent me into orbit. Although the author understood our need to know McVeigh was dead, he didn't grasp why any sane, moral person would want to watch it occur. This seemed, to the writer, to be out of the realm of human decency. Darlene and I discussed our feelings of outrage, and on Monday morning she wrote the following reply to the paper:

To the Editor:

I feel I must write in regard to your editorial of Friday, April 13, addressing the issue of almost three hundred people expressing desire to attend, and witness, the execution of Timothy McVeigh. You somehow think you have the right to criticize our decision to view this process. There has been some controversy in the media about this as well. I would like to address some of the key points I feel you are missing.

1. The decision to attend, or not attend, is a personal one made by those most intimately affected. Although a minority have elected to witness this administration of justice, we do not criticize those who choose not to attend.

2. It is most certainly not the right of the media to determine the appropriateness of our attendance.

3. "The circus" you refer to is not the families of the victims, or those who survived, but the media—of which there are 1400+ planning to attend at Terre Haute. Why don't you all get together and send five or six representatives to report to the world? Don't you trust each other to report accurately what happens there? Wouldn't it be enough to know that it happened from a few chosen witnesses? Do you actually have to be there? Can't you just read about it after it happens?

4. I personally attended both trials in full either at the FAA or Denver at great personal expense and burden to me and my family. The reason for this is simple. Someone we loved was stolen from our family. The fact that she was dead, and could not stand up for herself, made it imperative that someone from her family was there representing her.

5. As evidence and testimony was presented during those trials, most of the media reporting was skewed or misrepresented to the public. The only way we could factually know what occurred in that court room each day, was to be there and hear for ourselves what was presented. Do you think, at this point, I would trust the media representatives to report on McVeigh's death? I think not.

6. We are no different from any other murder victim's family. Some people handle this type of tragedy by withdrawing, avoiding, or not facing it. Some people do better by facing the reality head-on. Each person has to make this determination for themselves. Some choose to attend the executions, some do not. There is no right or wrong decision. I don't recall this much criticism when Brooks Douglas attended the execution of his father and mother's murderer. Why do you think we are any different?

7. There is some healing that may occur by being able to stand and face your enemy. This was seen over and over again in the courtroom in Denver as people faced McVeigh and Nichols. There is a need in some to stand and face evil and let them (or it) know you will not be defeated, that you will not go silently away, i.e., "We are still here, in spite of your actions."

8. We all know only too well that the execution will not bring back our loved ones. The editorials, and comments, made by the Oklahoman *and contributing writers only serve to condescend, judge, and try to shame us.* Shame on you!

9. This man deserves to die for his crimes. One hundred and sixty-eight people and three unborn babies died in that bombing. No matter how you add this up, it is beyond comprehension, the amount of lives and families that were affected by this horrific act. Life in prison does not always mean life in prison. We all too often hear of escapes.

The "Texas Seven" broke free to murder a young police officer in Ft. Worth. I wonder how his family could reconcile in their minds how someone who had already murdered could be out again. What about the two men from Stringtown who escaped, kidnapped and terrorized an elderly couple and others? Our society has the right to protection from sociopaths such as these. We live in man's world by man's laws. Certainly we would be in paradise if all humankind lived by God's laws. Unfortunately, we live in this world with God's granted "free will," and some prefer to impose their will on us. As long as McVeigh is alive, he will continue to champion his cause. According to his book, he still, after six years, has no remorse or regret, except that more weren't killed, that the building didn't completely collapse, and that the deaths of the children actually took attention away from his message.

10. I personally don't want Tim McVeigh to be the next "Elvis" or UFO sighting. I don't want to hear from some radical reporter or conspirator group that Tim McVeigh was seen in Brazil or Canada five years from now and wonder if the government actually served him what he deserved. I want to know personally, and for a fact, he is dead.

11. McVeigh's recent book and previous letters to the media have only added to our pain. Ashley was not just collateral damage. She was a beautiful, caring, loving little girl. She did not die for a cause. She was murdered. As long as McVeigh is alive, he will continue to send out his sick philosophy and rhetoric. Yes, we know he plans to say "hurtful" things to us at the time of his execution. Our solace in this is that it will be the last we have to hear from him—ever!

12. Most of us will feel no joy in watching McVeigh die. This is not what we are seeking. We seek justice for our loved one. We have a right to witness this. Some of us feel an obligation to attend. Whatever our motive, what we need from our neighbors is understanding and a little empathy, but most of all their prayers to help us through this time. No one knows how they might react when tragedy strikes. I hope no one else ever has to know the many heartaches we've had to endure.

Darlene Welch

Aunt of Ashley Megan Eckles—Age 4

I was proud of my sister. Over the last six years she'd been an incredible source of strength for me. Battles I didn't have the ability or time to fight she waged for me. I was glad she was on my side, and I was glad she had the internal fortitude to write our feelings down in such a clear and concise manner. For a while it seemed to restore some perspective to our paper.

Soon the execution was six days away, and I was grateful. Finally this man would be brought to justice. Then another shock wave hit. The FBI had discovered thousands of pages of documents relating to the bombing that had not been turned over to the defense team. What did this mean? Rumors of a stay of execution, and possibly even an overturned sentence, began to circulate.

The media contacted me again. What would I say? I was shocked, horrified. This wasn't just a little mistake; this was a huge error. This could mean we'd have to start all over again. This could mean I'd have to face years of McVeigh's vindictive statements to the press and publicized letters.

There was no doubt the FBI had failed us. In the past I'd been a staunch supporter of their investigation into this crime. I now had to face the fact I could be wrong about a greater conspiracy. Could there really have been others involved? Someone needed to take responsibility for this mistake immediately.

The very next day Attorney General Ashcroft made the dreaded announcement. There'd be a stay of execution. My eyes fixed on the television as he spoke. "Yesterday I was notified, documents in the McVeigh case, which should have been provided to his defense attorneys during the discovery phase of the trial, were not given to Justice Department prosecutors by the FBI. In most criminal cases, these FBI documents would not be required to be given to defense counsel during the discovery process. However, in the McVeigh case, the government agreed to go beyond the documentation required between prosecution and defense teams. While the FBI provided volumes of documents in this case, it is now clear that the FBI failed to comply fully with that discovery agreement that was reached in 1996."

He paused to catch his breath, then went on. "Today I have asked the inspector general of the Justice Department to investigate fully the FBI's belated delivery of documents and other evidence created during this investigation. When Justice Department prosecutors received the documents from the FBI, they notified the district court trial judge, Richard Matsch, and Timothy McVeigh's defense lawyers. These FBI documents were delivered to defense attorneys yesterday. The FBI is continuing to review its files, to ensure full compliance with the courts' discovery requirements.

"Career attorneys at the Department of Justice are confident, these documents do not create any reasonable doubt about McVeigh's guilt, nor do they contradict his admission of guilt for the crime.

"Over the past twenty-four hours, I have carefully considered the facts of this situation. Timothy McVeigh, by his own admission, is guilty of an act of terrorism that stole life from 168 innocent Americans, and these documents do not contradict the jury's verdict in the case. However, I believe the attorney general has a more important duty than the prosecution of any single case, as painful as that may be to our nation. It is my responsibility to promote the sanctity of the rule of law and justice. It is my responsibility and duty to protect the integrity of our system of justice.

"Therefore, I have made a decision to postpone the execution of Timothy McVeigh for one month from this day, so that the execution would occur on June the eleventh, 2001, in an effort to allow his attorneys ample and adequate time to review these documents and to take any action they might deem appropriate in that interval."

I leaned back into the couch and let out a long sigh of frustration. Although I agreed with Mr. Ashcroft, I was furious with the FBI for their inexcusable mistake. This error placed us right back in purgatory. The ball was now hopelessly in McVeigh's court. Although I resented the fact he was given further options, I agreed the process was more important than the end. I decided to wait with patience, just as the attorney general asked.

So on June 1, when McVeigh requested a stay of execution, I wasn't a bit surprised. However, I refused to offer any comments until Judge Matsch had spoken. I knew him to be a hard-hitting but fair judge. From the very beginning of the trial, he'd had a no-nonsense approach. Although at times I disagreed with him, he always seemed to have the interest of a fair and impartial trial at heart.

On June 6 he spoke. First, he seemed to take a poke at the FBI, but he finished by saying that McVeigh was not their appointed watchdog. "It's a good thing I was in quiet chambers, and not in court, because my judicial temperament escaped me when I read it. It was shocking," he said. "As the twelve jurors believe it [the verdict] is justified under all circumstances and executed their moral judgment as a conscience of the community, whatever may in time be discovered about the possible involvement of others does not change the fact that Timothy McVeigh was the instrument of death and destruction."

He went on, "It is clear Timothy McVeigh committed murder and mayhem as charged. McVeigh was at war against the United States government, but the United States government is not some abstraction, not some alien force. It is the American people, people in the Murrah Building who were there in service to their fellow American people."

He left no doubt that delaying McVeigh's execution would be equivalent to delaying the jury's "reasoned, moral judgment." I breathed a huge sigh of relief. Judge Matsch had not failed us. Justice would prevail.

I realized McVeigh could appeal to the Supreme Court, but so far the higher courts had upheld this judge's decisions. I listened carefully to the legal analyses on both radio and TV. All were in agreement. McVeigh's chances of winning were slim to none.

By Saturday the eighth, after losing in the Fifth District Court of Appeals, McVeigh decided to succumb to the judge's decision. It made me mad that he considered it *his* decision, and not the court's. But in the end it didn't matter—the battle had been won.

With the decision finalized, I had less than three days to prepare. But how does one prepare for an execution? Well, I can't answer that question for anyone else, but my family went on a vacation. Yes, that's right, a vacation. The boys were preparing to go to Falls Creek, a Baptist church camp in southern Oklahoma, and we wanted to have a few days with them before they left. So we loaded up the truck, hitched on the boat, and headed for our favorite lake.

As it turned out, I was glad I was inaccessible for a while. When I came home my answering machine had over fifty messages from reporters requesting interviews. I didn't mind talking to all of them, but I was relieved to know the frenzy would soon be over. There was a circus developing, and I resented the attention being directed at this man. I had to keep reminding myself, God was using me to share how such evil affects others. I needed to gather my composure for the final moments. Several reporters I'd come to know over the previous six years opted to come to my home to discuss the execution. I tried to relate my thoughts. What exactly were my feelings on the death penalty? How had this execution ballooned to such huge proportions? I realized intimately that this was a controversial issue but felt bound by my convictions. I wanted McVeigh to be forgotten. I said to my friend the reporter Betty Ann Bowser, "Do you remember the scene in the movie *The Ten Commandments* when Ramses banished Moses to the desert? Ramses made a declaration: 'Let the name of Moses be stricken from every tablet and every temple. Let the name of Moses never be spoken again.' That is what I want for McVeigh. I want every aspect of him to vanish from the face of this earth. I don't ever want to see him, to hear of him, or speak of him again." Betty nodded in understanding.

The night before the execution, I tried to get a few hours of sleep. I'd set the alarm for 2:00, knowing it would take a while to dress, have breakfast, and go to the U.S. marshals' hangar near Will Rogers World Airport.

We dressed in the dark. While we were trying to get ready, Kassidy woke up. She seemed to sense the stress and wanted to be held. She'd insisted on sleeping with us that night and had tossed and turned constantly. Finally I got Zachary out of his bed and had him lay down with Kassidy so we could leave. With her big brother by her side, she calmed down immediately. I shut the door, and we were on our way.

Michael knew I would be speaking with the media after the execution, so he decided to take his motorcycle while I drove my car. I was nervous and tired as we pulled into the hangar area. I'd brought my Bible, as well as photographs of Luther, LaRue, and Ashley. I was surprised when the marshals told me I had to leave my Bible behind. I was certain the official letter had said religious materials would be acceptable. I didn't argue. I simply took it back to my car, removed the photos, and locked it in the trunk. We checked in and boarded the bus to the training facility where we'd view the execution.

The mood on the bus was respectfully quiet. I looked around for my sister and niece but didn't see them. I saw a few familiar faces and smiled warmly at Aren Almon Koch. I'd grown to know and respect Aren for her quiet dignity and thoughtfulness throughout the ordeal. We were like-minded on many issues, and I felt comforted by seeing her.

Within moments the bus came to a halt, and we were ushered inside. Each individual was offered juice and coffee. I couldn't eat; I was nervous and felt a headache coming on. I'd had to leave my purse in the car, so aspirin was out of the question. Mike quietly sat beside me, sipping his coffee. Just then my sister and niece showed up, and so did Mike's brother Brad and his wife, Lois. We sat together near the back of the room, with a clear view of one of the smaller video monitors. That was as close as we could get. We spent the remainder of the morning hugging friends and quietly greeting those we'd come to know over the years.

At about 6:00 A.M. the officials asked everyone to take their seats. We were told Attorney General Ashcroft was present and wished to address us. Although I was somewhat stunned he'd come to Oklahoma City, I was pleased.

When the attorney general took the stand, I observed the same look of anguish I'd seen on his face the last time he visited Oklahoma. The crowd gave him a standing ovation. He thanked us for receiving him so warmly, then asked us to sit down. It seemed he was almost embarrassed by the immense show of support. Then he began. "After my trip here a few months ago, I realized, this was where I needed to be, where it was most appropriate to be on this day. You are the reason I am here, because you helped me to understand intimately what your needs are." He apologized that he was unable to accommodate every request. Then he explained he'd be leaving shortly to enter a private chamber near a secure phone. Although he wouldn't be in the same room with us, he'd still be with us in spirit. With that he thanked us for our dignity and our example through such difficult times and humbly dismissed himself. Immediately the crowd rose again, offering him another ovation.

I was glad he was there. So much of McVeigh's action was an attempt to dehumanize the U.S. government, making it a huge, evil monster that he alone could slay. To me, Mr. Ashcroft's presence made it apparent, our governing authorities still listen to the people. After he left most chatted quietly, and a few began milling around the room. Within moments we were asked once more to take our seats. The Bureau of Prisons representative briefed us on what was about to happen.

I looked at my watch. It was a little after 7:00. It wouldn't be much longer. Suddenly the live feed came on. There before me was a full facial view of Tim McVeigh strapped to a gurney, wearing a plain white T-shirt, with a white sheet draped across his chest. He stared directly into the camera with the same expression I remembered when he walked from the prison in Perry, Oklahoma. It was pure angry defiance.

I heard the curtains open. I watched McVeigh as he turned to look at each of the rooms surrounding the execution chamber. He seemed to take his time looking at every individual. Then he came to the window where victims' family members were waiting. McVeigh couldn't see them through the privacy two-way mirror, but he seemed to give them one last icy stare anyway. Then he turned his attention back to the camera, fixing a haunting, steely glare on those in Oklahoma.

We heard the warden say, "Inmate McVeigh, you may make your last statement." I held my breath in anticipation of his final words. I'd given much thought to what he might say. I knew any apology he offered would be empty and a lie. In the end, what I'd imagined was harsher than reality. As the moments ticked away McVeigh stared tight-lipped at the monitor, saying absolutely nothing.

The warden read from a laminated card: "Timothy James McVeigh was found guilty of conspiracy to use a weapon of mass destruction, use of a weapon of mass destruction, destruction by explosive, and eight counts of first-degree murder. On August 14, 1997, the United States District Court for the District of Colorado imposed a sentence of death, which is to be carried out today by lethal injection."

He turned to U.S. Marshal Frank Anderson and said, "Marshal, we are ready. May we proceed?"

The marshal picked up a red phone—a direct line to Oklahoma City and Attorney General Ashcroft—to check for any last-minute stays.

"This is the U.S. marshal to the Department of Justice Command Center. May we proceed?" Anderson asked.

The marshal paused, then said, "Warden, we may proceed with the execution."

Although I was stunned McVeigh had chosen to remain silent, I was also relieved. I found myself transfixed by the television screen before me. At first his eyes drooped and fluttered but remained open. He drew in one deep breath and expelled it, as if succumbing to sleep. I carefully watched the rise and fall of his chest as it became more faint. Finally, I saw his lips turn blue. Moments later, at 7:14 A.M., Timothy McVeigh was pronounced dead. It was finally over. A sigh of relief washed over the crowd, but in spite of some harsh predictions, no one cheered or clapped. We simply sat in respectful silence, awaiting the warden's announcement to the media.

Just before we were dismissed, CNN was piped into the room. A collective chuckle went out from the crowd as we realized reporters didn't know if the execution had been completed. It was probably the first time we knew something before the media, and in some strange way we found it immensely amusing.

Slightly after 7:30 the warden made his announcement, that Timothy James McVeigh had been pronounced dead at 7:14 A.M. Shortly thereafter we were released.

Once I boarded the bus I discovered McVeigh, not relying on his own thoughts, had left another author's words for the world to read. The work was "Invictus," an 1888 British poem he'd proclaimed as his own. Its lines include: "My head is bloody, but unbowed" and "I am the master of my fate: I am the captain of my soul."

He signed his initials, "T.J.M.," and dated it June 11, 2001.

I was struck with how inappropriate it was. The master of his fate? The captain of his soul? Obviously he was neither. If he'd mastered his fate, he wouldn't have been executed. If he were the captain of his soul, he'd never have to face God for his acts of murder. I found it ironic he chose this poem. Once again he'd revealed his ignorance. *Invictus,* after all, is Latin for "undefeated." Despite his fantasy, he was not victorious. Reality spoke louder than words; McVeigh had been completely and totally defeated.

He considered himself a soldier. To me this was a huge embarrassment to all honorably discharged veterans worldwide, and it seemed ridiculous that he carried this fallacy to his grave. Whatever he'd done in years past was negated by his act on April 19, 1995. He gave up all the honorable and decent things he'd ever accomplished when he became judge, jury, and executioner to 168 men, women, and children, and three unborn babies. I thought of my husband, who'd served his nation proudly for over twenty years; my brother who served in Vietnam; my own father, who served in the Navy during World War II, and my aunts and grandmother who were Army nurses in World War II and Korea. My family had a proud tradition of service to their country. It sickened me to associate this man with them, and it sickened me McVeigh's attorneys grouped him with this patriotic assembly. It seemed to be one last jeer at our way of life.

Although I resented it, I knew it was the last time he'd inflict his thoughts on the world, or me. I rejoiced in the knowledge, this man could no longer hurt my family. I'd never again have to worry about what he'd say next, never again have to invoke damage control in my home, trying to comfort my children and protect them from him, never again. He was gone. Justice had been served. For me his death didn't represent closure but was simply the last page of a bitter chapter, a period at the end of a sentence.

As we got off the bus, I felt a tremendous wave of relief wash over me. It was finally over, done, finished. I walked up to the podium. "The first thing I need to say today is the most important. I wish to extend my condolences to Mr. Bill McVeigh regarding the loss of his son. No one more than I understands what it feels like to lose a child. I intimately understand, like us, he too is a victim of his son's actions. No one is sorrier than I am for those actions that brought us here today. I received no joy from watching this man die, but this morning, I did receive justice."

I looked out over the crowd and saw many faces I'd come to know over the past six years. They seemed to understand the real story was not in Terre Haute but here in Oklahoma City. I asked the media to remember that fact instead of glorifying McVeigh and his actions any further, to turn their stories to the true heroes, those in Oklahoma City who'd given their lives for no good reason. Many reporters asked if the execution had brought me closure. Like many in Oklahoma, I'd come to hate that word.

"I'll have closure," I said, "when I stop grieving the loss of my daughter, when they lay me cold in my grave, and not a second before."

I stepped down from the podium, slowly walking away from the crowd of Oklahomans I'd come to know, love, and respect. Only this time I felt lighter, almost free. I knew instinctively where I had to go.

One of the news crews drove me to the memorial. I walked over to Ashley's chair and kissed the back of the seat. "Today, you can rest," I promised. I went to Luther and LaRue's chairs and did the same.

I ran into Constance Favorite, LaKesha Levy's mother, and hugged her tightly. LaKesha was a young army sergeant who'd been killed that day. Just like me, Constance had had to face the horror of burying parts of her daughter separately. She'd been grieving and sobbing incessantly. I'd seen her on several TV monitors as she was collapsed in front of her daughter's chair. I knew her anguish but tried to offer a measure of comfort. "Today, Constance, this man will no longer be able to steal any more of our joy."

"It's too easy," she said. "He got off too easy. Death is too good for him."

"No, Constance. Today he will face God for what he did to our daughters. And you and I both know, God won't deal kindly with him. He will punish this man. That's the best we can hope for." She nodded in understanding. I hugged her tightly, and we went our separate ways.

Later that afternoon, as I was descending the risers from a CNN interview, I ran into McVeigh's attorney Steven Jones. I'd grown to resent this man for his intensely vocal defense at the Denver trial. Yet over time, I grew to understand the uphill battle he was waging. As angry as I was about his defense of McVeigh, I came to accept he was a necessary part of the judicial process. Steven Jones did exactly what he had to. He attempted to change public opinion, and to sway people from convicting his client before he'd had a fair trial.

I leaned over as the words slowly came forth. "Mr. Jones, there's something I have to say to you." I watched closely as apprehension crossed his face.

"All right," he whispered, "I'll listen."

"I just want you to know, I understand the struggle you must have gone through. I realize you're an essential part of the process. I thank you for your contribution in bringing us to this day. This hasn't been easy for me. There were times I hated you for what you've said and done on your client's behalf. But I've come to understand your motives. And I forgive you."

For a moment he seemed taken aback, then he thanked me for my understanding. "You know, Kathleen, I once asked McVeigh what justified Ashley's death. I told him, 'She was innocently there in the arms of her grandmother.' And you know, he couldn't answer me."

I turned to Steven's wife, waiting quietly in the background. I took a few steps, then reached my hand out to greet her. She thanked me for my kindness, then told me her husband had suffered a great deal of anguish over the case, and she hoped my forgiveness would help him to heal.

For me this was the final release. Steven was the last person I needed to forgive. I was able to walk away feeling cleansed. I got back to my car and drove to my home, my oasis, my refuge, and my family.

The minute I walked through the door, I scooped Kassidy in my arms, and headed straight for Ashley's garden. With the loss of 168 people still weighing on my heart, I sat down amid the foliage. Running my fingers through the water, I gazed at the beauty before me. A colorful array of life reached out in fragrant glory. Deep inside my soul, I seemed to hear a whisper: "Just as the blossoms made their way from the dark, difficult soil, so will your life spring forth anew."

Yes, tomorrow would be a new day. Justice had been served, Ashley's blood avenged, and for the first time in six years, I would find peace.

Epilogue

After years of anticipation, prayers, and multiple cries for justice, Oklahoma District Attorney Wes Lane announced on September 6, 2001, that the state of Oklahoma will go ahead with a second trial for Terry Nichols, seeking the death penalty.

For some, a second trial represents an unnecessary expense. For others, it represents old wounds reopened. But for me, the death penalty sends a powerful message to anyone plotting to maim and destroy innocent people for the sake of their cause.

Terrorism, both foreign and domestic, is a cancer in the heart and soul of our world. As a people, we must diligently eradicate all traces of this evil or face the untimely death of what we love most as a nation—our freedom. Without a doubt, we have a moral and ethical responsibility to ourselves, our children, and our grandchildren, to fight terrorism with whatever means we have at our disposal.

In the aftermath of the terrible attacks on September 11, 2001, my simple prayer to share healing with a hurting world was answered in a way far beyond my imagination. In October 2001, I was sent to New York City, along with two others who'd lost loved ones in the Oklahoma City bombing, as a representative of the Red Cross and the Oklahoma City Memorial. Together, we were able to reach out to the grieving people of New York. There I shared my story with many anguished individuals as we brought them, one by one, to ground zero. Each trip to the devastation became a journey through sorrow and personal loss. For many, it was, as it had been for me, a release of their loved one. Through the sharing of tears, those who were once strangers are now precious friends. I pray my presence offered a living example of hope, that despite such horrific circumstances, in time they too will emerge from their difficult and dark journey into the light of tomorrow.

As for now, I await the second Nichols trial with faith that ultimate justice will prevail.

Ten Ways to Cope with the Loss of a Loved One

1. Give yourself time to grieve. No one can tell you the appropriate duration, since grief, on some level, will last for a lifetime. Remember, you'll have good days and bad. Do not apologize for your tears, and, most of all, don't hold them in.

2. Analyze your support structure. Your faith, family, and friends are vital to helping you get through a crisis. If any two of these support structures are firmly in place, you will find it easier to cope.

3. Don't be ashamed or afraid to ask for professional help. There is a great deal of comfort in knowing you are not going insane, especially in the early stages of grief. Most people seek professional help when, after an extensive period of time, they are still unable to rebound from the intensity of grief or are unable to cope with the basics of day-to-day life. This is a fairly good guideline.

4. Don't make any sudden, drastic changes in your life. For example, avoid making impulsive decisions to sell your home, leave your job, get married, or get a divorce. Major, abrupt changes may add to your stress level and cause you deep regret in the future.

5. Attitude is everything. Discover something each day you're grateful for. Take a moment away from your sorrows to count your blessings.

6. Find opportunities to talk about your loved one. Friends and family are good sources, but also seek out others who've lost someone in a similar fashion. Group therapy is one way of finding kindred souls.

7. Stay physically and mentally busy. It sounds like common sense, but most people who are struggling with grief tend to stop all their activities while they dwell on their loss. As much as possible, try to maintain

your routine. If you are incapable of that, take up a hobby or perform volunteer work to occupy your time.

8. Keep a journal or audio recording of your journey through grief. By doing this, you'll be able to see the healing process is taking place, even if it appears at times not to be.

9. Don't blame yourself for the loss or for past failings. It is not your fault. Forgive yourself.

10. Spend a little time alone each day meditating or praying, or just in quiet solitude. If you enjoy gardening, walking, or music, use these to your benefit. Surrounding yourself with beauty will allow you to grieve privately as you make your way through your journey.

Five Ways to Honor and Preserve the Memory of a Loved One

1. Collect all photographs, videotapes, voice recordings, honors, and awards and create a treasure box in which to place them. You can also add poetry or personal writings, as well as funeral gifts, pressed flowers, and newspaper clippings.

2. Write down memories of your loved one. Talk with others who knew him or her and consider making audiotapes of their remembrance as well. This will become a personal history not only for you but for generations to come. After you have the first two items ready, be sure to contact your local preservation agency for tips on making sure they do not deteriorate.

3. Make a remembrance button that says, "In Memory Of . . ." Wear it whenever you feel you need to talk about your loved one. Believe me, people will ask.

4. Plant a tree or garden in memory of the person you lost. On special days, such as birthdays or holidays, hang a yellow ribbon in their honor. If you don't have space for a tree or garden near your home, donate it to a church, school, day care, or hospital, but be sure to let them know who it represents. You might want to purchase a small placard for the personal memorial.

5. Perform an act of charity in honor of your loved one. Don't just stop at monetary donations. Go out and spend time with the charity as part of their workforce. Try to find one that focuses on the cause of your loved one's death, e.g., the American Cancer Society, Mothers Against Drunk Driving (MADD), or a foundation that helped you in your time of need. Be sure to wear your photographic pin. This will give you the opportunity to talk about your loss with others who may share a similar experience.